The
Crystal
Bible 3

The
Crystal
Bible volume 3

Judy Hall

**Featuring over 250 new generation, high-vibration rare
and esoteric stones for healing and transformation**

WALKING
STICK
PRESS

Published in the U.S. by Walking Stick Press, an imprint of F+W Media, Inc.
10151 Carver Road, Suite #200, Blue Ash, OH 45242
(800) 289-0963

First published in Great Britain in 2012 by
Godsfield Press, a division of Octopus Publishing Group Ltd
Endeavour House
189 Shaftesbury Avenue
London
WC2H 8JY
www.octopusbooks.co.uk

ISBN 978-1-59963-699-3

A CIP catalogue record for this book is available from the British Library.

Printed and bound in China.

10 9 8 7 6 5

NOTE: An asterisk* placed after a word indicates that the word or term may be looked
up in the Glossary section (see page 378–383) for a full explanation.

CAUTION: No medical claims are made for the stones in this book and the information
given is not intended to act as a substitute for medical treatment.
The healing properties are given for guidance only and are, for the most part, based on
anecdotal evidence and/or traditional therapeutic use. If in any doubt, a crystal healing
practitioner should be consulted. In the context of this book, illness is a disease, the final
manifestation of spiritual, environmental, psychological, karmic, emotional or mental
imbalance or distress. Healing means bringing mind, body and spirit back into balance
and facilitating evolution for the soul, it does not imply a cure. In accordance with
crystal healing consensus, all stones are referred to as crystals regardless of whether or
not they have a crystalline structure.

CONTENTS

CRYSTAL REFERENCE

CRYSTAL INNOVATIONS

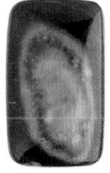

Eclipse Stone

Crystal lore says that the earth produces all the crystals we need and over 250 more have come to my attention in the three years since I wrote The Crystal Bible II. *New crystals appear on the market every month. Some are unique combinations of known crystals, others entirely new. Certain stones have generated enormous controversy. Some are abundant, others are rare and difficult to source. Knowing the effect of what you are wearing as well as how to apply crystals for personal, environmental or multi-dimensional healing and spiritual alchemy makes good sense.*

New generation esoteric stones have exceedingly high vibrations* but, as each physical body varies in its energetic resonance*, some of these crystals may have a different, or no effect on you. You'll find alternative choices here that resonate with your own unique energies. As well as these, we need earthier, grounded stones for balance and ones to protect you when assimilating new frequencies.

There is no right way to use the new

Lemurian Aquatine™ Calcite

Galaxyite

Kambaba Jasper

10

stones or a specific effect to anticipate; only the way that is right for you and the experience that is appropriate. Some crystals will jump out at you and these are the ones to start with. Bear in mind that biggest isn't necessarily best nor most beautiful most potent. Empathy nicks* may not look pretty but add to a crystal's power. These new crystals pack a great punch in a small stone. Find them by the intuitive resonance of your heart. Take time to look out for and touch these new crystals. You will know when a crystal is meant for you.

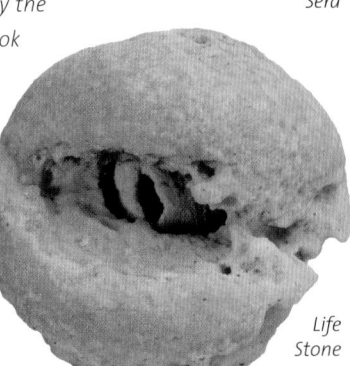

Que Sera

Life Stone

The Crystal Directory (see pages 34–359) describes the crystals' qualities – more may become apparent to you as you work with them. Knowing their qualities helps you to cooperate with them to expand your consciousness, enhance energy, protect your space, open chakras* and subtle energy meridians*, and journey safely into the multi- and inter-dimensional worlds that enfold us. In the context of this book healing means bringing back into balance rather than curing. The Directory also includes rare stones whose esoteric properties are not described elsewhere. Essential Quick Reference material is at the back of the book. A Glossary assists with unfamiliar terms marked * in the text. There is also an index to assist in finding exactly the right stone for your needs. Further chakras are opening up to facilitate the assimilation of new energies and you'll find information on these, traditional and higher dimensional chakras on pages 364–372.

Tantalite

Rainbow Mayanite

11

CRYSTAL BEINGS

Crystals are alive with a unified field of consciousness that connects them wherever they are. The awareness of this, and of the healing properties of crystals, was incorporated into esoteric knowledge from time immemorial. That knowledge fell largely into disuse although it never disappeared entirely. The old stonebooks (lapidaries) are still around if you know where to find them, as are the crystal oversouls*.

   As part of the current upsurge of natural healing and expansion of consciousness, people are once more connecting with the crystal oversouls. These immense beings bring about personal and collective awakening. The more we align our vibrations, expand our awareness and interact with higher dimensions, the more information encoded within crystals is revealed. Higher vibration crystals resonate with the journey of our soul and the process of enlightenment, literally bringing light into our inner being and the fabric of our physical body, reminding us that,

We are part of the Earth and the Earth is part of us. CHIEF SEATTLE

CRYSTAL STRUCTURE

All energy needs a structure to contain it and allow it to function, whether it be a wave, a particle, a frequency or amplitude, a physical matrix*, a subtle structure within the mind or the energetic bodies, or a grid (see page 374). Crystals and their crystalline matrixes naturally provide a structure that generates energy and into which energy anchors itself. However they, as with the physical or subtle bodies*, may hold on to detrimental patterns or negative energies which is why crystals need to be cleansed regularly and why energetic structures may need to be de-energized* and rebuilt more constructively.

HIGH AND LOW FREQUENCIES

Crystals have a measurable frequency. Some crystals have a low, earthy frequency and others an extremely high vibration and some exhibit both. The effect of a crystal differs according to how its vibrations interact with those of the recipient. Research has shown that people in lower vibrational states are grounded and connected to their ego, emotions and the material world. Lower vibration states are concerned with biological and physiological processes and survival needs. Higher vibration states are characterized by a transcendent *knowing*, increased creativity and mystical awareness. They connect with the higher mind and Divine Intelligence, encompass All That Is*, and create expanded awareness. In most people, there is a continuum of vibrational frequencies with spikes of activity along the spectrum. The optimum state is to have both grounded energy and high vibrational awareness, which is where crystals come in.

If you are not grounded in the earth-plane, nothing that happens in expanded awareness has relevance in everyday life. Such people are spaced out and eventually suffer from physical dis-ease*. Grounded energy is typically located in the feet and lower torso and is anchored to the Earth Star chakra. Ungrounded energy is in the upper torso and head where it shoots out of the crown chakra. When both are present an 'infinity loop' forms. If you are grounded and simultaneously operating at a high frequency, you can put your insights to work and appropriate energetic exchanges take place. Crystals provide grounding, smooth transition between higher and lower vibrations and ameliorate the effect of 'phase shifts' when the amplitude or power of a vibration suddenly increases or decreases.

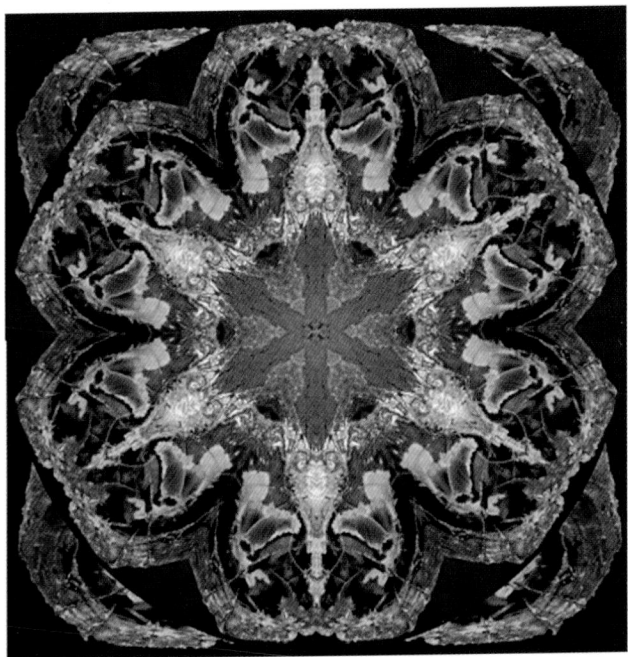

The energy field of a Petrified Wood crystal consciousness.

BIOSCALAR WAVES

Bioscalar waves* are one of the most exciting discoveries in healing. Many new crystals, such as Anandalite™ and Rainbow Mayanite contain concentrated bioscalar energy. It is probable that all healing crystals have this energy within their matrix, and that crystalline structure actually produces bioscalar energy. A bioscalar wave is a standing energy created when two electromagnetic fields interact from different angles and counteract each other so that the electromagnetism reverts to a static 'vacuum state of potentiality'. It would seem that bioscalar waves assist cell membranes in switching on the most beneficial genetic functions and switching off detrimental patterns encoded within ancestral DNA.

Electromagnetism has measurable frequencies, wave action and motion but bioscalar energy is stationary and is not measurable with current scientific instruments - although it has been demonstrated to have a powerful, beneficial effect on the human organism. It's postulated that bioscalar wave

Laying crystals out in a grid creates a matrix into which energy is anchored or from which it is manifested.

energy exists at the microscopic level in the nucleus of an atom or a cell and creates a bioenergetic source, cellular matrixes and other physiological processes. It links into the finding that cell walls contain an integral membrane protein that responds to energy signals from the internal or external environment, switching genetic potential and chemical processes on or off accordingly.

The internal structure or external shape of a crystal creates, contains or amplifies an energy field.

Bioscalar energy can be activated with focused intent, returning an energy field to optimum equilibrium, and so forms a basis for healing. Bioscalar waves directly influence tissue at the microscopic level, bringing about balance. They energize the extracellular matrix of the body and protect against electromagnetic emanations that otherwise detrimentally affect cells and tissue. Bioscalar waves activate the meridians* and facilitate the healing of the etheric blueprint* at the energetic interface between spirit and matter. The healing moves from there into the physical body. Research has shown that bioscalar waves increase circulation, unclumping blood cells and increasing their mobility, and reduce swelling. Demonstrated to enhance the immune and endocrine systems, they stabilize chemical processes, improve the coherence of the biomagnetic field and accelerate healing at all levels. They release stored emotions and ingrained thoughts from the cellular structure of the body, removing a root cause of psychosomatic dis-ease* and thus facilitating healing.

HIGH VIBRATION CRYSTALS

*If the head and body are to be well,
you need to begin by curing the soul.* PLATO

High vibration crystals have a light, refined vibration that connects to higher dimensional realities and your core spiritual identity, bringing about multi-dimensional healing and spiritual alchemy. The new generation high vibration crystals work at a soul level and beyond and at the molecular level of experience to bring body and soul into balance. They transform the cellular matrix* – physical and subtle – so that it is ready to receive an influx of new-frequency information, having previously released out-dated patterning. In soul matrix healing they repair or reprogram damaged patterns. Many high vibration stones work slowly to bring about physical change although with some it can be instantaneous. The impact is at the level of the soul and the etheric blueprint* which then filters into the physical body.

These crystals stimulate 'higher' chakras* such as the alta major, soul star and stellar gateway, and mediate the conventional seven chakras to accommodate high frequency energies. High vibration crystal work should be undertaken only when your vibrations are in harmony with the crystal. It is important to have completed your psychological healing and evolutionary work before moving on to multi-dimensional work. Not every high vibration crystal will resonate with you and it is vital to find the stones

Mangano Vesuvianite

18

to which you are attuned. If a high dimension crystal provoces a healing challenge*, remove it and hold a Flint, Smoky or Chlorite Quartz or one of the newer equilibrium stones between your feet to stabilize your energies. Return to the crystal when you have recalibrated your vibrations, or choose another. If you feel a strong aversion to a high vibration crystal, put it aside and choose another type. It may have the wrong vibration for you or it may be stirring up unresolved issues that will need working through before trying to attune to that crystal again. Be sensible! Don't push it.

Terraluminite™

ATTUNING TO HIGH VIBRATION CRYSTALS

- Open your palm chakras by rapidly opening and closing your hands several times until your palms become hot and tingly.
- Hold the crystal gently and sit quietly. Your body may vibrate as it attunes to the crystal or you may be instantly transported to another energetic dimension, which means it will work with you. If not, try again later when your vibrations have shifted having released toxicity or outmoded conditioning.
- Once you have established contact with the crystal, ask it to show you how to work with it for best results. Open your intuition to receive the answer.

Rosophia™ (Azeztulite)

Rainbow Mayanite

EXPLORING CRYSTAL POTENTIAL

All crystals have limitless potential. These esoteric stones subtly expand awareness, whether personal, planetary or multi-dimensional. This book introduces some of their possibilities but a crystal will interact with you according to your vibrational potential. Exploring for yourself precisely how crystals work with you reveals their full potential. The more sensitive you become to a crystal's resonance and how it engages with your own frequencies, the wider the possibilities become. This exercise helps attune your vibrations to those of a crystal. Remember to note any body sensations, thoughts or emotions you experience as you attune as well as chakra* activations and after-effects.

CRYSTAL ATTUNEMENT
- Open your palm chakras by rapidly opening and closing your hands several times until your palms become hot and tingly.
- Sit quietly holding your cleansed and dedicated crystal (see page 362). Breathe gently and allow yourself to relax and focus your attention on the crystal. State your intention to get to know this crystal better and to feel its energy.
- Allow your eyes to go into soft focus and gaze at the crystal. Note its shape, its colour and its size. Follow its contours and craters, if it has a 'window' look inside. Feel how light or heavy it is in your hand. Feel its vibrations and its energetic resonance. You may feel your energy jump or tingle (like getting an electric shock), or slow and pulse as it connects. Allow the energy of the crystal to travel up your arms and into your heart and mind so that it reveals itself to you. Be aware if

the crystal makes special contact with any part of your body – take it up through your chakras and all around your body, pausing over specific organs or sites where you feel tingling or pain, and see if there is an energetic response.

- Ask the crystal oversoul* to make itself known to you.
- When you have finished, put your crystal down and consciously break off contact with its energies. Take your attention down to your feet and feel their contact with the floor. Picture a bubble of protection going all around you. Keep a record of your results.

Meditating with your crystal assists you in exploring its potential and properties.

21

CRYSTAL SKULLS

Skulls have rapidly become something of a legend in the crystal world and many myths and practices have grown up around them. Some beautiful – and some downright ugly – stone and crystal skulls are being carved. Much older skulls are reputed to have been carved by the ancients as receptacles for their esoteric knowledge. These skulls are said to be inhabited by higher beings and extra-terrestrials that are vehicles for profound teaching. It is claimed that some skulls are between 5,000 and 30,000 years old and are remnants of the lost continent of Atlantis with exceedingly magical powers.

As a result, skulls have taken on an aura of magic and mystery like no other crystal artefact. They excite the imagination and are an amazing tool for personal and planetary evolution if used with the right intention and metaphysical awareness. But! As with all things esoteric and crystal, careful discrimination and personal responsibility are required when interacting with these skulls. It cannot be assumed that the beings inhabiting them are necessarily working for the highest good, nor should it be taken for granted that all is as it seems. There may be trickery and deception as well as the highest guidance. Truth often lies in the mind of the beholder rather than in the facts. This is what mythology – and the power of belief – is all about.

Crystal skulls are carved from a variety of materials.

There is, however, no denying the seductive qualities of crystal skulls

A crystal earth healing master who holds much knowledge about our planet and the changes it is passing through.

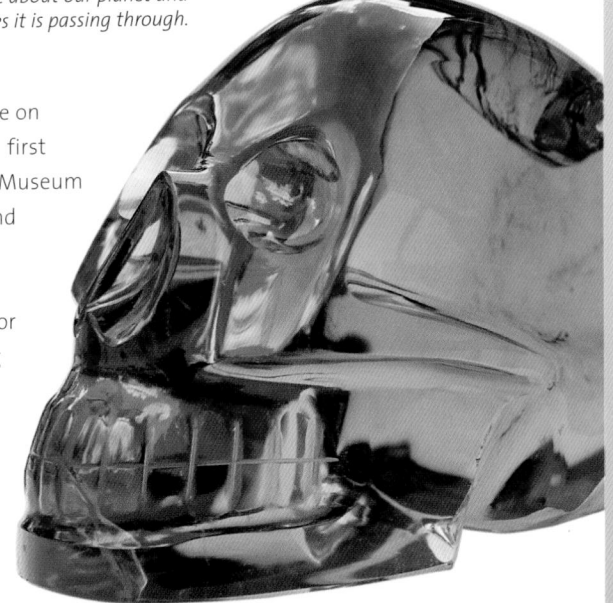

and the impact they have on your spiritual evolution. I first faced one in 1976 in the Museum of Mankind in London and have never forgotten the experience. I stood entranced in front of it for two hours while viewing the far past. However, it took 35 years before I purchased my first skull. Now I have a growing conclave that present me with information about how to skillfully navigate the energetic changes we are currently passing through and which enable me to change my vibrational frequency and journey* through multi-dimensions. An excellent focus for meditation and kything*, they assist communication with other skulls around the world.

THE LEGEND OF THE 13 SKULLS

A Mesoamerican myth carried forward from the Maya and Aztec civilizations tells of 13 crystal skulls belonging to the Goddess of Death. Known as 'the mothers and fathers of wisdom', each was carved from a single piece of crystal and had a moveable jaw. Rather than symbolizing

Thirteen crystal skulls in conclave

death in the way that a skull does in the modern world, they reflected the view that death was just a passing phase, a doorway to another dimension. Through death the spirit would rejoin the ancestors and the body would return to fertilise Mother Earth. According to at least one modern Mesoamerican teacher, the ancient skulls not only carried hidden wisdom but had the gift of telepathy and healing.

Each skull was kept at a different sacred site, guarded by keeper-priests. However, in other versions of the legend there are 13 major skulls within a total of 52 spread throughout the world. The Cherokee people are said to have a similar legend in which each skull belongs to one of twelve inhabited planets within the cosmos, with the thirteenth acting as a bridge to the different worlds.

Today these ancient skulls are believed to be emerging from hiding to share their wisdom once humankind has evolved sufficiently to understand the spiritual implications. In the meantime, keepers with appropriate training and sensitivity communicate with the skulls and pass on their message of assistance in the evolution of humanity. But you can work with modern skulls and receive great insights yourself.

THE MITCHELL HEDGES SKULL

Perhaps the best known, and one of the most controversial, skulls is that allegedly found by the late Anna Mitchell Hedges at a dig in Central America carried out by her archaeologist father. She claimed that, on the day of her seventeenth birthday in April 1927, she discovered a crystal skull under a ruined altar which, at the time, lacked its lower jaw. The jaw was later found close by and was a perfect fit having been carved from a single piece of Quartz.

Anna Mitchell Hedges maintained up to her death that she had discovered the skull at Lubaantun: The Place of the Fallen Stones. However, there is evidence to suggest that her father purchased the skull at an auction at Sotheby's in London in 1943. Opinions vary and it is hotly contested as to whether it is a fake or an authentic ancient artefact. It hardly seems to matter. The skull took on a life of its own. It was reputed to speak, to have a distinctive aura around it and to contain images of past, present and future. As did similar skulls that have opened an energy network which acts rather like a crystal internet. These skulls are communicating to people right around the globe the need to honour Mother Earth.

ACCESSING YOUR CRYSTAL SKULL

If you own a crystal or stone skull and it has not yet started to
communicate with you, activate it with a simple attunement that
harmonizes your vibrational frequency to that of the skull.

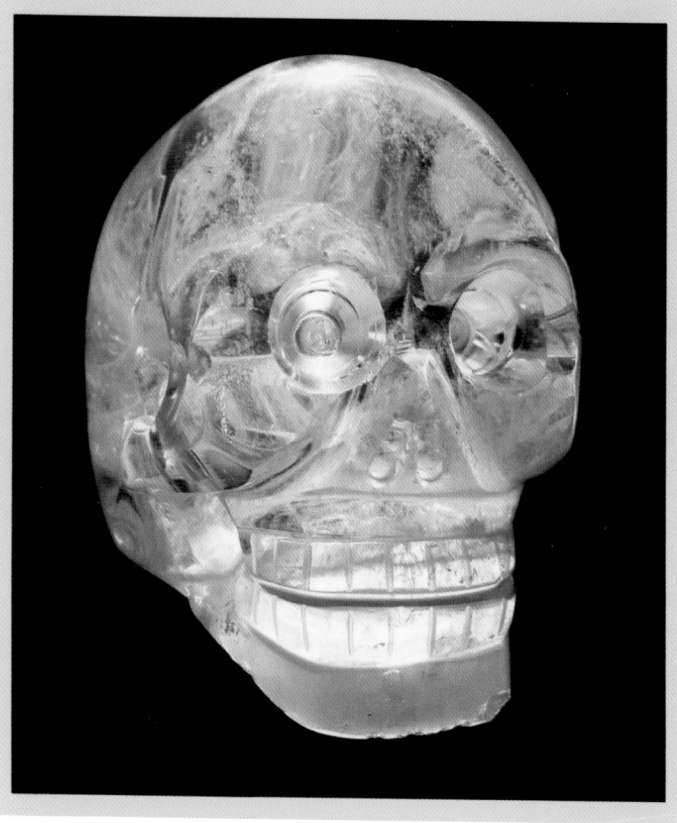

1 First cleanse your skull *As with all crystals, skulls take on the energy and beliefs of everyone who handles them. If you have a genuine higher being within the skull, cleansing it will not dissolve the contact. If you have a lesser being the information you receive is unlikely to be of any value. So, either use a proprietary crystal cleanser or immerse the skull in salt or running water (unless friable or delicate in which case place it in brown rice overnight). If the skull needs recharging, place it in sunlight or use a proprietary recharger.*

2 Invite your skull to activate *Place your hands on either side of the skull and, if the skull feels 'empty', invite the highest possible being to enter the skull and communicate with you. If the skull feels 'full', invite the being within it to awake and make itself known to you.*

3 Attune to your skull *Place the skull in front of you, preferably level with your eyes. With softly focused eyes gaze into the eye sockets. Ask that the skull communicate with you in a language you understand. Notice any sensations around your head, prickling or buzzing is quite common. Acknowledge thoughts or pictures that spontaneously rise up into your awareness.*

4 Kything* *If your skull is clear crystal, gaze into it to see pictures or to receive communications. If it is opaque, place your hands on the skull and allow images to form in your mind's eye or words to be heard in your inner ear. Always ask that what you are shown will be for the highest good of all.*

Left: 19th century crystal skull at the Musee du quai Branly, Paris.

BUILDING IN STONE

For thousands of years human beings have used whatever building materials were to hand but stone has been the most prized of all. To the ancients it was permanent, immutable and incorruptible and linked to the beginning of time in direct contrast to the frailty of human life. It was regarded as the primeval god become manifest which meant that, although indigenous and vernacular architecture relied on local stone, certain rocks were moved hundreds of miles to honour or represent the gods at sacred sites. Such rocks created an interface* between the visible and divine worlds.

However, the underlying geology has an energetic effect on the inhabitants of the land above. In some parts of the world, the geology is widespread but in others it is specific to small areas. In England, living in a Cornish granite stone house, for instance, is energetically different to living in a flint home set in chalkland in East Dorset or a sandstone house on clay in West Dorset, yet they exist within a hundred miles of each other. Granite is a highly resonant stone that magnifies and conveys geomagnetic energies. It is strongly grounding and enduring, resistant to change and some people find it 'heavy'. Sandstone allows energies to pass through it fluidly and so

Bluestones were moved 150 miles from their source in Wales to form an integral part of one of the world's most iconic sacred sites: Stonehenge.

29

encourages adaptation – although claggy clay is often beneath it so energies may get stuck below the surface. Resources could trickle away. The flint and chalk combination acts as a grounding and energizing battery for transformation and for metaphysical work.

Whether a rock was created rapidly – as with those fired out of a volcano; was created from living creatures, eroded and laid down again slowly or subjected to enormous pressure affects how we function when we inhabit a building constructed from the stone, as does the geology of the landscape on which we live.

IGNEOUS ROCKS

Created out of the internal tension of the earth, igneous rocks such as Granite, Gabbro and Basalt are formed from molten magma extruded, or exploded, into the crust of the planet. The primary material of creation, they are some of the oldest rocks on the planet although the process continues today. Such rocks stimulate humanity's spiritual yearnings and encourage personal growth and development. These plutonic stones assist with the process of apoptosis, cell death that allows the biological cycle of renewal and regeneration to continue. They have a strong healing power with a grounded, shielding vibration that supports evolution although they also have a serious, melancholic humour*. Having undergone extremely harsh and stressful conditions during their own evolution, they are a stable companion through change.

SEDIMENTARY ROCKS

Sedimentary rocks such as Limestone, Chalk, Flint and Sandstone are secondary rocks created from particles cemented together over aeons of time. Many of these rocks are the remains of sea creatures or of rocks that were eroded only to be reborn again. These fluid, transmuted rocks have enormous reserves of patience, they have seen it all during their incredibly long lifetime and they know that one thing forms out of another and something must die for something new to be born. So sedimentary rocks deal with issues of survival, adaptation and the stages of life needed to gain maturity and they have a sanguine, hopeful, humour. They help you to understand the exceedingly long cycle of the soul's journey and to peel away the layers that hide your true self.

METAMORPHIC ROCKS

Modified by heat, pressure and chemical processes, metamorphic rocks such as Marble were transformed while buried deep below earth's surface. The nature of the rock was polished, refined and dramatically altered. Metamorphic rocks help you find survival strategies and ways of coping with constant stress. They have a phlegmatic, pragmatic humour. Many of the most energetic healing crystals were formed by metamorphic processes.

Marble has undergone enormous chemical changes in its metamorphosis.

31

THE MADAGASCAR STONES

Madagascar is a huge island off the coast of Africa that is reputed to be one of the original colonies of Lemuria, an ancient civilisation predating Atlantis. Many of the specialist Madagascan crystals are thought to have been programmed with knowledge from that time and Madagascar Quartz is helpful for past life healing involving issues from Lemuria and Atlantis and for bringing forward that knowledge.

Madagascar has produced some astonishing and very powerful crystals, such as the wonderful Ocean Jasper, delicate Candle or Celestial Quartz, and the metaphysically fabulous Labradorite. Yet little is known in the wider world about the island or the mining there. The Ocean Jasper seam was found at low tide and is reported to be mined out but, as one Madagascan crystal dealer pointed out, another seam may be revealed a few feet away buried, for the moment, under rock until the sea erodes its covering and reveals its beauty.

Today the Chinese take almost all Madagascan crystal production. They are hungry for minerals and for beautiful crystals. But ethically produced, hand-mined crystals are still available and some of the milky Madagascar Quartzes are extremely powerful. Graphic Smoky Quartz takes you journeying into multi-dimensions and keeps you grounded at the same time, enabling you to be both *'here'* and *'there'* simultaneously.

Madagascar Cloudy Quartz

While there is strip mining in Madagascar with the use of blasting to obtain crystals such as Labradorite, ethical mining is carried out by families at their own small sites in between harvesting rice and planting the next crop of vegetables. The crystals are carefully hand-mined from holes in the ground and dealers have to travel for days, sometimes weeks, to collect them. The Madagascans are a spiritual people with deep beliefs about the earth. When a mining company wanted to access a particularly bright blue Labradorite in a sacred place, the villagers held a meeting and asked the spirits who replied that it would be alright as long as no dynamite was used. As hand mining was costly, the company had to relocate over the next ridge where the quality was poorer but the land not quite so sacred.

Ocean Blue Jasper

Polychrome Jasper

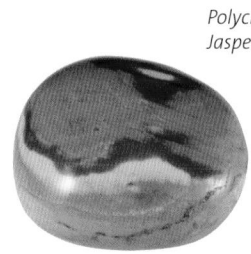

Graphic Smoky Quartz (in Feldspar)

Madagascar Finger Quartz

CRYSTAL DIRECTORY

Every day new crystals come onto the market, fresh combinations offer exciting synergies, old ones are rediscovered and enduring favourites reveal fresh properties. Crystals, as with humans, are evolving. Many make themselves known to assist us ascend into a higher vibration of consciousness, an expanded awareness that offers a new way of being here on the earth. Several are 'stones for the New Age' with a part to play in our spiritual evolution.

Certain crystals create an earthy energetic structure into which new vibrations anchor. Others offer a more refined, highly energetic frequency that facilitates healing at subtle and multi-dimensional levels. As the planet's vibrations are shifting, it's not surprising that crystals are keeping pace. In this directory you will find new tools and esoteric stones perfect for crystal aficionados who want to move beyond the mundane and crystals for beginners just starting out on an exciting journey of exploration.

AFGHANITE

Raw

COLOUR	Blue, white and colourless combination
APPEARANCE	Opaque stone
RARITY	Rare
SOURCE	Afghanistan

ATTRIBUTES A high vibration stone that enhances multi-dimensional journeying*, Afghanite facilitates bringing back guidance from the highest sources. It opens and aligns the brow, soma, alta major, crown, stellar gateway and soul star chakras* so that the soul is fully aware in whatever dimension it is operating. This stone assists reading the Akashic Record* for the soul's journey on earth and other planes. Facilitating soul retrieval* for fragments that are held outside earth time and space, it integrates the full spectrum of soul and spirit.

Afghanite encourages communication of your deepest thoughts and feelings, promoting empathy and intuitive understanding of another person's point of view. Excellent for facilitating group harmony, especially when the group is scattered and needs to focus on its purpose in coming together. Telepathic communication is strengthened so that the group mind operates with one accord.

The crystal oversoul* of this stone wishes to dissolve the war-gene encoded within the human DNA system and it is particularly effective combined with Trigonic Quartz as an essence for dissemination in the waters of the planet. Gridded on a map if necessary, it brings about peace and reconciliation in areas of ethnic conflict or ancient territorial disputes. Afghanite assists in resolving conflicts within your own psyche and teaches that external peace cannot be achieved until inner peace is firmly anchored at the core of your being. Once this is in place, Afghanite assists in radiating peace out to the world.

HEALING Afghanite may be helpful for headaches and migraines that arise from psychic blockages.

POSITION Hold, grid or place as appropriate. Disperse gem essence around the head. Place the essence or stone in water sources.

ADDITIONAL STONE

Lazurite The blue component of Lapis Lazuli and also from Afghanistan, Lazurite has a high vibration that opens metaphysical abilities and expands your awareness. This is a perfect journeying stone for stellar and multi-dimensional exploration and it can take you back to your star home. Ground Lazurite was used as a cosmetic in ancient Egypt to prevent diseases of the eyes.

Lazurite

AGATE: **BLUE HOLLY**

Raw

COLOUR	Blue/violet
APPEARANCE	Prickly, opaque stone with sharp edges
RARITY	Rare
SOURCE	United States

ATTRIBUTES The ethereal blue of Holly Agate stimulates the higher crown chakras*, connecting them with the heart and third eye chakras to increase your intuition and spiritual sight. Opening the alta major chakra, this stone assists in grounding high vibrational energies so that they are applied within the material world.

A mentally calming and clarifying stone, Holly Agate helps you to recognize and release the deeply repressed emotional traumas and blockages that have shredded your psyche in the past. This stone facilitates rapidly completing the soul scouring process that assists you in recognizing the gifts in all your experiences. Use for scarifying the outer layers of the biomagnetic field* to remove karmic* encrustations and outdated ancestral or other implants. Once this has been accomplished, awareness expands to encompass the breadth of your soul.

HEALING Blue Holly Agate reportedly assists headaches, especially those resulting from blocked psychic abilities, and improves or stabilizes brain function in dementia and degenerative conditions. It is reportedly used for jaundice, debilitating conditions and disorders of the heart or liver, and has been suggested as a panacea against typhoid fever.

POSITION Hold or place as appropriate. 'Comb' crystal or disperse gem essence around the outer edges of the aura.

AGATE: WIND FOSSIL

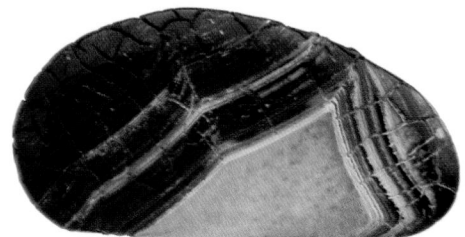

Shaped

COLOUR	Grey-black-brown and white
APPEARANCE	Banded, eroded stone
RARITY	Easily obtained
SOURCE	United States (may be manufactured)

ATTRIBUTES Teaching that you are an eternal incarnated soul* who happens to be on a human journey at this moment in time, Wind Fossil Agate appears to have been laid down in water and then created by currents and the wind carving through layers of Agate, leaving the tougher portion prominently displayed. Carrying the fires of transmutation, it brilliantly assists with the process of soul scouring, clearing away karmic* encrustations, beliefs and emotional baggage that the soul no longer needs on its journey. What remains is what the soul must face up to and resolve before moving on and the resilience and karmic strengths that the soul has built up over lifetimes of experience. But Wind Fossil Agate also contains the power of the Karma of Grace which says that, when sufficient work has been done, the soul can let go and is no longer bound by karma and so can move on.

Helpful in past life regression work, Wind Fossil Agate highlights lessons yet to be learned, gifts that have gone unrecognized, and promises, situations and relationships that have passed their sell-by date and need reframing. Meditating with a Wind Fossil Agate, especially on the past life chakras* behind the ears, reveals the soul contracts, pacts and promises that must be left behind, pointing the way forward. It also highlights the survival skills that have been learned in the past and how to apply them to the present moment to create a bright future in the here and now.

This stone is helpful during traumatic or challenging situations where strength and endurance are needed to overcome situations over which the soul, seemingly, has no control. It offers the confidence needed to quietly wait until the moment for change arrives and the courage to make a move.

HEALING Wind Fossil Agate may be beneficial for bones, teeth, cysts, calluses and encrustations of the skin such as psoriasis. It energetically assists osteoporosis and arthritic conditions and may provide pain relief.

POSITION Hold, place, position or grid as appropriate.

AMETHYST: **AMECHLORITE**

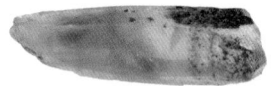

Natural points

COLOUR	Clear, purple and green
APPEARANCE	Clear Quartz point with coloured inclusions
RARITY	Rare
SOURCE	Russia, Brazil

ATTRIBUTES A cleansing combination of Amethyst and Chlorite, Amechlorite is a highly effective detoxifier on many levels. It is particularly useful for gently pulling emotional blockages and mental implants out of the biomagnetic field* and for releasing stress related dis-ease*, infusing healing light into the site to prevent a recurrence. Amechlorite opens a blocked third eye or soma chakra and energetically detoxifies specific organs.

HEALING Amechlorite may be helpful for hormone production, detoxifying and boosting the endocrine, metabolic and immune systems. It energetically purifies the blood and encourages the proliferation of helpful bacteria.

POSITION Grid, place or position as appropriate.

AMETHYST: RED AND CANADIAN RED CAPPED

Red Amethyst

Tumbled Canadian Red Capped

COLOUR	Red-purple
APPEARANCE	Clear to opaque with visible inclusions and phantoms
RARITY	Fairly easily obtained
SOURCE	Canada, Madagascar, India

ATTRIBUTES Carrying ancient wisdom, Red Amethyst unites sky and earth. Highly protective with its Hematite cap it provides grounding for the soul* and anchors the lightbody*. It shields during metaphysical work, assisting journeying*. Powerfully energetic, Red Amethyst captures high frequencies and grounds them in the physical body via the alta major and Earth Star chakras*. Highly protective, it assists during meditation and out-of-body experiences. Red Amethyst amplifies all metaphysical activity, enhancing telepathy and communication with

Auralite 23™

guardian beings. If high vibration crystal or ascension work is physically challenging, Red Amethyst adjusts your physical body to accept expanded awareness. Keeping your feet firmly on the ground, it guards against spiritual egoism or delusions.

A purifier for the aura, Red Amethyst assists insomnia from psychic-overload or electromagnetic pollution. It helps ascertain and release soul causes of addiction and obsession, reframing spiritual connections and karmic* contracts.

HEALING Hematite-rich Red Amethyst may assist the blood and blood rich organs and relieve stress.

POSITION Place over the third eye and soma chakra or grid as appropriate.

ADDITIONAL STONE

Auralite 23™: Mined in Canada and similar to Thunder Bay Amethyst, Auralite 23™ is said to be a powerful synergistic combination of different minerals including titanite, cacoxenite, lepidocrocite, ajoite, hematite, magnetite, pyrite, pyrolusite, gold, silver, platinum, nickel, copper, iron, limonite, sphalerite, covellite, chalcopyrite, gialite, epidote, bornite, rutile, and smoky quartz in amethyst. Balancing all the chakras, Auralite 23™ has a sedative effect on the mind, stilling it so that profound healing and conscious connection with higher dimensions occurs. It deepens meditation and enhances metaphysical abilities of all kinds. This crystal is said to be an extremely potent tool for the New Age, amplifying the effect of all other high vibration crystals and rapidly accelerating spiritual development.

Thunder Bay Amethyst

44

AMETHYST: CRYSTAL CAP

ALSO KNOWN AS SNOW CAP

Raw

COLOUR	Lilac with white topping
APPEARANCE	Amethyst crystal with white drusy crust
RARITY	Rare
SOURCE	Brazil

ATTRIBUTES With extremely high vibrations, Crystal Cap Amethyst is excellent for opening the higher crown chakras* and the alta major and connecting to expanded consciousness. Meditating with it creates a tunnel of light to the highest realms and opens the soma chakra to bring you back to your body when the experience is complete. You retain full awareness of all you see and hear during the journey.

Crystal Cap Amethyst assists in exploring the multitude forms that life encompasses, not just the physical and material reality. It connects you to the immensity of life and consciousness and attunes you to the most profound guidance. Crystal Cap Amethyst takes you into civilizations not as firmly corporeal as our present one. You connect to

45

Lemuria and live beyond the stars in other galaxies and universes, bringing back the wisdom and skills you garnered there. The stone conveys you to the start of our present universe and beyond to experience what went before.

This combination lifts the healing properties of Amethyst to a higher frequency, working mainly from the etheric blueprint* into the physical dimension to heal dis-eases* of the soul and subtle causes of addictions, eating and brain-based disorders. It has a profound effect on the harmony of the brain spheres, encouraging integration of the various parts, and activating neurotransmitters and new neural pathways.

HEALING Crystal Cap Amethyst reputedly reduces swelling and bruising. Energetically, it purifies blood, lymph and blood-rich organs such as the liver and spleen, and reorganizes cellular disorders. Placed under the pillow, it may assist insomnia and, on the back of the neck, cognitive disorders and mental confusion.

POSITION Place or hold as appropriate, especially to the third eye and soma chakra, or disperse gem essence around the aura.

ANDALUSITE

Faceted

Raw

COLOUR	Bluish-white with yellow and orange-brown
APPEARANCE	Translucent to transparent gem-quality crystal
RARITY	Rare in gem-form
SOURCE	Spain, Brazil, Sri Lanka, Austria, Brazil, Germany, Australia, Canada, Russia, Switzerland, Mozambique and United States

ATTRIBUTES Dubbed 'the stone of surrealism', Andalusite may attract bizarre or dreamlike situations in the external world or induce dreams to help you understand the deeper meaning of your life. If you are ready to listen with an open mind, it reveals the wisdom hidden at its core – and teaches how to remain serene and focused even if the experience takes on a nightmarish quality. You need a quirky sense of humour and a strong sense of self to work with Andalusite. This is a crystal to use with due care facilitated by a crystal practitioner who is skilled in receiving and interpreting crystal messages, no matter how black the humour seems or how deep an illusion is being projected.

A form of Chiastolite, gem-quality Andalusite is trichroic, meaning it shows three different colours when viewed from various angles, and polymorphic (a combination of Sillimanite and Kyanite) and so synergizes the qualities of both these crystals. Its colour changes show best when intricately faceted. It helps you to see new perspectives and all possibilities. Used by an experienced practitioner Andalusite assists clients journeying through an inner landscape that reflects their inward state of mind, so that deeply held beliefs and traumas are reframed through the power of the imagination. It stimulates insights in both the giver and receiver of counselling. Andalusite under the pillow activates profoundly revelatory dreams.

During moments of stress or psychological trauma Andalusite slows down the situation so that you have time to assess all that is occurring at the different levels of your being. It allows you to review situations as though in slow motion, catching significant pointers you would otherwise miss and so finding a positive, and peaceful, way through.

HEALING Andalusite provides a quiet calm centre in which the stressed soul can recuperate rather than working physically.

POSITION Grid, hold or position as appropriate. Wear faceted gem. Disperse gem essence around the aura, environment or therapy room.

ANDARA GLASS

*Raw Lavender
Andara Glass*

COLOUR	Rainbow range of colours
APPEARANCE	Clear, glasslike
RARITY	Rare
SOURCE	Northern California (man-made but described as 'volcanic glass' and also claimed to be 'found' in Indonesia and South Africa)

ATTRIBUTES Not a crystal in the true sense of the word, few 'crystals' generate such intense controversy as Andara Glass. Opinions are sharply divided and many claims made. Some people believe it to be the Philosopher's stone, a master cure-all with the highest vibration of any 'crystal' yet found and powerful transformative qualities that stimulate channelling and access universal wisdom through connection with the highest levels of consciousness. To others it is scrap glass from a rubbish heap. It depends on how your personal frequencies resonate or dissonate with the Glass.

Said to contain the prima-materia of the ancient alchemists, a combination of 70 minerals, Andara Glass was apparently found by a Native American shaman on a dump – claimed to be an ancient sacred site – near a vortex point in the High Sierra Mountains. Allegedly Andara Glass is infused with monoatomic elements of gold, silver, iridium, rhodium, chrome and platinum and trace elements of iron, manganese, selenium, cobalt, copper, nickel, titanium and uranium: essential elements for health, well-being and spiritual activation.

A protective stone, Andara Glass guards against electro-magnetic smog and environmental pollution. In those who are attuned to it, it clears negativity, activates and aligns all the chakras and rapidly accelerates spiritual growth. Increasing the flow of energy around the meridians, it strengthens the biomagnetic* field.

Myths have rapidly grown around this Glass. It is postulated to be an ancient healing stone of Atlantis and Lemurian imbued with crystal codes and that considerable knowledge can be obtained about those civilisations. It facilitates a link to Archangel Michael, other archangels and ascended masters. A stone of paradox and contradictions, it should be called the 'make-up-your-own-mind' stone – or 'try-it-and-see' as it is said to overcome doubts. An invaluable aid for assessing how you interact with a crystal rather than believing what you are told by an 'expert', it reminds us that we each have an equally valid opinion and that there is no right or wrong in crystal work, just different experiences according to how our awareness functions. Andara Glass is a useful receptacle for manifestation rituals.

Andara Glass has a central core of tranquillity that deepens meditation and, placed on the back of the neck, acts as an alta major and soma chakra* connector. Past, present and future become one and you move with ease through time and beyond. Each colour carries separate properties. Green is a renewing stone that contains the fountain of youth while lilac or lavender connects to St Germain and Archangel Zadkiel, linking to the violet flame of transmutation and opening metaphysical gifts. Yellow-brown Shaman Andara resonates particularly well with those attuned to Reiki.*

Andara glass is available in many colours

HEALING Andara Glass is reputed to be a master healer restoring health and equilibrium. It works from the subtle bodies and the etheric blueprint* to balance the physical body but may do whatever is asked of it.

POSITION Hold, place or meditate with the stone as appropriate or disperse gem essence around the aura.

ANDESCINE LABRADORITE

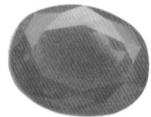

Faceted

COLOUR	Red to honey-red, orange, yellow, champagne and green
APPEARANCE	Iridescent coating
RARITY	Rare
SOURCE	Laboratory enhanced Labradorite

ATTRIBUTES Enhancing with copper brings the naturally high vibrations of Labradorite to an even more refined frequency. Encouraging spiritual visioning and kything*, Andescine Labradorite protects while you journey through multi-dimensions. Gazing into the stone when scrying enables you to access the future and see where your dreams take you. It connects to the Akashic Record* to check out how your soul's purpose is progressing. Facilitating transmission of healing energy to the site of dis-ease*, it assists in letting go of psychosomatic conditions.

HEALING Andescine Labradorite works mainly at the metaphysical level to bring the etheric bodies* into alignment. It may reduce cholesterol.

POSITION Wear, grid or position as appropriate or disperse gem essence around the aura.

ANGELINITE™

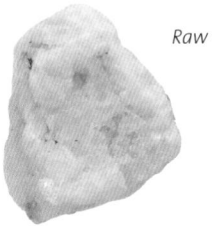

Raw

COLOUR	White
APPEARANCE	Shimmering, opaque crystalline stone
RARITY	Rare
SOURCE	United States

ATTRIBUTES Ethereal Angelinite™ connects to multi-dimensional worlds. Meditate with it on the third eye, soma or higher crown chakras. Quartz and Calcite with trace elements, it expands awareness, activates metaphysical gifts and puts you in touch with guidance from guardian angels and ascended beings. The crystal brings healing from higher dimensions, anchoring it into the light*, subtle* and physical bodies but may need balancing with a grounding stone if you are new to high vibration crystal work.

HEALING Angelinite™ brings healing light into the etheric blueprint* to rebalance and realign the subtle bodies.

POSITION Hold or place as appropriate, particularly over the third eye and soma chakra, or disperse gem essence around the aura.

ANGLESITE

Raw

COLOUR	White
APPEARANCE	Metallic sheen
RARITY	Rare
SOURCE	United States, Mexico

ATTRIBUTES High vibration Anglesite blends your consciousness with that of higher guides and the earth. It facilitates channelling, kything* and communication with other realms, assisting in speaking about such matters with sceptical people. This gentle stone promotes sensitivity and tenderness helping you become more relaxed. It releases blocked or negative energy.

HEALING Anglesite stimulates neural transmitters, energetically treats disorders of the nervous system and is reported to enhance circulation of blood and lymph.

POSITION Wear, hold or position as appropriate or disperse gem essence around the aura.

ANTHOPHYLLITE

Raw

COLOUR	White, brown, yellow, green, blue
APPEARANCE	Lumpy or veined, vitreous to dull or translucent
RARITY	Rare
SOURCE	United States, Canada, Germany, Sweden, Czech Republic

ATTRIBUTES Anthophyllite helps you get to the bottom of things whether it be through the ancestral line, karmic* connections or academic research. Attuned to serendipitous synchronicity and facilitating rapid retrieval of information, it acts as a 'library angel'

55

ferreting out sources seemingly by luck. The right book or website will fall into your hand when Anthophyllite assists in your search. Ask the stone to point you towards what is relevant – and to assist in understanding the deeper meaning of what you find. By taking you to a higher level to recognize the bigger picture, this stone integrates fragments of insight so that all becomes clear.

Anthophyllite facilitates exploring core beliefs* that keep you mired in outdated patterns and old ways of behaving. It helps you to recognize where you 'people please*', whether that be parents, authority figures or significant others. Meditating with this stone shows you the wider picture and assists in releasing that which no longer serves you, putting a more beneficial pattern in place through a Higher Self connection. With the assistance of Anthophyllite you align to your soul's plan and attract the people and experiences needed to play that out with ease.

The stone provides grounding and stamina. It is concerned with the assimilation and digestive processes that extract the nourishment your body and soul requires and excrete that which is no longer needful. It works with the blood-brain barrier, facilitating information retrieval and autonomous physiological processes by correct firing of neurotransmitters.

HEALING Anthophyllite reputedly assists digestive processes and aids breathing. It supports the cerebellum and anecdotal evidence suggests it may reverse degeneration in the brain, assisting Parkinson's, dementia and allied conditions.

POSITION Hold over the abdomen, at the back of neck or grid as appropriate. Disperse gem essence around head. *NOTE: Handle with care, avoid breathing the dust.*

ARFVEDSONITE

*Natural crystal
in matrix*

COLOUR	Black and grey
APPEARANCE	Striated black crystals in gritty grey matrix
RARITY	Medium rare
SOURCE	Canada

ATTRIBUTES Arfvedsonite helps you to see things from both sides and to reconcile difficulties. Opening the crown chakra, it stimulates journeying* and assists energetic downloads. Helpful for transitions of all kinds, this is a stone of birth, death and rebirth. At a mental level, it de-energizes* and restructures habitual patterns.

HEALING Arfvedsonite assists well-being by removing energy blockages in the physical or subtle bodies*.

POSITION Hold, position, grid or place as appropriate.

ARSENOPYRITE

ALSO KNOWN AS DANAITE

Raw

COLOUR	Steel grey to silver white-brown
APPEARANCE	Metallic opaque stone
RARITY	Rare but easily obtained
SOURCE	Portugal, Germany, Czech Republic, U.K., Bolivia, Russia

ATTRIBUTES Arsenopyrite is an Arsenic Sulphide. Under the principle of like heals like, it draws toxicity or blockages out of the body or environment. Useful when you have done all you can to overcome a dis-ease*, especially if underlying fears keep you mired in the situation, it overcomes fear of death. A conductive stone, Arsenopyrite facilitates telepathy and tuning into collective thought.

HEALING Arsenopyrite is reputed to dissolve blood clots and disperse fungal infections.

POSITION Place, position or grid as appropriate. *CAUTION: Wash hands thoroughly after use. Make essence by the indirect method only, do not take internally.*

58

ASTRALINE™

Raw

COLOUR	Grey-white with pale pink or yellow
APPEARANCE	Sparkling, opaque stone
RARITY	Rare
SOURCE	United States

ATTRIBUTES Gentle Astraline™ has very high resonance. A unique combination of Quartz, Muscovite and Crostetepite, it opens and aligns the higher chakras*, connecting them to the soma chakra so that you return safely to your body when journeying*. It heightens metaphysical abilities to link to your Higher Self and journey beyond the stars. This is the perfect stone to explore your stellar origins or to meet beings from other galaxies. Useful for those beginning high vibration crystal and multi-dimensional healing work, it never accelerates the process beyond what you are ready to handle.

Meditating with Astraline™ allows you to objectively recognize imperfections in yourself and all humanity and yet embrace those who are on the human path. Encouraging dynamic unconditional love, it helps to suspend judgement, teaching that we cannot know the soul reasons why someone treads what appears to be a destructive path. It points out that this may be for a purpose beyond our limited understanding while still in incarnation. This stone teaches that our greatest enemy may be a soul teacher in disguise, whom we will one day thank for the part that they played in our spiritual evolution or that of humanity.

Astraline™ opens the throat chakra so that you speak your truth and share your visions with those who empathize. It shows when it is appropriate to speak and cautions when to hold back. It helps you to work in the spaces between the layers of the etheric body*, restoring harmony and equilibrium during energetic changes.

HEALING Astraline™ clears the etheric blueprint* so that effects are felt in the physical body. Anecdotal evidence suggests Astraline™ is beneficial for blood sugar management through revealing past life or soul reasons for a condition. It may assist dis-eases* or distress with a psychosomatic or past life component.

POSITION Hold, place or meditate with Astraline™ as appropriate or disperse gem essence around the aura.

AURICHALCITE

Natural crystal in matrix

COLOUR	Turquoise-blue
APPEARANCE	Drusy crystal on matrix
RARITY	Rare
SOURCE	United States

ATTRIBUTES This gentle stone helps raise the consciousness of humanity and the planet as a whole. Lifting the soul to a higher perspective, it assists in knowing your purpose in incarnating. Meditate with Aurichalcite to facilitate downloads of information and high vibration energy into the physical body. Hold to the back of the neck to activate the alta major chakra.

HEALING Aurichalcite brings body, mind, soul and subtle bodies* into alignment.

POSITION Due to Aurichalcite's fragile nature it is best placed where it can radiate its energy into the environment. *NOTE: Make essence by the indirect method.*

AXINITE

Raw

COLOUR	Brownish-red, violet or brown
APPEARANCE	Flat, wedge-shaped tabular crystal with lustre
RARITY	Rare, may be faceted
SOURCE	Brazil, France, Mexico, California, Russia, Sri Lanka, Tanzania and Pakistan

ATTRIBUTES Opening the Earth Star chakra, Axinite brings out the positive in everyone. It is an extremely helpful stone for personal growth, encouraging you to let go and surrender gracefully to necessary change. Meditating with this stone promotes friendship and harmonizes all your relationships. It deepens intimacy at all levels and enables you to be totally open about who you are at your core being.

HEALING Axinite is reputed to be beneficial for disorders of the adrenal glands, motor function and bone fractures.

POSITION Wear, place, position or disperse gem essence around the aura as appropriate.

AZEZTULITE: **ROSOPHIA**™

Raw

COLOUR	Pink-red, grey
APPEARANCE	Opaque, mottled stone
RARITY	Rare
SOURCE	California and Colorado, United States

ATTRIBUTES Specialist high vibration Azeztulites for the New Age are usually from one location. Each has a slightly different combination of minerals and is given a separate name. Azeztulites have had their vibrations raised by an influx of energy from the Azez, a race of beings who wish to assist the spiritual evolution of the earth. They carry strong bioscalar wave* energy and effect multi-dimensional healing and spiritual attunement.

Rosophia™ grounds spiritual energy as it has a very profound earth connection. It links to Sophia, divine feminine wisdom. The pinkish-red portion is feldspar with inclusions of Quartz and particles of Biotite. Biotite helps you take an objective overview on what is happening in your life and shows how you are creating situations and what will result. Strengthening your rational and analytic thought processes, it helps you discard what is irrelevant and concentrate on the important detail. So, Rosophia™ facilitates assessing what is spiritual truth and what is illusion. Although a gentle stone, Rosophia™ has a powerful intensity when necessary.

All Azeztulites have been imbued with additional spiritual energy and coded information and so are stones of guidance and insight. This one is particularly helpful for strengthening and raising the energies of the lower chakras* so that you feel more comfortable in incarnation and adapt to the energetic changes, maintaining constant equilibrium. It helps you to open the Earth Star and send a shamanic anchor* deep down into the planet to securely ground and protect your body, but it also sets your mind and spirit free to explore infinite possibilities.

Rosophia™ is a pure stone of the heart and opens all the heart chakras. In ancient Egypt, and other cultures, the heart was the home of the soul and of consciousness itself. Placed over the heart seed chakra, Rosophia's energy rapidly travels through the heart and higher heart to open a spiritual connection to All That Is*. When these chakras are united, the soul works from a place of pure love. There is no room for fear, animosity, jealousy or resentment. You live from your heart in love.

At a psychological level, Rosophia™ dissolves self-doubt and a negative self-image. De-energizing old wounds and destructive beliefs, it enables you to love yourself, showing deep compassion for all you have been through on your soul's journey. It also assists you to identify the strengths you developed along the way and apply them to your life now. If you fear the future, wearing this stone helps you be more positive and shift to a spiritual outlook in which you take each day as it comes, living fully in each moment.

Rosophia™ helps to channel the dragon energy* of the earth into more appropriate forms to accommodate raised frequencies. Healing and reconnecting the earth's grid, it de-energizes stuck patterns and revitalizes the earth's subtle etheric body*.

Containing powerful bioscalar waves*, Rosophia™ facilitates self-healing for body and soul as it restores wholeness. Placed under the pillow, it helps to overcome insomnia, ensuring deep sleep and insightful dreams. The Biotite component may be beneficial for disorganized cell patterns.

HEALING Rosophia is excellent for healing the heart and circulatory system. Said to stimulate regeneration in the kidneys, lower intestine, bowel and bladder and restore elasticity to muscle and tendons. Anecdotal evidence suggests it overcomes cellular-disorganization and auto-immune dis-eases*, muscular dystrophy and gout, growths, bile regulation and dis-orders of the eyes.

Himalayan Red Azeztulite

POSITION Place, hold, wear or grid as appropriate. Disperse gem essence around the aura.

ADDITIONAL AZEZTULITES

These stones carry the core essence of Azeztulite but are attuned slightly differently according to their location and mineral content.

Himalayan Gold™ Found in the Himalayas, this golden Azeztulite and the vibrant red accelerate spiritual development and open the third eye and higher crown chakras to download higher vibration energies and assist with assimilation of the lightbody*.

Himalayan Gold™

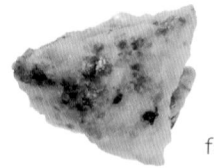

*Sanda Rosa
Azeztulite™*

Sanda Rosa Azeztulite™ An Azeztulite from North Carolina, Sanda Rose combines Quartz with mica and Spessartine Garnet inclusions. An excellent chakra unblocker and higher chakra activator, gentle Sanda Rosa purifies and raises the frequency of the body's entire energy system preparing it for an influx of higher vibration divine light. Facilitating multi-dimensional journeying, Sanda Rose expands awareness and is a useful stone for contacting angelic guidance and for all ascension work as it connects the heart and third eye chakras. Offering multi-dimensional healing to body and soul, Sanda Rosa aligns the subtle bodies with the physical and repatterns the etheric and karmic blueprints. It is used to energetically restore balance to cells. This particular Azeztulite assists children who are already attuned to the new, higher frequencies to be more comfortable in incarnation and helps them to feel the love that their Higher Self has for them.

Rhodozaz™ (Pink Azeztulite) Another heart-centred Azeztulite, this time from the Rocky Mountains, Rhodozaz purifies all the chakras and fills them with light and love. The stone is thought to be a synergistic combination of Quartz and Rhodochrosite, a powerful heart healing stone that is taken to another level by the infusion of Azez light. Rhodozaz links the three heart chakras with the higher crown chakras to bring about divine connection and channel higher guidance to the earth. Perfect to heal feelings of abandonment and rejection and bring inner peace, it assists if you suffer from 'imposter syndrome'* as it shows you your true worth and helps you to have confidence in your abilities.

*Rhodozaz™
(Pink Azeztulite)*

AZEZTULITE WITH MORGANITE

Raw

COLOUR	Pinkish
APPEARANCE	Translucent, opaque crystal
RARITY	Very rare combination
SOURCE	Unconfirmed

ATTRIBUTES This unusual combination brings together the high vibrations of Azeztulite with its bioscalar wave healing capability, and the gentle releasing properties of Morganite with its inbuilt dynamic unconditional love. It is excellent for bringing up the past and releasing repressed feelings that have never before been spoken about. It encourages forgiveness once the memory has been liberated, for yourself and for others. If you feel angry at yourself for allowing something 'bad', sleep with this gentle stone under the pillow to be less judgemental of yourself and find release. Giving you insight into situations of physical and emotional abuse, this stone helps you to forgive the perpetrator, recognizing the pain that may have underlain their own experience.

The combination helps you to connect to and embrace your shadow energies, healing shame and ancient abuse and transmuting the energy to self-love and profound acceptance. It promotes self-esteem and confidence in your own abilities. A powerful heart cleanser and healer, Azeztulite with Morganite clears the emotional body, dissolving blockages and encouraging free expression of feelings.

Gridded in areas of ethnic or environmental conflict, Azeztulite with Morganite assists in resolution and reconciliation and de-energizes* the memory from the earth.

HEALING Azeztulite with Morganite is excellent for healing psychosomatically based sexual difficulties. It assists with the fluid balance in the body and may bring the endocrine and nervous systems into greater harmony.

POSITION Wear, place or grid as appropriate or disperse gem essence around the aura. *NOTE: If the combination stone is not available, use individual stones and ask them to harmonize their action.*

AZOTIC TOPAZ

Faceted

COLOUR	Multi
APPEARANCE	Rainbow kaleidoscope on faceted stone
RARITY	Rare, available as jewellery
SOURCE	Laboratory enhanced clear Topaz from Brazil and other sources

ATTRIBUTES Azotic Topaz is presented as young, fun and highly fashionable, suitable for those with a rebellious mind or who wish to set a trend. With its bright, funky look, Azotic Topaz is decorative and uplifting. Confidence boosting, it feels great to wear and helps you to feel good about yourself and your appearance. Making you stand out from the crowd, it asserts your individuality. It is perfect for the young-at-heart. Wear Azotic Topaz if you want to express your own unique thoughts and beliefs.

The coating is titanium which uplifts the Topaz and it would be a pity if the full potential of this crystal were not recognized. Titanium opens your metaphysical abilities and Topaz promotes clear sight and insight. The combination is powerful. Meditating with Azotic Topaz takes you deep into yourself or into the multi-dimensional worlds. Imparting invisibility and protection, it allows you to safely traverse the shamanic underworld. This crystal rapidly raises your consciousness and yet grounds the experience into everyday reality. Titanium brings anything blocking your soul's plan to the surface and insists that you deal with it. It helps to skilfully negotiate your spiritual pathway. Wearing this stone continually harmonizes your mind and intention.

Anecdotal evidence suggests that titanium can assist with psycho-somatic and psychological conditions such as anorexia and this stone could improve the self image of anyone with body-based issues, helping them to see a truer picture. Used by a qualified therapist, the stone supports exploring the deeper issues behind eating disorders and body dysmorphia and sexual issues such as premature ejaculation, impotence, anorgasmia and infertility. Azotic Topaz facilitates exploring karmic or psychosomatic roots of other dis-eases* and emotional blockages.

HEALING Topaz is traditionally used to impart well-being and good health. Azotic Topaz may enhance cellular memory* and regeneration, strengthen nerves and blood vessels and support oxygen assimilation.

POSITION Grid, place or position as appropriate. Wear over the higher heart chakra*, on a finger or wrist.

BASALT

Raw Basalt

*Shaped
Basalt*

COLOUR	Black to greyish
APPEARANCE	Somewhat shiny, granular rock
RARITY	Found throughout the world
SOURCE	Worldwide

ATTRIBUTES A volcanic rock formed from molten lava, Basalt is strongly magnetic. It has undergone metamorphosis, so aids transformation and provides a solid support during life challenges. Basalt facilitates flowing fluidly while remaining grounded, and brings about realization that the conflicts and traumas we encounter help to polish the soul. Basalt erupts quietly in gentle flows of magma, forming shield-shaped

71

volcanoes, and so is a protective stone. A powerfully magical stone, in ancient Egypt it was associated with the Underworld and restoration of life. Healing statues carved from Basalt transferred their potency to water poured over them. It was drunk or used for bathing.

Basalt is useful for exploring your inner self. Facilitating emotional detachment from what you discover, it imparts strength of mind and stabilizes emotions and mood swings. It helps you to be more resilient under pressure, bounce back from life's challenges and achieve a more positive perspective on your situation. Basalt transmutes anger, particularly that held at a very deep level.

Gridding Basalt in areas of environmental unrest or instability realigns the earth's meridians and provides for free flow of energy, although living on it may impart an air of melancholy to sensitive people. Grounding 'floaty' people, this stone anchors the physical body into the earth and the soul into the physical body. A de-stressor, it works to maintain and realign, where appropriate, the structure of the body giving its motor function muscular strength and cohesion. Use it wherever there is tension in the body as it enables letting go at a profound level. Basalt also helps to bring your energy levels to optimum.

HEALING Basalt may assist muscles, releasing tension, and activates the intestines. It has long been used to ensure fertility of land and body.

POSITION Grid, place or position as appropriate or disperse gem essence around the Earth Star and base chakras. Keep a piece in your pocket during upheaval or energetic change.

BASTNASITE

Raw

COLOUR	Yellow, brown
APPEARANCE	Vitreous to greasy flat translucent crystal
RARITY	Rare
SOURCE	Sweden, Pakistan, Madagascar, France, United States

ATTRIBUTES A high vibration stone, Bastnasite powerfully stimulates the base and sacral chakras, activating your creativity and ability to manifest your dreams and plans. It helps you to recognize what is beneficial for your long term soul growth and to release unrealistic goals or expectations that get in the way of expressing your true self.

This stone facilitates releasing fear of the unknown. It acts as a catalyst for change enabling you to feel and express emotions without being overwhelmed by them and helping you to become less sensitive to the things that have previously caused upset. This stone may assist in stabilizing bi-polar disorder and personality or anxiety disorders, addictions and eating disorders by revealing underlying causes.

73

Bastnasite is beneficial for all dis-eases* that arise out of blockages in the base or sacral chakras*. These dis-eases are typically low level or flare up suddenly, or are toxic and psychosomatic. Placing Bastnasite over the blocked chakra regularly for several weeks cleanses the chakra, opening the way for the dis-ease* to rectify.

HEALING Bastnasite reputedly is beneficial for stiffness in joints, chronic back pain, renal, reproductive or rectal disorders; fluid retention, irritable bowel and constipation or diarrhoea. Supporting detoxification of the lymph or liver, it may assist varicose veins or hernias, glandular disturbances, auto-immune diseases, PMT and muscle cramps, reproductive blockages or diseases such as impotence and infertility. Bastnasite is said to be helpful for allergies, diabetes, urinary infections, liver or intestinal dysfunction.

POSITION Place over the abdomen or disperse as gem essence, especially the base and sacral chakras.

BENITOITE

Raw

COLOUR	Blue, pink, purple, white, clear
APPEARANCE	Transparent or translucent, tabular or pyramidal crystal, sometimes banded
RARITY	Rare
SOURCE	San Benito, California

ATTRIBUTES With extremely high frequency, Benitoite was thought to be a form of Sapphire but microscopy revealed its unique structure. This exceptional stone has concentrations of barium, titanium, fluorine, cesium, niobium, manganese and lithium which have a profound effect on the human organism. Formed in fractures in serpentine rock, Benitoite comes from an area that was once part of the ancient continent of Lemuria. A stone of lightness and joy, it facilitates astral travel and reveals the journey of the soul, helping you to know that you are in the appropriate place at the right time to fulfil your soul's mission. Promoting self-awareness, Benitoite will show you the beauty within yourself and others. It helps you to accept them – or yourself – exactly as they are now.

A psychic activator, Benitoite assists visualization and transmission of thoughts between partners or a spiritual group and has been used to contact extra-terrestrials. Experienced practitioners use it to view the bio-energetic* field and rectify areas of dis-ease*. As with all fluorescent crystals, it shines a light into inner darkness.

Benitoite helps to overcome psychological ennui, sharpening the mind and dissolving emotional blockages that drain energy. It releases anything that makes you feel weighed down. Great for helping you to walk lightly on the earth, it reputedly is particularly helpful for dancers and athletes as it facilitates physical and mental flexibility. Grid Benitoite to absorb negative energies and replace them with joyfulness.

HEALING Benitoite works at the psychosomatic level of healing, assisting in understanding and rectifying the underlying causes of dis-ease or aligning to the soul's purpose in taking on a dis-ease. It reputedly assists veins and blood disorders and to enhance the body's self-healing mechanism.

POSITION Hold or grid as appropriate or disperse gem essence around the aura.

BERYLLONITE

Raw

COLOUR	Colourless, white, yellow, peach
APPEARANCE	Opaque translucent stone
RARITY	Rare
SOURCE	United States, Afghanistan, Finland

ATTRIBUTES Beryllonite helps determine the cause and path of a dis-ease* as it manifests physically within the body. Aiding in intuitively recognizing the treatment required, the stone points to other crystals to assist healing. Beryllonite facilitates seeing the different layers of the biomagnetic sheath* and the auric bodies to determine at which level the healing process needs to commence and where blockages must be released before harmony is restored.

HEALING Beryllonite may assist reproductive functions and reduce PMS or menopausal symptoms.

POSITION Hold, position, place as appropriate or disperse gem essence around the belly.

BIOTITE

Raw

COLOUR	Bronzy-golden brown, black, grey, dark-green
APPEARANCE	Small metallic mica-flakes
RARITY	Common as a component of rock but rare as a healing stone
SOURCE	United States and worldwide

ATTRIBUTES Biotite offers an objective overview on what is happening in your life and shows how you create situations and your future. Strengthening rational and analytic thought processes, it helps discard what is irrelevant and concentrate only on the important. In particular Biotite shows you the impact you are having on the environment. Ferrous Biotite is slightly radioactive and may assist in bringing cell processes back into balance.

HEALING Biotite is said to assist restructuring disorganized cell patterns. It is traditionally used to heal eyes and growths and to regulate bile.

POSITION: Place, position or grid as appropriate.

BISMUTH

*Laboratory grown
Bismuth*

COLOUR	Metallic, rainbow-like tarnish. Natural: pinkish silver-white
APPEARANCE	Square or pyramidal metal shapes piled on each other or opaque crystalline stone
RARITY	Easily available
SOURCE	Natural: Russia, Germany and elsewhere (Also laboratory grown or amended crystal)

ATTRIBUTES Most often found in its geometric laboratory-grown form, Bismuth is having a renaissance as it settles in the new high-energy vibrations, and helps the adjustment to higher frequencies. Activating the crown and higher crown chakras, it sends kundalini* energy back down through the body to energize the base and earth star chakras. Use Bismuth if you need to move easily between the physical plane and

Bismuth
(natural)

the spiritual realms. It strengthens your connection to universal energies, drawing these down into the base and sacral chakras to create a clearer, more cohesive energetic field and help you to connect to All That Is*. Bismuth facilitates changing complex thought patterns that have become obsolete so that a more constructive pattern is imprinted. It assists with cells that need to be raised in frequency to accommodate new energies. As is suggested by its interlinked shapes, laboratory-grown Bismuth is excellent for ensuring group cohesiveness. It assists people who are isolated or who have become institutionalized to move into a caring, accepting community.

HEALING Bismuth is traditionally used for stomach and intestinal disorders. It energetically strengthens muscles and reduces fevers. Bismuth overcomes extreme exhaustion and helps to find new ways of healing chronic conditions such as M.E.

POSITION Grid, hold or place as appropriate or disperse gem essence around the aura.

BLUE EUCLASE

Raw

COLOUR	Blue
APPEARANCE	Transparent, veined crystal
RARITY	Rare
SOURCE	Zimbabwe, Columbia, Russia, Brazil

ATTRIBUTES Blue Euclase is perfect for a potent medicine pouch. This journeying stone takes you deep into the recesses of your own psyche, the shamanic underworld or the furthest reaches of creation. It assists in soul retrieval*, forgiveness and reconciliation. Enhancing metaphysical abilities, Blue Euclase facilitates deep meditational states by harmonizing brain waves and opening the subtle endocrine system. It helps you to speak only truth and brings clarity to your mind and your intentions.

Grid Blue Euclase to bring deep peace into your home or your neighbourhood. It draws together like-minded people to create a spiritually-orientated, co-operative community whose members look out for each other and whose fundamental motivation is that of sharing. Blue Euclase is known as the Stone of Happiness and it instils deep peace and inner clarity, a quiet calm centredness that easily copes with change or trauma. This stone promotes a love of truth. Physically, it realigns energy fields and harmonizes new vibrations, reducing tension in the physical body. It is helpful if you tend to fall back into old patterns as it gently restrains you from endlessly repeating lessons or situations. It helps you to value your own achievements and true worth.

Blue Euclase facilitates female rites of passage such as puberty, pregnancy or menopause. This stone encourages serendipitous synchronicity. Life flows, bringing to you with ease and grace all you need. Blue Euclase helps to joyfully recognize that abundance does not mean having more, it is sufficient that there is enough. Helping you to reconnect to and read the Akashic Record*, this gentle stone helps you to show gratitude for the riches garnered by your soul.

HEALING Iron-rich Blue Euclase is a useful pain reliever taking the source of dis-ease* out of the subtle bodies* so that the physical body lets go. It assists arthritis, spasm and muscle tension or cramp. It is considered anti-bacterial and antiseptic and to reduce swelling and inflammation or constriction of blood vessels. Traditionally used to treat the reproductive organs and dis-eases such as endometriosis and infertility, it may assist speech disorders. Place over minor cuts or bruises.

POSITION Hold or grid as appropriate or disperse gem essence around the aura.

BOLI STONE

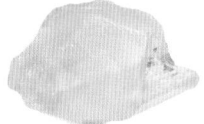

Raw

COLOUR	White, grey, brownish
APPEARANCE	Rounded, glassy crystals
RARITY	Rare
SOURCE	Rubal Khali Desert, Saudi Arabia

ATTRIBUTES Boli Stone assists a shift for earth into unity consciousness encouraging co-operation between all humankind, each part being equally valuable. An emotional teacher that digs deep into your subconscious mind to release anything outdated or outgrown, Boli Stone highlights soul contracts and promises that no longer serve. Raising you above emotional turmoil to gain an insight into why and how it came about, Boli Stone shows the part it played in your soul evolution, or lack of it. With Boli Stone's assistance, you move on.

HEALING Boli Stone works best at the spiritual and psychosomatic levels of healing.

POSITION Place, grid or position as appropriate or disperse gem essence around the aura.

BROCHANTITE

Natural crystal in matrix

COLOUR	Green
APPEARANCE	Long translucent crystals on matrix
RARITY	Rare
SOURCE	Namibia, Peru, Slovakia, United States

ATTRIBUTES Brochantite is copper-based and is a powerful purifier and realigner of the chakras and the energetic bodies. It is effective in chakra lay-outs, providing an interface* at the outer edge of the etheric body* at which healer and client can meet without the healer taking on the condition but retaining insight into its cause and manifestation.

HEALING Brochantite is reputedly helpful for arthritis and swelling of the joints. It may assist the release of fluid retention and remove free-radicals from the bloodstream and muscles and strengthen the blood-brain barrier. It energetically supports the spleen, pancreas and prostate.

POSITION Place over the site, wear or grid as appropriate. Disperse gem essence around the body. *NOTE: Make gem essence by the indirect method.*

BROOKITE

Raw

COLOUR	Black, light to dark brown, yellow-brown, white to grey
APPEARANCE	Translucent or transparent crystal
RARITY	Rare
SOURCE	Russia, Switzerland, United States, Italy

ATTRIBUTES Brookite packs a powerful energetic punch, activating the higher chakras. It contacts lost civilizations, universal knowledge, higher beings, multi-dimensional layers of reality and the Akashic Record*. Helpful if you seek a new direction or are stuck in an intractable situation, Brookite imparts courage to move forward without fear even if not knowing where you are heading. It energizes the environment or other crystals.

HEALING Brookite assists recovery after surgery, strengthening the chakras, biomagnetic* field and major organs. Said to assist the liver, kidneys, heart, bones, teeth and circulation and to dispel apathy and lethargy, it reverses debilitating conditions and infertility.

POSITION Place, grid or hold as appropriate or disperse gem essence around the aura.

BRUCITE

Raw

COLOUR	Blue, grey, white, yellow, brown
APPEARANCE	Opaque, fine grained stone
RARITY	Fairly easily obtained as mineral specimen
SOURCE	United States, Canada, Italy, Russia, Sweden

ATTRIBUTES Brucite helps deal with people who fluctuate or vacillate. It assists in breaking away from what is outgrown. Giving the mental flexibility to follow the twists of intuitive thought processes, it leads to 'aha moments' of great insight. It may stabilize multiple personality disorders, focusing on one personality at a time and exploring its roots or balancing out bi-polar highs and lows. This gentle stone unites a soul group* and assures cohesion of purpose. Brucite brings light to the environment.

HEALING Brucite is reputed to clear furred arteries and to overcome excess alkalinity in the body.

POSITION Hold, place or grid as appropriate or disperse gem essence around the aura.

CALCITE: **ALABASTER**

Raw

COLOUR	Creamy to pinkish white
APPEARANCE	Veined opaque, sparkling stone
RARITY	Easily obtained
SOURCE	Egypt, Europe, UK

ATTRIBUTES Alabaster connects the known with the unknown, the seen with the unseen, acting as a bridge to the future or alternative realities. It helps you journey through multi-dimensions and time-frames. The Egyptians crafted statutes and lined shrines with this sparkling material which they believed served as a bridge to the stars and the gods. Alabaster diminishes the internal anger and emotional blockages which underlie disease, particularly those of the heart and arteries.

HEALING Alabaster reportly helps with circulatory system disorders.

POSITION Place, grid or disperse gem essence as appropriate.

87

CALCITE: AJO BLUE

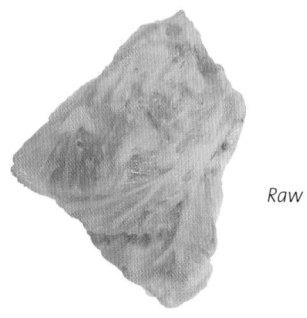

Raw

COLOUR	Blue-green
APPEARANCE	Translucent crystal
RARITY	Rare
SOURCE	United States

ATTRIBUTES Discovered in the Arizona desert near an Ajoite source, this gentle stone carries the same loving energetic resonance as that exceedingly high vibration stone. As Ajo Blue's base is gentle Calcite, it carries a nurturing energy that opens the heart chakras and connects you to All That Is* and the archangelic realms. This beautiful stone effects intercellular and multi-dimensional healing.

Placed over the solar plexus it dissolves old hurt and sorrow from any lifetime or dimension, releasing emotional blockages and traumas that have been hidden from view. Once these are acknowledged and de-energized* you feel deep love for yourself and everyone around you.

Lifting the spirits during depression, it is helpful for anyone who feels trapped on the earth-plane and who longs to return home to the celestial or star realms. It provides comfort and deep spiritual support, at the same time showing you why you are here and the part you are to play in the expansion of consciousness.

In a healing layout, Ajo Blue rebalances the entire energy field, bringing all the subtle bodies* into alignment so that multi-dimensional intercellular healing occurs. It repatterns emotional or spiritual beliefs that no longer serve and replaces them with emotional and spiritual equilibrium.

HEALING Ajo Blue works mainly beyond the physical, recalibrating the energy bodies to restore health and well-being. However, it may assist with backache and headaches that have a psychic cause.

POSITION Grid, position or disperse gem essence around the aura.

CALCITE: WITH AMETHYST AND GEOTHITE

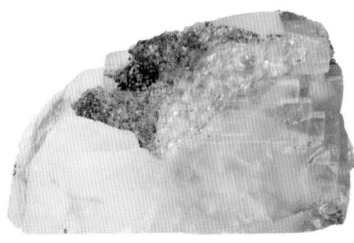

Amethyst and Geothite on Raw Calcite

COLOUR	White with purple and black
APPEARANCE	Translucent waxy crystal with drusy coating
RARITY	Unusual combination
SOURCE	Unconfirmed

ATTRIBUTES This gentle, nurturing combination has a soothing effect on the soul, emotions and mind. Drawing off angst and disharmony, it cloaks the aura in a protective coating within which you simply be. An excellent de-stressor, it absorbs negativity at any level and fills the space with loving energy. A companion through life changes that require skilful negotiation of your soul's path, you recognize the reasons why situations arise and underlying patterns to be de-energized*.

HEALING This combination is a de-stressor and etheric* cleanser.

POSITION Place where the stone can radiate its energy into the environment.

CALCITE: **ANGELS WING**

Raw

COLOUR	White or honey-yellow
APPEARANCE	Luminous, stacked layers of translucent crystal
RARITY	Rare
SOURCE	Mexico

ATTRIBUTES High vibration Angels Wing stimulates the soul star, stellar gateway and other higher crown chakras, bringing in spiritual light. It opens psychic abilities. Facilitates angelic contact and receiving guidance from the highest of levels. Harmonizes the brain hemispheres. Assisting in being comfortable in incarnation, it integrates the lightbody* and grounds higher dimensional energies in the physical plane.

HEALING Angels Wing Calcite works mainly beyond the physical to harmonize the etheric body* but anecdotal evidence suggests that it assists with psychosomatic dis-eases* and underlying causes of diabetes and conditions such as multiple sclerosis.

POSITION Hold, place, or meditate or disperse gem essence (make by indirect method).

CALCITE: ISIS

ALSO KNOWN AS BOJI STONE

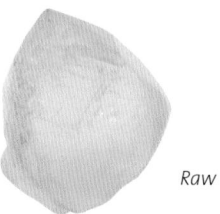

Raw

COLOUR	Clear to creamy white
APPEARANCE	Translucent, waxy crystal
RARITY	Rare
SOURCE	Saharan Africa

ATTRIBUTES Isis Calcite is attuned to the divine feminine and draws that energy to earth to bring light into the core. An excellent stone for goddess work, enhancing rituals and journeying*, receptive Isis Calcite awakens the third eye and soma chakras and facilitates intuitive vision on the inner or outer planes. Gently releasing emotional trauma trapped in the subtle* or causal bodies, it replaces it with healing light and compassionate love for yourself and others.

HEALING Working beyond the physical level, Isis Calcite heals the psychosomatic and karmic* causes of dis-ease*.

POSITION Hold as appropriate or disperse gem essence around the aura. Place on an altar to invite in the divine feminine or archangels.

CALCITE: **LEMURIAN AQUATINE**™

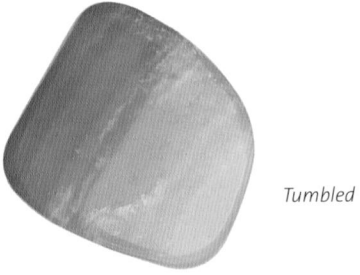

Tumbled

COLOUR	Blue, blue-green
APPEARANCE	Translucent, slightly waxy crystal
RARITY	Rare
SOURCE	Argentina

ATTRIBUTES Lemurian Aquitane Calcite™ ushers in a New Age and allows you to explore previous ages as it has a powerful connection with Lemuria and other ancient civilisations. It assists past life recall, reading the Akashic Record* of your soul's journey to expand awareness of just how vast that soul is and the breadth of its experience. Lemurian Aquatine Calcite™ has a strong resonance with water and with the creatures that inhabit the oceans of our planet, assisting telepathic communication with these beings.

A crystal of infinite love, Lemurian Aquatine Calcite™ promotes empathy and intuition on all levels. It opens the higher crown chakras* to facilitate communication with multi-dimensional higher beings and creates an energetic interface* through which information passes. This gentle crystal deeply nurtures the emotional and etheric bodies*. Encouraging 'dancing with the flow of life', Lemurian Aquatine Calcite™ assists in skilfully negotiating blockages in your path. Facilitating letting go of rigid control and fear for the future, it eases chronic anxiety, alleviates stress and worry ushering in core tranquillity and trust in the process. The crystal teaches you to look inside yourself to find the vulnerabilities that leave you open to psychic attack and ill-wishing. It assists in recognizing where you sabotage and attack yourself, revealing your inner enemy and how you project that onto the external world. Your apparent enemy may be your greatest soul ally who is helping you to complete lessons, unfinished business or soul imperatives* from the past. The crystal shows where it is appropriate to let these go and move on.

This crystal helps restructure emotionally-based programs held in the subconscious mind or the etheric blueprint* so that the soul no longer carries destructive constructs. It dissolves entity or ancestral attachments or imperatives, cords, implants, openness to energy vampirism and so on. The reprogramming goes way back into the soul's history to heal the original source so that there is no longer a subtle energy structure through which dis-ease* invades in the present life.

Lemurian Aquatine Calcite™ combines well with Satayaloka™ Quartz to bring light and insight into situations that have a soul-based, previously hidden, agenda. It takes you to a higher dimension for an overview of the situation and how it may be resolved.

HEALING Lemurian Aquatine Calcite™ works best at the subtle level of healing, bringing the etheric blueprint* into equilibrium and effecting multi-dimensional and intercellular healing for the biomagnetic* and physical bodies.

POSITION Hold, place or grid as appropriate or disperse gem essence around the aura. Hold to the soma or past life chakras during meditation.

ADDITIONAL STONE
Orchid Calcite helps you look forward with optimism, teaching how to manifest exactly what you need. Holding a positive vision of the future, it is the perfect antidote to premonitions of global destruction. If you glance longingly back to the past, it releases you to move forward confidently, gently dissolving fears and supporting your journey. It ensures sound sleep, calming anxiety and thought. Helping you settle comfortably into incarnation, it grounds you but teaches how to walk lightly on the earth. Orchid Calcite may assist vitamin and mineral assimilation and absorption of nutrients.

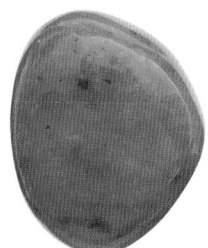

Tumbled
Orchid Calcite

CALCITE: **MERKABITE**™

Raw Merkabite Calcite

COLOUR	Brilliant white
APPEARANCE	Translucent, luminous milky crystal
RARITY	Rare, one location only
SOURCE	Kansas, United States

ATTRIBUTES An ascension stone, delicate Merkabite Calcite™ has an exceedingly high, angelic vibration that expands consciousness into an ever widening field, encompassing inner and outer multi-dimensions and all timeframes. Merkabite creates a ladder to the Higher Self upon which the soul ascends in awareness. It was given the name Merkabite to remind us that we have a rainbow body of light represented by the merkaba, a multi-dimensional Star of David. Transcending the limitations of the physical world, it assists in remaining grounded and operating efficiently in our current reality as it links higher dimensions with the earth-plane. Described as an elevator to higher consciousness, placed on the third eye it connects the soma, crown, soul star, stellar gateway chakras* and beyond so that spiritual knowledge is brought to earth and anchored in the lightbody*.

If you want to know your soul's purpose, meditating with Merkabite Calcite™ enables you to read the Akashic Records* for your current and future lifetimes. It connects you to the guides and higher beings that are assisting your soul evolution. If you have difficulty staying in the present moment, wear Merkabite to keep you anchored in the eternal now no matter which dimension you occupy.

Merkabite instils mental clarity and removes the confusion that often accompanies a change of energetic frequency. It stimulates the right brain, heightening intuition and helping you to successfully navigate your world.

HEALING Merkabite works mainly beyond the physical to create harmony in the etheric bodies* and the soul. However, holding it during healing sessions strengthens receptivity to healing energy and other crystals.

POSITION Hold, place or grid as appropriate or disperse gem essence around the aura.

CALCITE: **PHANTOM**

ALSO KNOWN AS PYRITE IN CALCITE

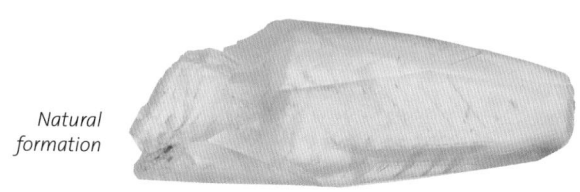

Natural formation

COLOUR	White
APPEARANCE	Pyramidal or feathery lines in clear/translucent stone
RARITY	Rare
SOURCE	United States

ATTRIBUTES Pyrite in Calcite forms a 'ladder to heaven'. Activating higher chakras*, it creates metaphysical gates to protect during higher dimensional travel. It takes you into expanded awareness to explore the wider reality of consciousness and ground the insights. Excellent for those beginning high dimensional work, it never proceeds too rapidly and activates the soma chakra to bring you back into everyday reality. On the back of the neck, it assists memory and mental reprogramming.

HEALING Phantom Calcite reputedly assists brain function, the nervous system and neurotransmitters, realigning to the lightbody*. May encourage mineral absorption and support joints, muscles and skeleton.

POSITION Place, or disperse gem essence particularly above the head to open the higher chakras.

CAROLITE

Raw Carolite in matrix

COLOUR	Light to steel grey
APPEARANCE	Opaque, metallic-looking stone, may be tarnished
RARITY	Rare
SOURCE	Congo, Zaire, United States

ATTRIBUTES Teaching that love overcomes fear, Carolite gently dissolves deeply ingrained negative beliefs and past life causes that underlie phobias and shows how you create your own reality. It offers a positive take on life and helps shape your future, enhancing your ability to manifest exactly what you need for your spiritual and personal growth.

HEALING Carolite works beyond the physical to remove the psychosomatic causes of dis-ease*.

POSITION Place, grid or disperse gem essence as appropriate.

CATLINITE

ALSO KNOWN AS PIPESTONE

Raw slab

COLOUR	Reddish-pink
APPEARANCE	Dense, clay-like stone
RARITY	Rare, one source
SOURCE	Minnesota, United States

ATTRIBUTES Catlinite or Pipestone has been sacred to Native Americans for thousands of years and as such must be treated with due deference and respect. It is what ceremonial 'peace pipes' and other talismans are created from and is highly protective. A potent mix of diaspore, pyrophyllite, muscovite and hematite, it is the perfect stone for healing and reconciliation ceremonies. Always ask permission before using this stone and, where possible, seek instruction in its use from a Nation member. However, you don't actually need to have a piece of Catlinite to access its properties. Simply tuning into the stone at an energetic level, especially if you psychically journey to the quarry to connect to 'your' stone, allows you to work with its energy.

Catlinite is laid down in plates. Plate-like crystals are helpful for working on several levels at once as they spread their energy out in layers. Catlinite assists in getting to the bottom of things. The white flecks in the clay symbolize the vast infinite night sky and the stone plays an important role in North American cosmology.

Catlinite promotes a profound connection with All That Is*, or Great Spirit, and unites the physical with the spirit world. It grounds prayers and rituals into the everyday world showing that everything is sacred and cannot be set apart. It is perfect for medicine wheel ceremonies and has traditionally been used to contact spirits and ancestors. Use this stone to reconnect to the wisdom of the Native American Indian past and its deep interconnection with nature and the presence of the divine in the everyday. Or, use the stone to connect to your own ancestral line and communicate with the spirit world.

The stone has an incredible ability to bring everything into the now. There is a holistic vibration with this stone, it wants to reconnect us to

Pipestone in situ at Pipestone Quarry

the 'universal self'. To help us see that the universe isn't an external mechanism working around us but instead is an integral part of our inner construct and consciousness and exists in every cell in our being.

In many respects, Catlinite brings you far more than you anticipate and strengthens the manifestation process. It is an excellent stone to mediate with if you wish to create your own deep inner peace, a stillness that cannot be ruffled by outside influences. When you have a calm centre, you radiate that peace out to the world. Place Catlinite over your base chakra to root and ground yourself on the earth so that you walk lightly upon it, honouring its sacredness. Grid Pipestone to bring peace to areas of discord or environmental damage. It draws from the physical body any past life dis-ease* and induces a deep sense of peace and ease.

Catlinite has been used in past life healing, particularly for dealing with guilt around genocide and mistreatment of people or animals in the past, and for the sadness and resentment of those who were the victims of abuse or racism, or who perpetrated such abuse. With its power to promote forgiveness and bring inner peace, it is a useful stone to assuage past life guilt, shame or anger. Placing it over the Earth Star chakra during such healings absorbs the negative feelings and de-energizes them, sending dynamic unconditional love into Mother Earth and to the incarnated soul. Grid it to bring about healing for an environment in which such things took place.

HEALING Catlinite brings about profound healing by creating inner peace. Traditionally said to be a healer for the lungs and to carry the healing power of the Great Spirit, so helping every ailment or dis-ease.

POSITION Place over the base or earth star chakras or grid as appropriate. Disperse gem essence in a room or environment.

CELESTOBARITE
ENFOLDED IN CALCITE

Raw chunk

COLOUR	Orange, grey and white enfolded in white
APPEARANCE	Banded, opaque stone
RARITY	Rare
SOURCE	UK

ATTRIBUTES This rare combination has emerged from the quarry that is a source of English Celestobarite. It may make itself known in other Celestobarite deposits as it carries deep peace and the core stability to ride out vibrational changes and stabilize the earth. The combination represents the multi-dimensional layers of our being. This is a stone that has been through enormous pressures. The Celestobarite layer was thrust up and folded in on itself, and peaceful, purifying Calcite was then laid down around it to calm and heal the transformation. The combination facilitates rapid spiritual expansion. If you are seeking your own transformation, meditate or sleep with this combination under your pillow.

Celestobarite cuts through blockages and takes you to the edge and beyond. With strong shielding energy, this excellent journeying* stone creates shamanic and cosmic anchors* holding you between the core of the planet and the centre of the galaxy. It shows you both sides of an issue, elucidating what is not clear but leaving you to decide what to believe or put into practice. Reminding you that nothing stays the same, it teaches how to laugh at yourself and the absurdities of the human condition. If you feel as though an answer or insight is just out of your grasp, holding Celestobarite brings the answer to the surface.

A powerful purifier of energy, Calcite stimulates higher awareness and opens metaphysical abilities. This powerful combination helps your psychic abilities take off, facilitating journeys deep into yourself or into the furthest reaches of the galaxy and beyond to seek wisdom and a way forward for humanity. The Calcite component offers you the discernment to distinguish true wisdom from wishful thinking or deliberate deception.

HEALING Celestobarite in Calcite brings about multi-dimensional healing beyond the physical but assists in being more integrated in the physical body. It encourages energetic elimination of toxins and helps to reorganize neural pathways.

POSITION Hold, grid or place as appropriate or disperse gem essence around the aura.

CERVANITE

Raw

COLOUR	Bluish
APPEARANCE	Flaky and brittle
RARITY	Rare
SOURCE	Unconfirmed

ATTRIBUTES This toxic stone contains antimony as a product of decomposition. However, it can fill the environment with spiritual vibes, lifting depression and dark moods both personal and in the greater whole. Program it to bring joy into your life and work but handle with care.

HEALING Should only be used under the direction of a qualified healer.

POSITION Grid or position with care. *CAUTION: Toxic, contains antimony. Handle with care and wash hands after use. Make gem essence by the indirect method and do not take internally.*

CHALCANTHITE

Raw

COLOUR	Brilliant deep blue
APPEARANCE	Fibrous mass or botryoidal crust on matrix
RARITY	Rare
SOURCE	United States, Chile, Spain, Portugal, Poland, Namibia (may be laboratory grown)

ATTRIBUTES Created through oxidation of copper sulphate, Chalcanthite is water soluble. It stimulates psychic attunement and insight, enhancing clairvoyance and intuitive assessment of people or situations and opens the throat chakra*, aiding communication. This stone assists with making choices that lead to fulfilment of personal desires and goals. Releasing feelings of abandonment or constriction, if you've been held back it de-energizes* the pattern so you move forward without restraint.

HEALING Chalcanthite may be beneficial for arthritis, blocked arteries and fluid retention. It may assist disorders of the reproductive system and act as an anti-oxidant.

POSITION Grid, hold, place as appropriate. Disperse essence around the aura. *NOTE: Make essence by the indirect method.*

COMBINATION STONE
Chalcanthite with Coquimbite Lilac-purple Coquimbite contains the violet flame of transformation and carries the energy of Archangel Zadkiel. Transmuting negative energy, it raises vibrations to an extremely high level and assists lightbody* integration. It prepares the nervous system and neurotransmitters to receive high vibrational energy downloads. Coquimbite with Chalcanthite enables you to purify your spiritual self and to transform your psychic vision so that you access multi-dimensional levels while remaining grounded.

Raw

CHALCEDONY AND APOPHYLLITE

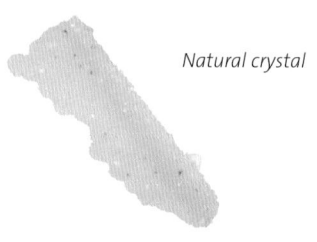

Natural crystal

COLOUR	White
APPEARANCE	Drusy points
RARITY	Rare
SOURCE	Unconfirmed

ATTRIBUTES This beautiful combination stone lifts spiritual vision to a very high level, accessing multi-dimensions and numerous timeframes. Opening the third eye and the higher crown chakras*, Chalcedony and Apophyllite channels guidance and insight from higher guides, linking into All That Is*. If you need metaphysical stimulation, this is the combination for you.

HEALING Chalcedony and Apophyllite works mainly beyond the physical to heal the etheric blueprint* but can clear headaches and migraines caused by psychic blockages.

POSITION Hold, place or grid as appropriate. Disperse gem essence into the aura or the environment.

CHALK

Raw

COLOUR	White
APPEARANCE	Powdery stone
RARITY	Easily obtained
SOURCE	UK, Northern Europe

ATTRIBUTES Chalk has a coherent information field that connects to the far past. Many sacred sites are on chalk because of its receptivity to spiritual energies and the fluidity it imparts to metaphysical working. Combines with Preseli Bluestone to create a battery that powers the environment, overcoming energetic depletion. It supports during changes, aiding your survival instincts. Highly absorbent, it draws off toxicity, cleansing the aura and releasing fluid from the physical body.

HEALING Containing a high degree of calcium, Chalk reputedly energetically assists with the skeletal system and to detoxify the organs of elimination. Chalk facilitates earth healing*.

POSITION Grid with Bluestone to create an environmental battery, hold or position as appropriate.

CHROME DIOPSIDE

Raw

COLOUR	Intense green
APPEARANCE	Faceted stone or translucent crystalline mass
RARITY	Rare
SOURCE	Russia

ATTRIBUTES A stone of intense energy transmission, Chrome Diopside revitalizes the chakras and physical body and heals disorders of the mind and psyche. A clearing stone, it instils deep peace and tranquillity, balancing and healing subtle bodies* and the soul. Believed to have fallen from the Tree of Life, Green Diopside was buried with the dead to ensure renewal. It connects your heart to that of Mother Earth, teaching how to care for our planet and all upon it. Helping you to remember forgotten knowledge, it reconnects to the healing energies of the plant and animal kingdom.

HEALING Chrome Diopside is reputed to overcome physical weakness and muscular spasms during physical exertion. The trace element chromium supports normal glucose metabolism and breakdown of fats and proteins. This stone may assist in maintaining a correct blood sugar balance.

POSITION Grid, place or position as appropriate. Place on the forehead to ensure sweet dreams, over the pancreas to stimulate insulin utilization or disperse gem essence around the aura.

ADDITIONAL STONE

Enstatite and Diopside A stone of great determination and decisiveness, iron-based Enstatite encourages a spirit of competition and imparts courage to succeed. Upholding fairness and justice, this combination creates a deeply compassionate nature. Aligning the personal will to the Higher Self, it encourages you to be of service to the planet. Enstatite and Diopside assists when you need to be frank and direct yet tactful. The combination cleanses and activates the base chakra and links it to the sacral chakra activating creativity, which it moves to the throat to be expressed and the crown to be put into action. This lively stone lifts a depressed mood and re-energizes body and mind. It helps you to release grief and put down your burdens, taking up joy instead.

Assisting with the normal cycles of decay and new growth within the body essential for homeostasis, it supports cellular memory* and overcomes physical weakness. Rebalancing the nervous system when the chakras have been raised to a new vibration, it supports recovery from surgery or serious illness. Enstatite with Diopside works mainly beyond the physical to bring energetic balance to the body. It supports iron assimilation and utilization and may bring an alkaline body to a more acidic condition.

Enstatite and Diopside

111

CHRYSOTILE IN SERPENTINE

ALSO KNOWN AS STONE OF LIFE

Tumbled

COLOUR	Black in white, grey or green
APPEARANCE	Bi-coloured opaque layered stone
RARITY	Easily available
SOURCE	Unconfirmed

ATTRIBUTES Carrying great strength and power, Chrysotile in Serpentine clears the debris of the past and emotional baggage carried in the energetic bodies so that the core self is accessed. Facilitating telepathy and psychometry, it programs a more positive approach to life. Use to facilitate shamanic journeying to ascertain the past life and emotional causes of dis-ease* or soul blockages. It clears entities*, attachments or cords that no longer serve from the aura, chakras, etheric* or physical bodies. This stone helps you to be in touch with your true self and align with your destiny. If you are being manipulated or controlled by others, or are doing this to others, it helps to release and let be. The stone opens your mind to infinite possibilities.

112

HEALING This energizing combination reputedly assists those who suffer from chronic fatigue or multiple sclerosis. Said to heal throat conditions, emphysema and inflammation of the skin, it strengthens the energetic meridians* of the body, supports the parathyroid and brain stem, and may rectify arterial and vein disorders and balance blood sugar.

POSITION Place, grid or position as appropriate or disperse gem essence around the aura. *CAUTION: Use tumbled. If making a gem essence use the indirect method as the stone contains asbestos. Wash hands after use.*

CLINOHUMITE

*Clinohumite
(tabular crystal)
and Chromite
in Calcite*

COLOUR	Orange, yellow, brown
APPEARANCE	Clear and bright when faceted
RARITY	Very rare gemstone
SOURCE	Tajikistan, Siberia, Tanzania, Italy, Cyprus, Pakistan

ATTRIBUTES Clinohumite was discovered in 1876 in limestone blocks that had erupted from Mount Vesuvius in Italy. It is one of the rarest gemstones in the world but new deposits have recently opened up. Clinohumite is a powerful activator for the sacral and solar plexus chakras*, stimulating creativity and removing emotional blockages. It links these chakras to the base, alleviating depression and instilling energy. Especially in its sunny yellow and orange form, Clinohumite is a stone of happiness that brings joy into your life. If you need an extra boost in the morning, place it over the solar plexus to awaken and revitalize your whole body.

HEALING Clinohumite reputedly increases the blood flow through the circulatory system.

POSITION Wear, hold or grid as appropriate. Disperse the gem essence around your aura.

ADDITIONAL STONE
Clinohumite and Chromite in Calcite This unusual combination from Pakistan combines sunny Clinohumite (brown inclusions) and powerful Chromite (black iron-based inclusions), within the pure energies of clear Calcite. Excellent for boosting your vitality and keeping depression at bay, it imparts strength, gentleness and optimism and is particularly useful for those who feel overwhelmed by life circumstances and loss of hope. Helping you to stay serene in the midst of turmoil, it assists in moving forward when you encounter setbacks. Keep one in your pocket and handle it often.

COPROLITE

ALSO KNOWN AS DINOSAUR POO

Polished

COLOUR	Grey, black, brown, blue
APPEARANCE	Mottled opaque stone
RARITY	Easily obtained, especially in polished form
SOURCE	UK, United States

ATTRIBUTES As may be expected from something so old, Coprolite, which is the fossilized remains of Dinosaur excrement, enhances memory and facilitates past life regression. It is particularly useful for getting to the bottom of survival issues and for finding the courage to continue what may prove to be a difficult journey through life. Mentally, it strengthens intelligence and increases intellectual stability, assisting with the assimilation of new information.

Enhancing mental flexibility and dexterity of thought processes, Coprolite opens the mind to new ideas.

HEALING Coprolite may assist the skeletal and digestive systems, stimulating the assimilation of nutrients and elimination of toxins.

POSITION Grid, place or position as appropriate.

ADDITIONAL STONE

Dinosaur Bone Fossilized Dinosaur Bone increases physical energy and strengthens memory and thought processes. It is an excellent stone for past life regression, taking you far back into the past to heal basic survival issues. It dissipates anxiety and instils confidence in the future. Dinosaur Bone is traditionally used for healing paralysis and broken bones and for restructuring disordered bone growth. It reputedly improves hearing, vitality and the assimilation of phosphorous. Dinosaur Bone is used for regulation of body temperature, reducing fever, and controlling growth processes within cells.

*Dinosaur Bone
(tumbled)*

*Dinosaur Bone
(raw)*

CRYOLITE

Raw

COLOUR	White
APPEARANCE	Translucent crystal
RARITY	Rare
SOURCE	Greenland (may also be laboratory-made)

ATTRIBUTES Officially sanctioned as a pesticide in the US, Cryolite is an aluminium based mineral that leaves a toxic fluoride residue: a surprising quality in a stone prized in the crystal world for its ability to raise consciousness. But natural Cryolite energetically purifies the subtle bodies* so higher states of awareness are reached with ease.

Used homoeopathically Cryolite can clear etheric pests, implants, parasites and block mind control. This crystal stimulates contact with your Higher Self and your soul* and assists you to align with your spiritual truth and live from your heart.

At an emotional level, Cryolite overcomes indecision. It helps you to make up your mind by freeing you from the constraints of an outmoded belief system or emotional conditioning. It facilitates knowing where you are going with your life and identifying the shortest route to get there.

HEALING At an energetic level, Cryolite may assist with brain function, stomach, intestinal and neurological problems, anaemia, thyroid, rashes and bone issues. It may be helpful for chronic indigestion, ulcers, IBS, Crohn's disease and for energetically dissipating an excess of fluorite.

POSITION Grid, place or position as appropriate or disperse gem essence around the aura. *CAUTION: Crysolite contains aluminium. Wash hands thoroughly after use and make gem essence by the indirect method.*

CUMBERLANDITE

Raw

COLOUR	Greenish-black with white inclusions
APPEARANCE	Granular stone
RARITY	Rare, one location only
SOURCE	Rhode Island, United States

ATTRIBUTES An ancient stone born of a volcano, Cumberlandite is the State Stone of Rhode Island and was sacred to the Nipmuck Nation. Magnetic and rich in iron and titanium, Cumberlandite was smelted to create tools and cannons during the War of Independence. It contains a high proportion of Olivine (Peridot) a protective and purifying stone that releases 'old baggage' and counteracts jealousy or resentment. This stone stirs your intellectual curiosity and links to the higher mind, stimulating your need to know.

Psychologically Cumberlandite strengthens mental acuity and balances nervous energy, being useful for hyperactivity, attention deficit disorder and similar conditions and is highly recommended for teachers. Said to activate and balance both sides of the brain, it provides calm when under mental stress.

Physically, Cumberlandite assists with motor function and flexibility, keeping the body supple.

HEALING Cumberlandite may assist with disorders of the brain, thyroid and parathyroid glands and energetically align the sympathetic nervous system. It is also said to help motor function.

POSITION Grid, place or position as appropriate.

CUPRITE WITH CHRYSOCOLLA

ALSO KNOWN AS SONORA SUNRISE

Tumbled

COLOUR	Turquoise and red combination
APPEARANCE	Opaque stone with distinct, vibrant colourations
RARITY	Rare but becoming more easily available
SOURCE	Mexico

ATTRIBUTES Two powerful stones, dynamic Cuprite, which infuses energy into the body, and purifying Chrysocolla, which encourages communication and speaking your truth, combine in Sonora Sunrise. Cuprite, a philosophical stone, teaches humanitarian principles and encourages helping others. The combination encourages service to the planet.

Use Sonora Sunrise to explore past lives and learn from experiences your soul has undergone. It is excellent for reframing destructive emotional or mental patterns from any timeframe and for feeling safe in all situations. Sonora Sunrise eases the mind with regard to worries and situations over which you have no control and strengthens trust that all is well. Overcoming difficulties with a father, guru, teacher or other authoritarian figure, present or past, it releases rigid 'oughts and shoulds' and mind control. Aligning your personal will with that of your Higher Self, it aids in taking responsibility for your life. The combination attracts a positive mentor when required.

Physically, Sonora Sunrise offers great vitality and strength. It provides support where there is fear of having a terminal condition and encourages overcoming a terminal diagnosis, attracting what you need to survive psychologically. With strong vitality, it rejuvenates the physical body. Placed over the heart, it restores energy to the blood. Cuprite helps the body take in Qi* or prana from the air you breathe. Through the blood, Qi passes to the cells of the body which are invigorated restoring normal functioning. Sonora Sunrise revitalizes the base chakras, grounding the physical body, activating creativity and restoring libido and sexual functioning.

HEALING Cuprite with Chrysocolla reputedly strengthens and oxygenates the heart and blood, muscle tissue and skeletal system and overcomes metabolic imbalances. Helpful for the throat, it is said to balance the female hormonal system. This stone energetically treats AIDS, cancers, blood disorders, water retention, bladder and kidney malfunction, vertigo and altitude sickness. It is helpful to smokers and lungs.

POSITION Wear over the thymus or place over area of dis-ease* or low energy, or on base and sacral chakras. Place over the past life chakras for far seeing. Disperse the gem essence around the aura or environment.

DIANITE

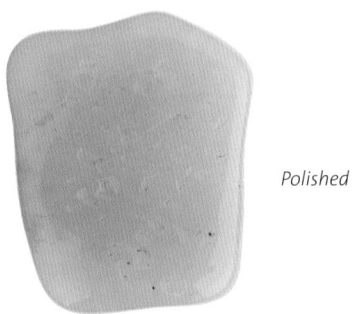

Polished

COLOUR	Sky to dark blue
APPEARANCE	Opaque stone, may have cloud-like markings
RARITY	Only available from one mine
SOURCE	Siberia

ATTRIBUTES Discovered in the year that Princess Diana died, Dianite is a blue nephrite-like stone named in her honour. Similar in energetic feel to Blue Violane from Italy, it is a mix of Quartz, Tremolite and blue Amphibole and has acquired a reputation as a profound healing stone for those who are troubled. It calms hyperactivity and infuses peace into body, mind and spirit, allowing you to listen to the voice within. A high vibration stone, it is an aid to deep meditation and communion with the cosmos. Enhancing spiritual growth and connection with your Higher Self, Dianite may be helpful in rectifying poor self-image and body dysmorphia. In healing, Dianite brings warmth to the extremities and to the heart of those who hold it.

HEALING Dianite may assist with arthritis and inflammation of the joints. It is reputedly helpful for asthma and bronchial conditions and to Raynaud's disease.

POSITION Grid, wear, hold or disperse gem essence around the aura.

ADDITIONAL STONE

Violane (Blue Dioptase) Light blue to purple Violane from Italy is similar in its energetic effects to Dianite from Siberia. The crystal powerfully enhances metaphysical abilities and heightens your insight. It creates and activates a link between the higher heart, soma and soul star chakras*. Violane forms an energetic matrix or web in the physical dimension that directly connects to universal energies. It creates an information field for healing and higher learning. This stone helps you to resonate more closely with your guides. An effective karmic* healer, it cleanses the past life chakras then recalibrates the energy to the present moment. Wear Violane constantly if you need to support your vitality as it stimulates the flow of Qi*. Violane may assist muscles and the genitals.

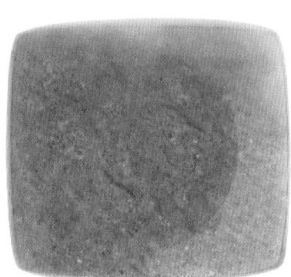

Polished

DIASPORE

ALSO KNOWN AS ZULTANITE

Raw

Diaspore facets

COLOUR	Green and yellow changing to pink depending on light source
APPEARANCE	Translucent layered raw crystal, or faceted gemstone that changes colour
RARITY	Rare
SOURCE	Turkey (gem quality), Russia, New Zealand, United States, Brazil, Argentina, UK, China

ATTRIBUTES One of the rarest gemstones, high vibration Diaspore (gem quality sold as Zultanite) opens the crown and higher crown chakras and grounds high vibration energy to earth. The raw stone is used for metaphysical and healing work. Placing this stone on the forehead promotes lucid dreaming and enhances metaphysical abilities. It is useful if you psychically read for others as it enhances your connection. The colour comes from manganese which absorbs the ultra-violet

126

spectrum and appears different when viewed from two directions. You literally see things in a different light with this stone.

An important physiological constituent with a powerful antioxidant and metabolic function, manganese is required for correct bone development, tissue repair and assimilation of minerals within the body. Correct balance of manganese is essential and Diaspore delivers an energetic boost or sedates as required.

HEALING Diaspore is reputed to assist the body to maintain the correct acid-alkaline balance and to remove free radicals and toxins or pollutants. It energetically releases water retention, promoting weight loss and body reshaping. In crystal healing Diaspore is used for Parkinson's disease, for stimulating the production of T-cells in the immune system, and encouraging wound healing and correct bone development.

POSITION Wear, grid, hold or disperse gem essence around the aura as appropriate.

DRAGON STONE

ALSO KNOWN AS BASTITE

Tumbled Bastite

Australian Dragon Stone

COLOUR	Green and red
APPEARANCE	Opaque, bi-coloured stone
RARITY	Rare
SOURCE	Australia, South Africa

ATTRIBUTES Dragon Stone, found throughout the world, stimulates kundalini* rise, activating the chakras* and creativity on all levels. It activates Dragon energy, the earth's kundalini, assisting earth healing and bringing order out of chaos. It enhances fertility and puts meridians back on line. Helpful in past life healing where ancient abuse blocks sexual response. Placed on minor chakras located in the knees, Dragon Stone helps you be more centred and grounded on earth.

HEALING Reputed to help infertility and conditions arising from a blocked base or sacral chakra. Dragon Quartz shares its properties.

POSITION Grid, position or place as appropriate or disperse gem essence around the base and sacral chakras.

ECLIPSE STONE

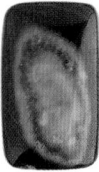

Polished

COLOUR	Yellow and black
APPEARANCE	Opaque stone with distinct areas of colour
RARITY	Rare
SOURCE	Indonesia

ATTRIBUTES A mysterious stone, Eclipse Stone appears to be a powerful combination of Orpiment in Black Agate or Jasper. It is excellent for the Crone phase of life. The Crone is the wise woman, the old priestess who holds ancient wisdom and who used to be honoured within the tribe. With this stone the menopausal woman reclaims her power and her place in society. In men who have had a mid-life crisis or been made redundant in later years, it stimulates a new start.

Black Agate or Jasper is profoundly strengthening and Orpiment is a great support during times of change. Enhancing clarity of thought, it helps you to plan ahead and yet be flexible enough to go with the unfolding flow if circumstances show that the plan is inappropriate for your soul growth. Eclipse Stone dissolves hatred, jealousy and resentment and fills your heart with joy and love.

This stone stimulates intellectual abilities, encouraging analysis and logical thought. Keep one in your pocket when studying or taking examinations. It rolls away whatever is hiding the truth and brings the shadow into the light. If one parent has been overly dominant Eclipse Stone mitigates the influence so that the subconscious effect of the eclipsed parent is understood. The stone purifies the solar plexus, releasing emotional blockages, memories and ancestral patterns.

Spiritually, Eclipse stone stimulates both inner sight and insight, leading the way to enlightenment. A stone of wizardry and magic, it takes you deep into yourself to explore the sacred, set-aside and taboo areas of life.

HEALING Eclipse stone is reputed to ameliorate menopausal symptoms and mid-life conditions in men and women. It may assist disorders of the intestines, circulatory system, alimentary canal, ears, nose, and throat.

POSITION Place over the solar plexus or sacral chakras or grid as appropriate. *CAUTION: Orpiment is toxic. Wash hands after use and do not make gem essence by the direct method.*

EKLOGITE

Raw

Polished

COLOUR	Green and grey
APPEARANCE	Opaque stone
RARITY	Rare
SOURCE	Germany

ATTRIBUTES Eklogite nurtures your inner energy, especially when you need courage or endurance. This piece of oceanic crust was pushed up from the depths of the earth under great pressure. It helps to maintain your Qi*, the life-force that sustains body, mind and spirit and reinforces healing by opening energy meridians* in the body. Eklogite activates the higher energy centres in the body so that your lightbody* and your consciousness awaken further.

HEALING Eklogite sustains body and the soul and encourages cell membranes to manifest the most beneficial genetic code possible.

POSITION Place, grid or hold Eklogite. Wear amulets or jewellery for long periods.

EOSPHORITE

Raw

COLOUR	Pink, clear, white, brown, red-brown, peachy-orange
APPEARANCE	Transparent to translucent crystal
RARITY	Rare
SOURCE	Brazil, Canada, Pakistan

ATTRIBUTES Offering you protection while exploring previous lives, Eosphorite transports you to the core situation that set up a karmic* pattern de-energizing it at source, so that the effect no longer carries forward. It helps overcome long held feelings of anger or inferiority, replacing them with self-confident assertion. Pink Eosophorite is particularly helpful for opening and cleansing the heart chakras* so that joy is felt.

HEALING Eosphorite is reported to assist repairing RNA and DNA structures, activate 12 strand DNA and facilitate assimilation of the minerals necessary for correct cellular functioning.

POSITION Hold, grid or disperse gem essence around the heart and aura.

FLUORAPATITE

Natural crystal

COLOUR	Pink, white, yellow, blue, purple, green, brown
APPEARANCE	Translucent, striated crystal
RARITY	Easily obtained
SOURCE	United States, Pakistan, Switzerland, Czech Republic, Germany, Mexico, Russia, Canada

ATTRIBUTES A catalyst for change, Fluorapatite is a useful tool for conflict resolution, inner or outer. This stone of grace and harmony helps to remove aggression between people or conflicting interests. It synthesizes a group, ensuring harmony. Program it as appropriate.

Hydroxyapatite, a component of the crystal, naturally occurs in the pineal gland. The pineal monitors the effect of electromagnetic fields and regulates the body accordingly. It is believed by mystics to be the third eye and Fluorapatite stimulates metaphysical abilities. A structure with no blood-brain barrier, the pineal produces melatonin, regulating bio and circadian rhythms. Fluorapatite resonates with hydroxyapatite

133

sand in the pineal, activating inner sight and connection to All That Is*. It is postulated that the pineal secretes DMT, the 'spirit molecule': a neuro-chemical looking glass. DMT is a natural psychedelic involved in out-of-body, near-death and other exceptional human experiences that take the soul into multi-dimensions.

Fluorapatite has long been used as a fertilizer and it seeds new vibrations and ideas into your life. Inducing equilibrium, it blocks out the demands of the external world so that you find inner peace. Psychologically it eases irritability. Grid it to promote harmony in the home.

HEALING Fluorapatite has been used in the energetic treatment of cancer, disorders of the eyes, lungs and extremities and to reverse loss of sense of smell. It may assist bones and teeth.

POSITION Hold, grid, position or disperse gem essence around the head.

ADDITIONAL STONE
Fluorellestadite shares many properties with Fluorapatite.

GABBRO

*Polished
Gabbro*

COLOUR	Deep green to grey, blue
APPEARANCE	Opaque, coarse grained, gritty stone
RARITY	One of the most common rocks
SOURCE	Worldwide

ATTRIBUTES A plutonic rock formed when molten magma cooled into a crystalline mass, Gabbro underpins most of the world's oceans and much of the land surface. Gabbro is low in silica and high in calcite. Minerals such as feldspar, chlorite, serpentine, muscovite, pyroxene, hercynite, and magnetite in a matrix, it may contain olivine, chrome garnet, actinolite, and biotite. The synergistic effect is incredibly powerful. Gabbro helps to ride out energetic perturbations and puts you in touch with your Higher Self. Highlighting changes that are needed in your life, it dissipates confusion and instils strength of mind. The stone assists in releasing karmic* contracts and core soul beliefs that no longer serve you.

This peaceful stone is extremely supportive and deeply grounded. It plugs you into the earth and puts a protective shield around you, cutting out Wi-Fi and electromagnetic pollution and negative energies. Holding Gabbro filters downloads of information occurring within the

Gabbro with Pyrite

dimensional shift*. It stabilizes your contact with the earth bringing these into play at ground level. Gabbro makes you aware of the importance of experiences that you may have overlooked at the time, pointing you to the gift at their heart. The stone is an excellent stress buster. Gabbro may energetically regulate apoptosis, the essential biological process of cell death that allows the cellular lifecycle to continue as cells die, regenerate and renew themselves. When this process is disrupted dis-eases* such as auto-immune dysfunctions and cancer occur. Said to assist in locating energetic disharmony within the physical body, Gabbro defuses subtle energy* blockages and is profoundly detoxifying for all the bodies.

HEALING Gabbro is reputed to treat "hot flashes", cellular swelling and infections, disorders of the immune system, bruising and sprains. Gabbro may alleviate the effects of geopathogens* and fevers and balance alkalinity in the body.

POSITION Wear, hold, place, grid as appropriate. Disperse the gem essence into the aura or the environment.

ADDITIONAL STONES

Blizzard Stone™ Speckled with white on a black background, Alaskan Blizzard Stone™ is a combination of chlorite, serpentine, muscovite, pyroxene, hercynite, magnetite and white feldspar. Providing powerful protection against electromagnetic smog from computers etc, it strengthens the biomagnetic field*. This stone helps you to attend to your own business and let other people get on with theirs. Uniting opposites, it is useful for past life work and for recognizing how the past impinges on the present. Blizzard Stone™ removes from the

Blizzard Stone™

Akashic Record* and from the karmic blueprint any incidences of persecution, prejudice, racial hatred or discrimination, whether as perpetrator or victim, restoring peace to the psyche and the soul. Blizzard Stone™ is said to be a specialist metaphysical agent for the eradication of hatred, violence and oppression on our planet. It reverses anti-social behaviour and aggression and fosters forgiveness. Grid on a map or the environment in areas of conflict. Blizzard Stone™ clears blockages from the physical body, strengthens the immune system and increases your sensitivity to radionic treatment.

Indigo Gabbro

Gabbro with Pyrite is a powerful synergistic combination that keeps you protected and grounded during metaphysical working.

Indigo Gabbro takes you journeying into multi-dimensions and keeps you grounded at the same time, enabling you to be both 'here' and 'there' simultaneously. An excellent support, hold it during traumatic times to uplift and stabilize your energies.

Mystic Merlinite™ Madagascan, Mystic Merlinite™ is energetically similar to Merlinite. On the third eye, it is one of the fastest ways to open metaphysical abilities, move into expanded consciousness and contact elementals and devas. Useful in past life healing, Mystic Merlinite™ assists in gathering up fragmented soul parts, purifying them and returning them to the incarnated soul or to the Higher Self if it is not appropriate for the soul part to return to earth. It assists in exploring the hidden parts of the psyche and applying retro-cognition to better understand situations that have had *Mystic Merlinite™ (raw)*   a profound effect on how you live now.

Mystic Merlinite™ (polished)

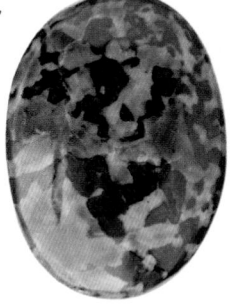

GALAXYITE

Polished

COLOUR	Deep blue-black with white sparkles
APPEARANCE	Opaque stone, looks like the night sky
RARITY	Rare
SOURCE	Canada

ATTRIBUTES A micro-Labradorite in Feldspar, Galaxyite's high vibrations connect to the entire cosmos and the immensity of creation. Assists studying astrology or astronomy, journeying with this stone takes you to the far reaches of our universe. Provides auric protection during metaphysical work, keeping you grounded. Galaxyite helps take an overview of spiritual development, attuning you to the soul's purpose.

HEALING Galaxyite may assist brain or metabolic disorders, and eyes. It reputedly helps digestion, colds, rheumatism and gout and dispels anxiety and stress-related dis-ease*.

POSITION Hold, place, grid or disperse gem essence around the aura.

GARNET IN PYROXENE

Tumbled

COLOUR	Red and purplish-grey
APPEARANCE	Clearly delineated colours in opaque stone
RARITY	Rare
SOURCE	Unconfirmed

ATTRIBUTES The highly energetic properties of Garnet are softened and grounded by Pyroxene. This unusual combination is helpful for clearing blockages from the base and sacral chakras so that creativity on all levels is stimulated. Placed over the base of the skull, it aligns and activates the alta major chakra and opens metaphysical abilities.

HEALING As with all Garnets, this combination may assist blood flow and the heart. It may also stimulate fertility and a sluggish metabolism.

POSITION Hold, place or grid as appropriate.

GLAUCOPHANE

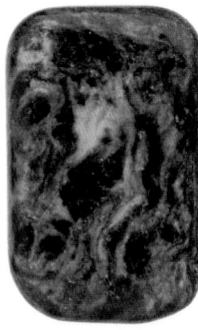

Polished

COLOUR	Blue-grey with white and gold
APPEARANCE	Mottled, sparkling opaque stone
RARITY	Rare
SOURCE	Mountainous regions of Europe

ATTRIBUTES A blue amphibole, Glaucophane looks like a galaxy hanging in outer space with twinkling stars. The name means 'blue appearing' and it is a sodium-rich metamorphic rock, which means that it has undergone great pressure in its long life. It positively fizzes in your hand. Placed over the third eye it opens metaphysical sight and over the throat chakra* it enables you to communicate what you see and to share your spiritual vision. Over the soma chakra this stone takes you travelling to meet star people and find your soul's home. It makes a useful anchoring stone for a cosmic anchor hooked in the centre of

140

galaxy which conveys you home safely to your body, no matter how far you may travel.

This stone is excellent wherever you need clarification and it can help in finding solutions to problems that have formerly been intractable. Meditate with it or place it under your pillow and ask for an insightful dream that shows you what underlies such situations.

HEALING Glaucophane is a powerful all round healer and well-being enhancer. It particularly assists the throat and dis-eases* that arise from repressed thoughts and feelings or experiences that have never been spoken about.

POSITION Hold, grid, place or disperse gem essence into the aura, especially around the throat and head.

GLENDONITE

Natural formation

COLOUR	Light to mid greyish-brown
APPEARANCE	Many knobbly points on opaque sphere
RARITY	Rare
SOURCE	Russia

ATTRIBUTES This stone of guidance and spiritual purpose helps you discover your soul intention for the present life. Meditate with it to check that you are following your present intention rather than an outmoded one that has become 'stuck' in your energy field. Glendonite de-energizes* the old pattern and helps you to access a more beneficial intention for your spiritual evolution.

Activating all the chakras* especially those at the higher level, Glendonite facilitates learning. It allows information to move freely through the body and facilitates rapidly processing thoughts and insights. Placed over the third eye, it transfers psychic downloads and opens clairvoyance and inner vision. Glendonite helps you to simplify your thought processes and speeds up information assimilation so that the most complex subject becomes easily understandable.

A useful stone for transmuting emotional patterns that no longer serve, Glendonite creates a loving environment and overcomes a dysfunctional family background to create a loving, supportive family life. With this stone, you live life as you are now rather than as a product of the past. It is a stone of personal learning and discovery, and assists in reuniting with your soul family.

HEALING Glendonite is reputed to ameliorate insomnia and headaches, especially where these have an emotional cause. Said to facilitate healing of broken bones, cuts and abrasions, it is also thought to strengthen teeth and bones and to assist cell regeneration.

POSITION Place, grid or position as appropriate or disperse gem essence around the aura. *NOTE: Make gem essence by the indirect method.*

GOLDEN CORACALCITE™

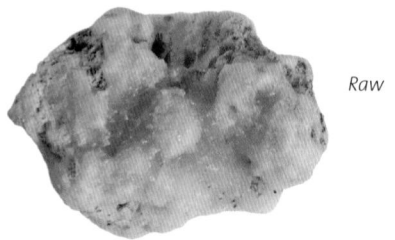

Raw

COLOUR	Golden to creamy yellow or white
APPEARANCE	Skeletal, opaque, coral-like crystal
RARITY	Rare
SOURCE	Florida, United States, Caribbean

ATTRIBUTES This high vibration fusion of coral with calcite connects the spiritual and physical aspects of your being and enhances your intuition. Golden Coracalcite™ activates the lightbody* and connects it to the physical body through the lower chakra system, and to All That Is* through the higher vibration chakras. It focuses your intention so that it manifests what you most desire in accordance with your soul's timing as you travel the evolutionary path to higher consciousness.

HEALING Golden Coracalcite™ facilitates multi-dimensional cellular healing. At a physical level it resonates with the bony structures of the body, connective tissue, teeth, nerves and neurotransmitters.

POSITION Place or grid as appropriate or disperse gem essence around the aura.

GOLDEN SELENITE

ALSO KNOWN AS SUNSET GOLD

Natural formation

COLOUR	Pale to golden amber or yellow
APPEARANCE	Transparent or translucent points on a bed
RARITY	Rare but becoming more easily available
SOURCE	Peru, Canada, South West United States

ATTRIBUTES One of the most refined forms of an already extremely high vibration crystal, Golden Selenite gently lifts you off to another dimension for an overview on life and your soul's path. This beautiful stone helps align your personal will to that of your Higher Self, your soul intention and the divine plan. An excellent crystal for manifesting, it ensures that what you bring into being is for the highest good of all and that the reality you create is joyful and evolutionary. This stone facilitates accessing the highest levels of guidance and soul learning, facilitating multi-dimensional travel and stellar exploration.

As Golden Selenite harmonizes the will, it is extremely helpful in overcoming addictions and obsessions of all kinds and in bringing harmony to mind, body and spirit.

All Selenite is crystallized divine light, but Golden Selenite also has a huge infusion of sunlight and unbounded energy that may assist with Seasonal Affective Disorder and the winter blues. Keep the stone near to you at all times to overcome depression or lethargy and bring in spiritual sunshine.

HEALING Golden Selenite may assist digestion but works mainly from the subtle energetic* levels to restore harmony to the subtle bodies*.

POSTION As Golden Selenite is delicate, place or grid with care as appropriate or disperse gem essence around the aura. *NOTE: Make essence by indirect method.*

GRAPHIC SMOKY QUARTZ IN FELDSPAR

ALSO KNOWN AS ZEBRADORITE

Polished

Raw

COLOUR	White-beige to cream with grey or brown
APPEARANCE	Translucent crystal streaks in a dense matrix
RARITY	Fairly easily obtained
SOURCE	Madagascar, United States

ATTRIBUTES Smoky Quartz has been powerfully compressed into a Feldspar matrix. Feldspar helps you to be grounded and balanced in physical incarnation and Smoky Quartz purifies your energies and opens your metaphysical abilities. The combination cleanses and opens all the chakras. This stone keeps you grounded in the here and now while you explore past lives and multi-dimensions. Its gentle, protective energy has been described as 'an angel stroking my hair'. Extremely useful if you want to travel unseen through the lower shamanic realms, it gives you the stealth of a cat and helps to conceal your true objectives, cloaking your activities at every level. However, it must be used with integrity or will backfire. It helps you find a more creative way to approach your goals.

Graphic Smoky Quartz instils infinite peace during physical or emotional trauma. Helpful for overcoming tragedy, it offers insight into group experiences. It helps to overcome low self esteem, inducing self confidence and emotional stability. It is useful if you need to learn to trust people again as to helps you to lower your psychological barriers. With a fizzy, invigorating effect on the body, it infuses dynamic energy and a feeling of well-being. Said to have been used to find lost objects.

HEALING Graphic Smoky Quartz supports structures in the body, especially spinal alignment, and may assist arteries, veins, nerves or compressed joints. A detoxifying stone, it removes debris and trauma from the body and is said to heal the lungs and tuberculosis.

Runic Feldspar

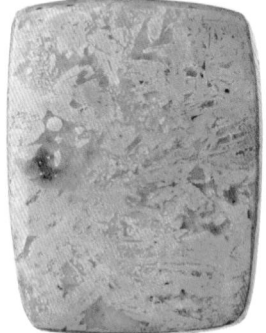

POSITION Hold, place or grid as appropriate. Grid in each corner of a room or at your feet to clear negative energies or disperse gem essence around the aura or environment.

ADDITIONAL STONE

Runic Feldspar is Hematite compressed in Feldspar. Although from the Southern Hemisphere, it contains runic symbols and can be used to access the mythology of the Nordic gods and the shamanic practises of Seid magic and its ancient healing culture.

GRANITE

*Raw Grey
Granite*

COLOUR	Grey, pink, black
APPEARANCE	Speckled, grainy, often sparkling opaque stone
RARITY	Extremely common
SOURCE	Worldwide

ATTRIBUTES With a high proportion of Quartz and Feldspar, Granite has light-catching crystal specks on its surface and this resonant stone emits powerful, measurable, paramagnetic frequencies. In stone circles and other monuments it earthed the power of the heavens. A strongly focused and grounded stone, it helps 'floaty' people earth themselves. High in Qi*, Granite passes this life force into the body so, if you live in a Granite house or landscape, your energy field is stabilized and energized. If prone to depression its harshness may lead to melancholy.

Plutonic stones such as Granite may energetically regulate apoptosis, the essential biological process of cell death that allows the cellular cycle to continue and cells to die, regenerate and renew themselves as appropriate. When this process is disrupted dis-eases* such as auto-immune dysfunctions occur. With its stabilizing effect on the human energy field, Granite realigns the subtle bodies* with the physical, activating electrical activity in cells and stimulating the immune response. The rock neutralizes the ill-effects of toxic earth energy lines and re-energizes the earth's magnetic grid. It is an excellent gridding stone to create a safe, sacred space in which to practice magical and transformational rituals and, when struck, is a powerfully resonant lithophone for sound healing. Granite helps you see the whole picture before making up your mind. It is useful for promoting diplomacy and tact and for maintaining balance in a relationship.

HEALING Granite speeds up healing by stabilizing the subtle bodies with the physical. Traditionally Granite heals eyes, rickets, rheumatism and infertility and is said to assist disorders of the hair, face and head.

POSITION Hold, place or grid it around the body to create a stable matrix in which healing is enhanced. Place a piece of Granite at each corner of your bed to attract transformational resonances that boost the flow of energy through all your bodies and open your heart seed chakra. Disperse gem essence around the aura or the environment.

Aswan Pink Granite

ADDITIONAL STONES

In addition to the generic properties of Granite, the following stones have further properties.

Aswan Pink Granite facilitates reconnection to temple lives and arcane knowledge from ancient Egypt. This Granite has the highest paramagnetic resonance of all and obelisks harnessed the power of the sun god Ra to fertilize the earth. The ancient Egyptians were aware of its transformational effect on the human energy field. It brings the bioenergetic field to a higher resonance and encourages humankind to look to the stars for their origins. The Egyptians utilized it to draw the power of the Gods to earth – and to assist the Pharaoh on his shamanic journey to the stars. Powdered Granite was used to treat white spots of the eye and to imbue strength and durability. An irritant, it is more usual to place a tumbled stone over the eyes.

Texan Pink Granite

Texan Pink Granite has a similar resonance to, although with a less powerful paramagnetic resonance than, Aswan. Its frequency can be permanently heightened by placing it on Aswan Granite for an hour or two.

Indian Granite

Indian Granite This gentle stone nevertheless has a powerful transformational and stabilizing effect on the human energy field or on the environment. It is a great companion to accompany you through traumatic situations and energetic changes.

Ruby in Granite and **Garnet in Granite** The powerful lifeforce of Ruby or Garnet is magnified and focused by its Granite matrix. It assists the transport of Qi* around the body, energizing every cell. Excellent for repairing a broken heart, physically or psychologically.

Ruby in Granite (tumbled)

Pink Granite

GREENSAND

Raw

COLOUR	Greenish-beige
APPEARANCE	Granular, grainy rock
RARITY	Easily available as a building stone
SOURCE	Worldwide

ATTRIBUTES This particular form of Sandstone has an iron bearing mineral within it that gives the rock a greenish tint. The high quantity of silica in Greensand emits high frequency energy and it was valued highly by ancient peoples. The edge of the Greensand belt, especially where it intersected with chalk, was a favoured place for stone circles and other monuments. This was liminal space: a magical portal to another dimension. The 'altar stone' at Stonehenge is a Greensand with Garnet inclusions brought from the Preseli Mountains.

As with all sedimentary rocks, the stone reflects the way that souls are scoured and character refined through the changes and pressures of everyday life. It is the perfect companion on the journey to maturity as it brings to the surface survival traits that may be useful, or may need to be laid aside, in order to evolve. It helps you adapt to current circumstances even if these are not ideal.

Environmentally, Greensand is used in the treatment of water to filter out impurities. It works the same purification on the fluid in the body.

HEALING Greensand may assist in regulation of the lymphatic and blood systems in the body, releasing water retention and de-energizing an accumulation of fluid in the lower extremities.

POSITION Hold, wear or place as appropriate. Use a polished stone to stimulate lymphatic drainage, working from the feet to the heart and from the head to the heart. Disperse the gem essence as appropriate.

GUARDIAN STONE™

Raw

COLOUR	Black, grey and white
APPEARANCE	Speckled, gritty stone
RARITY	Rare
SOURCE	Oregon, USA

ATTRIBUTES As the name suggests, Guardian Stone™ is extremely protective and it assists in feeling safe and comfortable within your body. A combination of aegirine, analcime, apatite, biotite, feldspar, nepheline, olivine and riebeckite-arfvedsonite, it aids recovery from trauma and dissolves fear and negative vibrations, so maintaining positive energy flow.

HEALING Guardian Stone™ enhances overall well-being.

POSITION Hold, grid or position as appropriate.

HAUSMANNITE

Raw

COLOUR	Silvery grey-black-brown
APPEARANCE	Metallic pyramidal shapes on grainy matrix
RARITY	Rare
SOURCE	South Africa, Germany, Sweden

ATTRIBUTES Formed under enormous pressure in hydrothermal vents, Hausmannite helps to stabilize energies during the process of transformation. This stone calls in the healing energies necessary for recovery from dis-eases* and disorders of the structure of the physical and subtle bodies*.

HEALING Hausmannite is reputedly used for dis-eases of bone and cellular structure and to support hair, skin and blood vessels. It has been used in the treatment of nose bleeds.

POSITION Grid, place or position as appropriate.

HILULITE

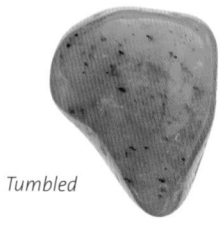

Tumbled

COLOUR	White-orange-black-red
APPEARANCE	Translucent stone with clear areas of colour
RARITY	Extremely rare
SOURCE	Sri Lanka

ATTRIBUTES An unusual, highly energetic combination of Garnet, Zircon Geothite and Quartz, Hilulite's energy is extremely positive, reaching high dimensions, and yet it acts as a grounding stone allowing you to be 'here' and 'there' at the same time during metaphysical and psychological work. Hilulite helps to value yourself more highly and recognize the part you are here to play in the evolution of consciousness.

HEALING Hilulite is reputed to assist the circulation.

POSITION Hold, grid or position as appropriate. Disperse gem essence into the aura.

HUBNERITE

Raw

COLOUR	Yellow-brown, red-black, black
APPEARANCE	Translucent to opaque 'ribbed' stone
RARITY	Rare as a healing crystal, obtainable from mineral dealers
SOURCE	Peru, Kazakhstan, United States

ATTRIBUTES Created in geothermal vents, Hubnerite has undergone enormous pressure and accelerated evolution and supports during rapid energetic changes, adjusting your physical body to adapt to the shifts. It has an endurance that helps you through prolonged challenges.

HEALING Hubnerite is reputedly used in the treatment of disorders associated with excess iron. Said to balance out blood sugar swings and strengthen weak vision, it may also help correct alignment of vertebrae.

POSITION Keep it with you at all times.

ILMENITE

Raw

COLOUR	Black
APPEARANCE	Chunky opaque tabular or rosette crystals, metallic lustre or faceted gemstone
RARITY	Rare as a raw healing crystal
SOURCE	Ontario, Russia, Norway, Switzerland, Zaire, Sri Lanka, India, Madagascar

ATTRIBUTES Ilmenite offers philosophic guidance on the deeper questions of life. Enhancing ritual working, placed over the third eye it stimulates psychic insight and on the soma chakra* promotes journeying*. Ilmenite dissipates illusions that arise from the past and is extremely helpful in exploring their effect on the present. It releases implants and entities*, especially those passing down the ancestral line.

HEALING Ilmenite is reputedly an excellent all round healing stone as it offers support to the subtle* and physical bodies.

POSITION Hold, place or grid as appropriate.

IRONSTONE

Polished

Raw

COLOUR	Deep brown, grey, black
APPEARANCE	Dense, opaque, gritty, sometimes banded stone
RARITY	Common
SOURCE	UK, United States, South Africa, Worldwide

ATTRIBUTES Geomagnetic and protective, Ironstone is extremely hard, iron-rich sandstone with grains of Quartz embedded. An excellent grounding stone, it stabilizes a grid or brings you back to earth after metaphysical working. The ancients used it for grave covers as a portal to the next world. Incorporated in churches it draws sacred power to earth. An energetic stone, gets things moving in a pragmatic, sensible way.

HEALING In earth or personal healing Ironstone restores vitality and stability to the energy matrix and can heal structures in the body.

POSITION Place, hold, grid as appropriate.

JADE: **AFRICAN**

ALSO KNOWN AS BUDD STONE

Tumbled

COLOUR	Blue-green
APPEARANCE	Opaque stone
RARITY	Rare
SOURCE	South Africa

ATTRIBUTES African Jade is excellent for grounding 'airheads' as it opens the earth star chakra* and helps you anchor to the core of the planet. Activating the alta major chakra, it assists in dealing with the practicalities of everyday reality and stimulates growth via the physical world. Placed behind the ears, Budd Stone opens the inner ear and attunes you to spirit voices, your Higher Self and your own intuition – helping you seek out the right path. It assists in understanding the noises your body makes when picking up subtle signals. Bringing order out of chaos, it clears environmental negativity. At your feet during meditation it suggests practical solutions. Sweeping the stone around the biomagnetic* field clears subtle impediments to growth. It clears

160

and purifies the energies, allowing you to progress at exactly the right pace. The stone helps with the flow of energy or fluid within the body, enhancing Qi* and circulation.

Effective if your soul's path entails working in the commercial world to bring in more light and promote ethical decisions, this stone facilitates business dealings and negotiations that require finesse and acute perceptions of hidden agendas. It unites a group into a common purpose. With Budd Stone's assistance you skilfully negotiate pitfalls to reach a successful conclusion.

HEALING As an essence, Budd Stone may assist degenerative or fungal conditions of the feet. It reputedly amplifies hearing.

POSITION Hold, position or place as appropriate. Disperse gem essence around the head and Earth Star. Use as a pressure wand in reflexology or metamorphic technique treatments.

ADDITIONAL STONE

Bowenite ('New Jade') helps release blocked or repressed emotions and find a solution through your dreaming mind. Place it under the pillow and ask for an insightful dream whenever you feel stuck or have an intractable problem. Tell yourself that you will remember the solution when you wake. Use Bowenite to deepen your meditation and ask your Higher Self for guidance. This stone is a powerful heart healer that stimulates kundalini* rise. It affords psychic protection against ill-wishers and negative forces. Said to encourage fidelity and bond your relationships, Bowenite reputedly assists diabetes and hypoglycaemia and treats disorders of the head and scalp.

Bowenite ('New Jade')

JAMESONITE

Raw

COLOUR	Grey-black
APPEARANCE	Fibrous, iridescent metallic
RARITY	Rare
SOURCE	Bolivia, Germany, Hungary, Slovakia, Mexico

ATTRIBUTES Jamesonite has a strong energetic charge that detoxes the physical and mental subtle bodies. If you need to distinguish truth from fiction, keep this stone in your vicinity. Clarifying your thoughts, it helps you to maintain harmony while standing in your truth.

HEALING Jamesonite is a cooling and stabilizing stone that assists the body to maintain its energetic well-being.

POSITION Grid, hold or position as appropriate. *CAUTION: Wash hands after use. Make essence by indirect method.*

JASPER: **CHOHUA**

*Dragon skull
Shaped Chohua*

COLOUR	White, blue, red, grey, brown
APPEARANCE	Opaque stone, often streaked or blotched
RARITY	Only one source but fairly easily available
SOURCE	Lijing River, China

ATTRIBUTES Chohua Jasper is an energetic stone that can stimulate kundalini* rise through the chakras, cleansing and activating as it goes. It stimulates love and passion. The various colours carry dragon energy*: red that of the fire dragon, white that of air, blue of water, brown of earth. If you have lost your integrity or if your honour has been besmirched, wearing Chohua Jasper helps you to regain your reputation and your trust in yourself.

HEALING Chohua Jasper assists the circulation and the heart, strengthening arteries and veins. It stimulates the immune system and kidneys and may ameliorate skin conditions. According to colour, it may help to balance blood pressure and lift depression. The red variety of the stone enhances vitality and well-being and can assist convalescence.

Guinea Fowl Jasper

POSITION Place, grid or position as appropriate. Disperse gem essence into the aura or around the bedroom to stimulate passion.

ADDITIONAL STONES

Guinea Fowl Jasper is gentle and protective. It is ideal for those who have been traumatized or who are too timid to interact with the world. Assisting meditation and connection to All That Is*, it calms emotional upheavals and mental anguish. It is helpful for nerve endings and scaly skin, calming inflammation and dis-eases* such as shingles or psoriasis. It may assist the spleen and liver.

Sea Sediment Jasper

Sea Sediment Jasper This soft Jasper-like stone was laid down on the ocean floor and is often colour-infused into multiple colours popular for jewellery. Its gentle energy is refreshing and calming. It may bring up past life issues for resolution and offers protection and reassurance during traumatic circumstances.

JASPER: **CINNABAR**

Tumbled

COLOUR	Deep red
APPEARANCE	Whorls and orbs of colour
RARITY	Rare
SOURCE	Unconfirmed

ATTRIBUTES This synergistic combination infuses the alchemical magic of Cinnabar into one of the most profoundly supportive stones, Red Jasper. As with all synergistic stones, the combination is more than the sum of its parts and this highly energetic stone turns your world upside down, inside out and gives you a whole new perspective on your life path and why you have undergone experiences that polished your soul. It teaches that everything is perfect exactly as it is.

Psychologically, Cinnabar in Jasper transmutes anger and resentment or psychological impotence into dynamic and charismatic assertion that powers life and manifests whatever you need. Helpful for calming people who have a short fuse, the combination protects you from other people's anger. Placed a hand's breadth beneath the right armpit, it removes cords and de-energizes* anger implanted in any lifetime.

Jasper has always been used to support healing and this is an excellent stone to carry if you feel physically or mentally exhausted and unable to face the challenges in your life. Keep it with you at all times.

HEALING Jasper enhances all the energy systems of the body and supports the sexual organs. Jasper and Cinnabar have long traditions of healing blood, the liver, spleen and circulatory system and may help in overcoming anaemia.

POSITION Wear, place or position as appropriate for long periods. Disperse the gem essence into the aura or rub over the liver. *NOTE: Cinnabar is toxic. Use in tumbled form and make gem essence by the indirect method only.*

ADDITIONAL STONE

Polychrome Jasper From close to the now mined-out Ocean Jasper source, Polychrome Jasper is highly protective when travelling between the worlds. It helps you to feel that you belong on earth as part of the clan of humanity, helping you reach out to others out of strength rather than need. Resolving dualities, it helps you integrate into the whole. A useful stone if you seek your power ally.

Polychrome Jasper

JASPER: **KAMBABA**

ALSO KNOWN AS GREEN STROMATOLITE, CROCODILE JASPER

Polished

COLOUR	Intense dark and light green
APPEARANCE	Orbs of darker or lighter colour on opaque stone
RARITY	Rare but easily obtained as jewellery or spheres
SOURCE	Madagascar

ATTRIBUTES This fossilized Jasper is also named Crocodile Jasper due to its resemblance to crocodile-skin. The three billon year old fossils, some of the oldest in the world, are stromatolites, created by a blue-green algae or cyanobacteria. It is believed that cyanobacteria were responsible for the creation of the earth's oxygen atmosphere and Kambaba Jasper holds an ancient and profoundly wise earth energy. Kambaba Jasper goes right to your foundations bringing stability – physically and of purpose. A deeply earthing stone, it harmonizes you with the cycles of the natural world, attuning your personal biorhythm to that of the planet.

Kambaba Jasper is beneficial for the lungs, not only of the human body, but that of the planet. This stone takes you back to your roots and reconnects you to the energy of Mother Earth and your purpose in incarnating here. It attunes you to the deeper cycles and rhythms of the natural world. Meditate with it to hear the wisdom that nature has to offer and to find a wise mentor for your spiritual path.

Kambaba Jasper resonates with the oldest part of the brain stem and the autonomic processes of the body. Placed in the hollow at the base of the skull, it removes blockages and programs that have been deeply ingrained and encourages assimilation of new patterns. It assists meridian*-based tapping therapies such as EFT, increases brain function and enhances neurotransmitters.

HEALING Kambaba Jasper is said to assist the digestive system, particularly the elimination of toxins and assimilation of vitamins and minerals. Controlling the flow of bile, it reputedly cleanses the gall bladder. Encouraging detoxification and healing at the cellular level, it strengthens the body's structures and assists recovery from serious illness or psychosomatic dis-ease*. Assisting the cerebellum, it may be helpful in diseases such as Parkinson's, and balance the body on all levels bringing about optimum well-being.

POSITION Hold, position or grid as appropriate or disperse gem essence around the aura, especially at the feet. Grid Kambaba Jasper around the bed to improve personal fertility and at the corners of a garden or field to improve crops.

NOTE: See also Stromatolite *pages 332-333*

JASPER: **OCEAN BLUE**

Polished

COLOUR	Light and dark blue
APPEARANCE	Blue orbs on an opaque stone
RARITY	Original seam is mined out
SOURCE	Madagascar

ATTRIBUTES Ocean Blue is a form of Ocean Jasper that has strong links to the ancient knowledge of Atlantis and Lemuria. It invokes orbs: the strange balls of light that appear in photographs; at sacred sites, around people's heads or close to high vibration crystals. Many theories are put forward as to what orbs actually are, suggestions including the lightbodies* of angels or departed spirits. Ocean Blue Jasper assists in transcribing the messages that these energy-beings bring.

If you met your death by water in a previous existence Ocean Blue helps you to reframe the experience and to feel at home in water. It helps release emotional trauma from the subtle* emotional body and heals psychosomatic dis-ease*. The 'eyes' in Ocean Blue offer protection and can be used as an amulet while travelling through dark places, environmental or psychic. They assist in grounding the information into a practical application for the earth.

Polished

HEALING All round healer that supports the immune, nervous and lymphatic systems and neurotransmitters. It may reduce bloating and oedema.

POSITION Grid, place or position as appropriate. Disperse the gem essence in the aura or environment.

ADDITIONAL STONE

Bumblebee Jasper Born in the fumeroles of an Indonesian volcano but also found in Australia, this startlingly coloured Jasper is an excellent healer for sacral chakra dis-ease. It is similar to Eclipse Stone and shares similar properties (see page 129). Encouraging total honesty with yourself, the stone represents triumph over the impossible as a bee is not aerodynamically designed to fly. One of its most obvious qualities is to support the at-risk bumble bee population but it also encourages the 'pollination' of new projects and, like all Jaspers, is supremely nurturing. *CAUTION: May be toxic, wash hands after handling.*

Bumblebee Jasper

170

JASPER: **SILVER LEAF**

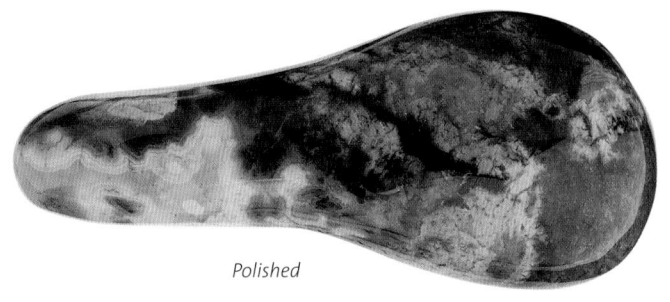

Polished

COLOUR	Black-silver-grey-green-red
APPEARANCE	Foliage-like swirls and spots on opaque stone
RARITY	Fairly easily obtained
SOURCE	India, Russia, France, Germany

ATTRIBUTES Silver Leaf Jasper puts a shield around the physical and subtle bodies* and keeps you grounded. Providing protection when you travel through dangerous places, it also protects you during out-of-body experiences. Carry one with you if the energies of an environment or situation adversely affect you, or if you need an amulet of safety. Having Silver Leaf Jasper with you during psychic or healing works helps you focus your intuitive powers and to work at interface*.

Wear Silver Leaf Jasper if you have difficulty in saying no or if you constantly put other people's needs above your own. It strengthens your willpower, helps state your needs clearly and find a way to get those needs met without infringing on other people's rights or requirements. With its help you find contentment in your relationships and provide appropriate care to those around you while receiving nurturing for yourself. This Jasper helps you to find mental clarity. Keep it with you if you have a tendency to confusion or lack a sense of direction as it helps you to focus.

HEALING Silver Leaf Jasper is an excellent stone for physical well-being as it gives you core strength and helps overcome dis-ease* at any level.

POSITION Wear, hold or place as appropriate. Disperse gem essence around the aura or in the environment.

ADDITIONAL STONE

Shell Jasper (Shell Marble) As befits a stone containing calcite and fossils this soft and gentle stone instils serenity and contentment, while at the same time providing grounding and protection. Paradoxically it invigorates at the mental, physical and emotional level and helps you to make a very practical and safe spiritual connection. Shell Jasper energetically assists the structure of bones and teeth and may help spinal alignment. Disperse gem essence up the spine.

*Shell Jasper
(Shell Marble)*

JASPER: **TRUMMER**

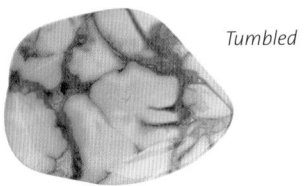

Tumbled

COLOUR	White and brown
APPEARANCE	Opaque stone
RARITY	Rare
SOURCE	Unconfirmed

ATTRIBUTES Trummer Jasper enhances core strength of the body. It energetically neutralizes anything in the environment, body or psyche that interferes with your well-being. Bringing the body back from a state of dis-ease* to equilibrium, it clears negative energy and replaces it with positive. Trummer Jasper assists in turning around a negative self-image, lack of confidence or doubt in your own worth so that you become a confident, optimistic person who feels good about yourself. This positive attitude manifests an all-round improvement in your life.

HEALING Providing support during chronic or severe illness, Trummer may assist dis-eases with an environmental or sick building syndrome cause. It reportedly counteracts viruses and bacteria and brittle bones.

POSITION Leave in place for long periods. Grid to keep the environment clear or place around sickbed. Disperse gem essence into aura or the air.

KEYIAPO

Raw

COLOUR	Greenish-grey-brown
APPEARANCE	Dense nodule
RARITY	Rare
SOURCE	United States

ATTRIBUTES A mix of Iron Pyrite and Quartz, Keyiapo grounds energy into the body, spirit into matter. Providing a protective shield while encouraging consciousness to reach the highest dimensions, it settles the soul deeper into incarnation, retaining a strong connection to the Higher Self. Channelling energy to the base and sacral chakras*, it strengthens and aligns them with the solar plexus and heart chakras giving emotional stability. Keyiapo assists reading the Akashic Record* and facilitates journeying to previous lives.

HEALING Keyiapo cleanses the auric bodies and the karmic* blueprint removing dis-ease*, detaching entities and instilling a sense of well-being.

POSITION Grid, hold or position as appropriate. Hold at the past life or soul star chakras to access the Akashic Record. Disperse gem essence around the aura.

KHUTNOHORITE

Natural formation

COLOUR	Pink, greenish-grey
APPEARANCE	Bubbly botroydal crust or ribbed translucent to opaque crystal
RARITY	Rare
SOURCE	South Africa, Wales, Czech Republic

ATTRIBUTES A major heart healer, Khutnohorite operates at a refined frequency that enables you to live from your heart. Working with the throat chakra*, it calms anxiety and clarifies how you express yourself. Although gentle, it carries masculine energy and unifies your inner male and female aspects to support each other, promoting and enhancing unconditional love and acceptance. This stone encourages community, joining people together to think about how they can help each other rather than just themselves. Connecting the heart seed chakra with the soul star, it infuses divine love into our world and the cells of the physical body. Ideal for those who are working at the highest levels of transmutation and soul healing, it brings about karmic* balance. Khutnohorite connects you to your soul's journey and the purpose of incarnation. It reveals how you operate in the multi-dimensions of consciousness where past, present and future are all one, pulling in spiritual gifts and wisdom from beyond time and space.

This gentle stone radiates peace and calm into an environment with disturbed earth or hyped-up human energy. A stone of forgiveness, it helps transmute grief, fear and resentment into acceptance and release.

Khutnohorite helps you to perceive the bigger picture. It dissolves emotional wounds, outmoded feelings and ingrained thoughts, especially those centred around past fears and trauma, that prevent your mind from expanding into its true potential. Khutnohorite is an excellent stone for rebirthing and soul retrieval* work.

HEALING Khutnohorite rectifies disturbed sleep patterns. It has a manganese base. A powerful antioxidant and metabolic regulator, manganese is essential for correct bone development, tissue repair and assimilation of minerals in the body. Khutnohorite is a useful pain reliever for arthritis, headaches or joint pain that has an emotional component. It may assist psychiatric disorders and brain malfunctions that arise from neurotransmitter glitches in the etheric blueprint* which impact on the physical. Khutnohorite acts at the subtle levels to correct the etheric and karmic* blueprints. Restores harmony to a site.

POSITION As Khutnohorite is delicate it is best placed in the environment or, with care, on the body rather than worn. Disperse gem essence around the aura. *NOTE: Make gem essence by indirect method.*

KIMBERLITE

Polished

COLOUR	Bluish-grey
APPEARANCE	Solid, heavy rock
RARITY	Common but may be difficult to obtain
SOURCE	South Africa, Tanzania, Zimbabwe, West Africa, Australia, United States

ATTRIBUTES Holding precious things safely within its grasp, Kimberlite delivers them to the surface when the time is right. The matrix for diamonds, it has learned how to survive and assists when you are undergoing trauma or transformation. Protective, Kimberlite teaches how to let go of resistance. It promotes deep meditation, out-of-body journeying to multi-dimensions, and strengthens visualisation. Kimberlite helps you to complete projects or your life purpose. It promotes flexibility and the ability to 'see round corners'.

HEALING Kimberlite is reputed to assist de-acidification and regulate the mineral balance in the body. It also sends distant healing.

POSITION Grid, position, place or hold as appropriate.

177

KINOITE

Raw crystal on matrix

COLOUR	Pure, light blue
APPEARANCE	Speckled onto transparent or translucent matrix
RARITY	Rare
SOURCE	Arizona, United States

ATTRIBUTES This stone has a much lighter vibration than most copper-based crystals. It opens all the metaphysical gifts, raises awareness and makes an excellent scrying or kything* support as it safely transports you through multi-dimensions. Meditate with this stone to release delusions and self-limiting beliefs.

HEALING Kinoite may assist arthritis. It reputedly increases stamina and physical vitality, and assists teeth, throat, and the nervous system.

POSITION Grid, place or hold as appropriate. Disperse gem essence around the aura.

KLINOPTILOLITH

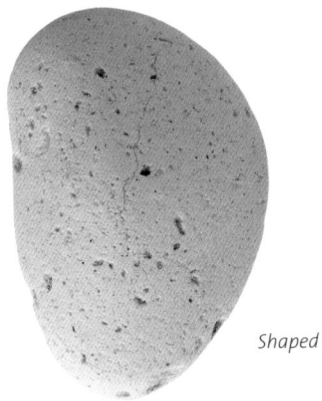

Shaped

COLOUR	Whitish-grey
APPEARANCE	Chalky with pinpricks on the surface
RARITY	Rare but becoming more easily available
SOURCE	Turkey, New Zealand, Australia, United States, Russia

ATTRIBUTES A powerful chemotherapy drug is made from Klinoptilolith. Research suggests that the pure stone absorbs electromagnetic pollutants, radioactivity and other forms of negative energy that disrupt cell function. It assists the digestive system to rid itself of toxins and regenerate its lining. This stone brings the body back into balance and enhances the immune system, supporting the production of T-cells, the body's natural immune system. Reputedly Klinoptilolith supplies the metabolic system with essential minerals required for optimum functioning.

Klinoptilolith energetically stimulates detoxification processes and enhances the body's self-healing mechanism. It reportedly mobilizes heavy metals and free radicals out of the body improving memory, brain and motor function. Overcoming psychosomatic dis-ease, it also mobilizes energetic toxins releasing implants, tracking devices, entities, hooks and negative constructs of all kinds so that the body energetically regenerates itself to a more appropriate level of functioning.

HEALING Anecdotal evidence suggests Klinoptilolith assists connective tissue, tumours and out-of-control cell processes, improves the uptake of nutrients and stimulates and detoxifies the digestive system. There is also evidence to suggest that it may shrink tumours and cysts. An antioxidant that reduces over-acidification, it is said to be beneficial for the liver and kidneys, balancing homeostasis and encouraging oxygenation of the cells. The stone or gem essence is an emergency measure for insect bites, light burns, wounds, skin impurities and fungal infections, especially on the feet.

POSITION Place as appropriate for long periods or disperse gem essence around the aura or onto the body.

KORNERUPINE

Raw

COLOUR	Green
APPEARANCE	Translucent stone, may be faceted gemstone
RARITY	Rare
SOURCE	Germany, Canada, Madagascar, Greenland

ATTRIBUTES Kornerupine is filled with dynamic unconditional love and acceptance. Placing it over your heart helps you to treasure each moment you spend on earth, recognizing its beauty and the part you play in its evolution. If you live with illusion or confusion, place it over your third eye to break through everyday reality into All That Is*. The possibilities you find may surprise you. Kornerupine is extremely effective at revealing hidden causes behind dis-ease* and life events.

HEALING A stone of holistic healing that restores well-being to mind, body and soul, Kornerupine reputedly assists connective tissue disorders such as Marfan Syndrome.

POSITION Grid, place or hold as appropriate. Disperse gem essence around the aura or environment. Place stone over the heart.

LARVIKITE

ALSO KNOWN AS NORWEGIAN MOONSTONE

Raw

Tumbled

COLOUR	Bright blue flash
APPEARANCE	Iridescent stone
RARITY	Fairly easily obtained
SOURCE	Norway

ATTRIBUTES A stone of magic and metaphysics that enhances soul journeying through multi-dimensions and different timeframes and the darkness of the shamanic underworld, Larvikite stimulates metaphysical abilities and facilitates visionary experiences. It sees behind the outer façade of people and situations. Helpful for past life regression and understanding the breadth of your soul's experience as well as connecting to your Higher Self, it has an earthing and grounding property that holds soul and body in harmony especially during visioning or kything* work. Helpful when working elemental magic, the stone is said to cancel spells and to repel negative energy. Historically, boulders of Larvikite were placed in the North of England to repel invaders. It still fulfils this function today, releasing attachments and spirit entities from the biomagnetic sheath and blocking reattachment.

Larvikite is excellent if you want to get in touch with nature in all its forms. This intense stone carries earth and water elemental spirits and has a powerful connection with water, especially rain and storms. In weather magic it brings rain to drought stricken earth, or dries out flooded areas. Water flows easily, bypassing obstacles or washing them away, and Larvikite helps you to deal flexibly with life encouraging you not to dwell on problems but to be adaptable. Supporting emotional healing, it goes deep into your self to find and release the causes of dis-ease*. Larvikite helps you to be the best you can be. Assisting in seeing behind the façade that people present, if you want to know what the true desires and agendas of yourself or others are, keep the stone in your pocket.

Although it has the power to expedite situations, Larvikite teaches the value of right timing and atunement to natural cycles. It assists in making decisions based on common sense and analytic reasoning rather than emotional conditioning. If you need assistance during intensive periods of learning or when working magic, Larvikite helps your mind to process and assimilate new information and may create fresh neural pathways in the brain.

HEALING Larvikite infuses the physical body with vitality and youthfulness. It has an energetically detoxifying effect on tissue, cells and lymph and anecdotal evidence suggests it lowers blood pressure. It is used for calming and stabilizing the nervous system.

Polished

POSITION Grid, place or position as appropriate or disperse gem essence around the feet.

LAVENDER ANGELITE

ALSO KNOWN AS LAVENDER ANHYDRITE

*Lavender Angelite
in matrix*

COLOUR	Delicate lavender
APPEARANCE	Crystalline mass in a gritty, grainy matrix
RARITY	Rare
SOURCE	Canada

ATTRIBUTES This high vibration stone calls in the protective and transformational qualities of Archangel Zadkiel and invokes this Archangel's presence. Use it if you want to discover what the Archangels require of you, but you must be prepared to be of service to the planet when doing so rather than accessing it for egotistical motives, no matter how cunningly disguised those may be.

HEALING Lavender Angelite works beyond the physical level.

POSITION Meditate with this stone. Hold, position or grid as appropriate or disperse gem essence into the environment and around the aura. *NOTE: Make essence by indirect method.*

LINARITE

Raw crystal on matrix

COLOUR	Brilliant azure blue
APPEARANCE	Crystalline mass in a matrix
RARITY	Rare
SOURCE	New Mexico, United States, UK, Namibia, Australia

ATTRIBUTES Linarite stimulates bringing out the best in you. A great support for fragile souls with little faith in their ability to function efficiently, it instils confidence and the ability to utilize talents brought forward from other lives. Showing the gift in the heart of traumatic or destructive experiences, Linarite helps to understand the reason for and how to live within limitations – and supports transcending them where appropriate. It acts as a guide and mentor through life.

HEALING Linarite works at the level of soul healing.

POSITION Place, hold or grid as appropriate. Disperse the gem essence around the aura to instil confidence and self-love.

185

LORENZITE

ALSO KNOWN AS RAMSAYITE

Raw crystal on matrix

COLOUR	Clear, grey, pinkish, brown, blackish-brown
APPEARANCE	Opaque lozenge
RARITY	Rare titanium mineral
SOURCE	Kola Peninsula, Russia, Greenland, Northern Canada

ATTRIBUTES Lorenzite, also known as Ramsayite, is an extremely useful stone of protection when you have tried everything else. It wards off repeated psychic attack from those who understand crystal working and can circumvent the protection afforded by more common stones. Lorenzite creates an impenetrable shield for the furthest and most subtle layers of your aura.

HEALING Lorenzite helps to stabilize and harmonize the mental and physical bodies.

POSITION Wear, grid or place as appropriate. Disperse the aura with gem essence daily.

MACHU PICCHU STONE

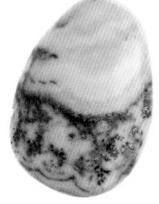

Polished

COLOUR	Greenish, various according to mineral content
APPEARANCE	Opaque stone with landscape markings
RARITY	Rare but available as cabochons
SOURCE	Peru

ATTRIBUTES This is a beautiful, gentle stone. Wearing it feels like a caress from powerful beings with your highest good in mind. It brings together in energetic harmony cuprite, manganese (rhodochrosite), psilomelane (merlinite), calcite and quartz and the effect is profound. Use it to journey to visit the Incas and ancient cultures of Mesoamerica. If you were involved in sacrifices or cultural upheavals, the stone provides healing and de-energizes* the memories to return your soul to peace.

HEALING Machu Picchu Stone heals the soul as opposed to the physical body.

POSITION Grid, place or position as appropriate. Disperse the gem essence into the environment or around the aura.

MAGDALENA STONE

ALSO KNOWN AS TUMBLED WITCHES FINGER

Tumbled

COLOUR	Clear with black, silver, gold and coloured inclusions
APPEARANCE	Rounded, tumbled stone with visible inclusions
RARITY	Rare
SOURCE	Zambia

ATTRIBUTES Tumbling Witches Finger totally transforms the energies of that stone, taking off the prickly edges. Magical and mystical, Magdalena Stone is highly effective for shamanic journeying* or earth healing*. Containing Smoky Quartz, rutile, tourmaline, chlorite, amphibole and smoky hematite, it has a profound cleansing effect for the soul, subtle and physical bodies. Clearing away all that is outgrown, rejected or dis-eased*, replacing it with the spiritual light of All That Is*, connecting to the sacred Magdalene archetype, companion to Christ.

HEALING Magdalena Stone works best at the metaphysical level of healing to bring the soul into balance.

POSITION Grid, hold or position as appropriate. Meditate with the stone to remove the dross from your soul.

MALACHOLLA

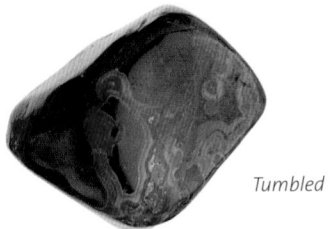

Tumbled

COLOUR	Green and turquoise
APPEARANCE	Swirling patches of colour
RARITY	Fairly easy to obtain
SOURCE	Africa

ATTRIBUTES Malacholla synergizes the energetic properties of Malachite and Chrysocolla into a powerful stone of communication, especially of what has been hidden. An excellent detoxifier on all levels, it regenerates the whole chakra and meridian systems of the physical and subtle bodies*. This stone helps you stand in your power and can be gridded in areas of environmental unrest.

HEALING Malacholla may assist spasms, infections, blood disorders, the excretory organs and insulin-blood sugar balance.

POSITION Hold, grid or position as appropriate. Disperse gem essence into the aura. *NOTE: Wash hands after handling. Make gem essence by the indirect method.*

MANGANO VESUVIANITE

Raw

COLOUR	Pink and blue-grey
APPEARANCE	Drusy crystals in crystalline matrix
RARITY	Rare
SOURCE	Unconfirmed

ATTRIBUTES This high frequency combination of Mangano Calcite with Idocrase takes love to an even more profound level. Mangano Vesuvianite provides an unshakeable link with your Higher Self and the angelic realm so that you feel an influx of compassion for your incarnated self. This love can be sent out to all of humanity and our earth. A wonderful stone for dissolving grief and heartbreak, it de-energizes* outworn emotional patterning.

HEALING Mangano Vesuvianite is a multi-dimensional cellular healer, assisting veins and dis-eases* that are the result of trauma or emotional turmoil.

POSITION Grid, hold or position as appropriate. Disperse gem essence around the aura. *NOTE: Make gem essence by the indirect method.*

MARBLE

Polished

COLOUR	Varies according to type
APPEARANCE	Veined, banded opaque stone
RARITY	Easily accessible
SOURCE	Worldwide

ATTRIBUTES Marble is a Calcite that has undergone immense transformation and passed through the harshest of conditions as it metamorphosed. An excellent stone to accompany you through soul-scouring challenges and traumatic or energetic changes, it stimulates your resilience and survival instincts so that you recognize that you are an eternal being who just happens to be undergoing yet another transformation. This calming stone teaches that everything must pass

191

away and that all will be re-formed so the only security is to be found in your inner self. Despite its earthy nature, this stone also helps you look to the stars and bring celestial energy to the earth.

With Marble's assistance, you polish your soul to a clear shining brightness that beams out into the world. If you are stuck in a rut, meditate with Marble to gain insight into the changes needed to bring about hope and joy, or to suggest coping strategies to help you gain the greatest gift from your present experience. If your life is chaotic, use it to gain stability of purpose. This uncompromising stone helps you to shake off lethargy and get on with life.

HEALING Marble is reputed to assist with stress and associated dis-eases.*

POSITION Hold, place or grid as appropriate. Keep a piece of Marble in your pocket during energetic or life changes.

Porphory

ADDITIONAL STONES

In addition to the generic properties of Marble the following stones have additional properties:

Porphory A type of marble, Porphory draws divine energy down to the earth which is why it was used for church decoration. With a Porphory floor, you literally stood on divine energy and were uplifted. It links to the ancient view that the divine was to be found in everything and facilitates connection to the divine within yourself. Meditating with Porphory helps you to recognize soul lessons in the smallest details of life and teaches that the soul is always free to make a choice, no matter what the external circumstances might be. It strengthens your connection to your inner guidance so that you trust your insights. Opening your inner vision, it also helps you to trust others because you can see into their heart and check out their integrity for yourself. With the assistance of Porphory you are able to inspire trust yourself by shining out your heart-light and displaying your spiritual integrity for the world to see. Porphory may assist the veins and structures of the body.

Picasso Stone is a form of marble that assists communication and encourages clarity of thought. Strengthening intuition and helping you connect to the higher mind, it puts you in touch with eternal wisdom. Meditating with its abstract symbols helps organize chaotic thoughts and overome challenges.

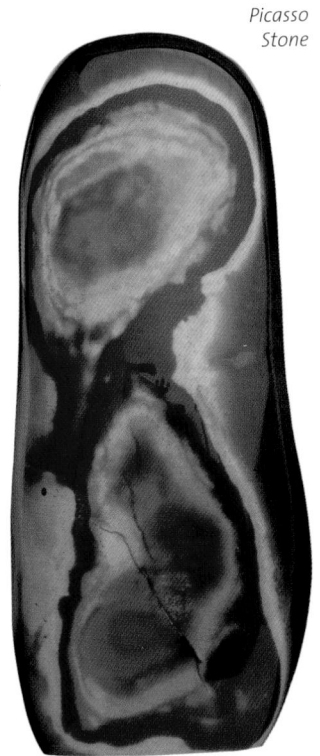

Picasso Stone

MARIALITE

Natural

COLOUR	Colourless, white, grey, purple, yellow, green, pink, brown
APPEARANCE	Vitreous, pearly opaque stone
RARITY	Rare
SOURCE	Madagascar, Tanzania, United States

ATTRIBUTES Marialite stimulates independence of thought and helps you to set achievable goals as you move confidently through life. It provides an impetus for assertive change and, if you feel that you have been scapegoated or martyred at any time, helps to de-energize* old patterns and move forward in life. Placed over the eyes, it helps see your way clearly.

HEALING Marialite supports post-operative recovery and is said to repattern cellular memory*. It is traditionally used to treat varicose veins, cataracts, glaucoma and bone disorders.

POSITION Hold, position, grid or disperse gem essence around the aura.

MAW SIT SIT

Polished and shaped

COLOUR	Green with dark veining
APPEARANCE	Jade-like, veined and mottled opaque stone
RARITY	Rare
SOURCE	Burma (Myanmar)

ATTRIBUTES Maw Sit Sit has a variable chemical composition of at least six minerals. The intense green comes from chromium. It shines like glass when polished and is helpful for inward reflection and meditation. Found in the foothills of the Himalayas, it has been subjected to enormous earth pressures. This energizing and uplifting stone shows you the joy of being alive and helps to lift depression. If you have a melancholic nature, wear it constantly.

HEALING The trace element chromium supports normal glucose metabolism and the breakdown of fats and proteins. Maw Sit Sit may assist in maintaining correct blood sugar balance.

POSITION Wear constantly or place over the pancreas. Disperse gem essence into the aura.

MOHAVE TURQUOISE

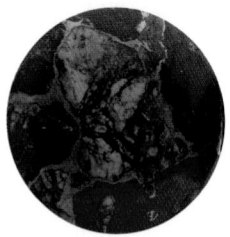

Polished

COLOUR	Bright blue-purple-yellow-gold-bronze-green
APPEARANCE	Mottled, polished stone
RARITY	Easily obtained
SOURCE	Laboratory made dyed American Turquoise

ATTRIBUTES Tiny pieces of natural Turquoise are dyed and compressed together to make this brilliant-coloured stone that is extremely popular for jewellery. In addition to the usual Turquoise properties of protection, metaphysical opening, abundance, solace for the spirit and healing for the body, Mohave Turquoise enhances your feeling of inner well-being and lifts your spirit.

Due to the way it is bonded, it helps to solidify groups or families. Assisting in knowing that you are a part of All That Is* and acting accordingly to everything around you, it expands unity consciousness. Wear this stone to remind you to walk lightly on the earth.

HEALING Mohave Turquoise retains the healing properties of Turquoise, although these may be depleted by the dying process.

POSITION Due to its fragile nature, Mohave Turquoise is best worn as jewellery set in silver.

ADDITIONAL STONE
Navaho Purple Turquoise is made in a similar way and both are very similar. The underlying stone is a powerful blue enhanced with red dye and Navaho Purple Turquoise is reported to help you stay in a place of loving connection with others.

*Navaho Purple
Turquoise*

MOHAWKITE

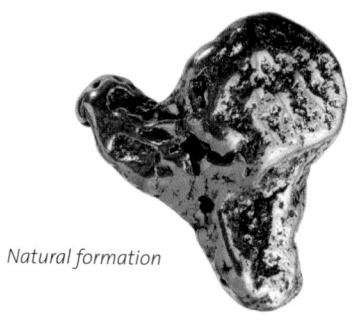

Natural formation

COLOUR	Silvery-coppery-goldish brown or grey
APPEARANCE	Pitted, metallic stone; occasionally cubic crystalline
RARITY	Found in only one location
SOURCE	Michigan, United States

ATTRIBUTES Copper-based with traces of nickel, iron, silver and cobalt, Mohawkite combines the stability and perceptiveness of metal with the transmutational possibilities of cobalt. Particularly useful for working at a higher dimension and within the earth's frequency at the same time, it grounds vibrational change and harnesses subtle energy fields*. Equally effective within the human body or that of the earth, it re-energizes and harmonizes the etheric* grid, chakras and meridians* to support the physical level of being. It is excellent for grounding and shielding, and is particularly useful for holding the space of a grid*.

Mohawkite facilitates unity consciousness and also creates an interface between your psyche and that of another person, so that you fully empathize without being overwhelmed by what you perceive whilst at the same time honouring your unity of spirit.

With its ability to move through time, Mohawkite is an effective healer for the ancestral line,* sending healing into the far past and forward into the future so that new generations are freed from the karmic* burdens and core beliefs* that have shaped a family's reality throughout time. An effective earth healer*, it cleanses and restructures areas of dis-ease* and anchors the earth's grid. It aligns your physical body to the earth. Instilling strength of mind and resolute purpose, Mohawkite is stabilizing and protective. It encourages openness to yourself and to others through feeling totally safe within your environment, inner or outer. If you hold outdated core beliefs and attitudes detrimental to your well-being, such as self-loathing, or are judgmental, it releases these and helps renegotiate with inner figures such as the saboteur or critic.

A stone of balance, Mohawkite stabilizes extremes of emotion, bringing about inner equilibrium. This stone encourages the free flow of energy through the meridians and organs.

HEALING This stone is strengthening for the whole body, particularly at an energetic level.

POSITION Hold or place as appropriate, particularly in grids or on maps for earth healing, or disperse gem essence around the aura. *CAUTION: Mohawkite is arsenate-based so handle with care and wash hands thoroughly after use. Do not make crystal essence by the direct method.*

MONAZITE

Raw

COLOUR	Yellow, brown, red-brown, orange, grey-green
APPEARANCE	Distinctive cross or lozenge shaped crystal
RARITY	Rare
SOURCE	Brazil, United States, Norway, India, Madagascar

ATTRIBUTES Monazite contains rare-earth elements that are much prized by industry, which means that it is rarely available as a healing stone, but it is very effective for earth energy work in areas of disturbance or disconnection of the grid. It repairs meridian* lines and re-establishes equilibrium.

HEALING Monazite works best for earth healing*.

POSITION Grid in the landscape or on a map. Disperse gem essence into the environment.

MONTEBRASITE

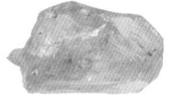

Raw

COLOUR	Grey, yellowish, blue, white
APPEARANCE	Translucent or opaque and vitreous
RARITY	Rare
SOURCE	France, Pakistan, Brazil, United States

ATTRIBUTES Montebrasite has a light, sunny vibration that heals depression and anxiety and stabilizes bi-polar swings. Creating a calm centre in which to serenely wait out changes or difficulties in your life, it helps recognize when action is appropriate. Strengthening willpower, if you suffer from procrastination or start but never finish projects, this is the stone for you. It stimulates creativity. Montebrasite aligns the whole chakra system, integrating the higher chakras into the body's energy field.

HEALING Montebrasite reputedly assists digestive problems such as IBS, heartburn and ulcers and genetic disorders and hyperactivity. It harmonizes the electrical systems of the body.

POSITION Place, position or grid as appropriate. Disperse gem essence into the aura.

MOONSTONE: **BLACK**

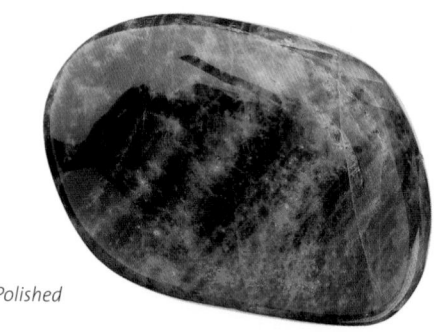

Polished

COLOUR	Black-grey
APPEARANCE	Streaky opaque to translucent stone
RARITY	Easily obtained
SOURCE	Madagascar

ATTRIBUTES The trade name for a type of Labradorite, Black Moonstone is excellent for metaphysical pursuits of all kinds as it protects and opens your energy field to higher vibrations. If you need a mentor or spiritual guardian, hold Black Moonstone and ask that a suitable guide comes to you from higher dimensions or in the physical realm. Holding a powerful connection to the divine feminine, it links to the transformative energy of the Black Madonna or the Magdalene.

Black Moonstone screens out the undesirable effects of electromagnetic emanations, especially mobile phones, computers and WiFi, and blocks radiation and X-rays. Assisting those who are emotionally over-sensitive, it filters the energetic information you pick up from other people so that you only perceive what is useful. Grid Black Moonstone around your home to attract abundance and to create a calm, serene atmosphere. It stabilizes rocky relationships and assists during teenage angst. This stone strengthens concentration so use it for study or creativity.

Physically, Black Moonstone increases your stamina and assists accident prone or dyspraxic children to be more focused with better co-ordination. It helps adults who have motor difficulties or who lack concentration to better focus their attention.

HEALING Black Moonstone is reputedly helpful for the colon, kidneys, liver, spleen, stomach and female reproductive organs. It may stimulate recovery from a stroke and be beneficial for Parkinson's and similar diseases*. Moonstone is traditionally used to balance the female hormonal cycle and assist during menopause.

POSITION Hold, place or grid as appropriate.

ADDITIONAL STONES
In addition to the generic properties of Moonstone, the following stones have further properties.

Adularia An Orthoclase Feldspar, gentle Adularia opens the third eye and assists your inner sight. A calming stone, it helps to dispel the illusions and hysteria that arise from over-sensitivity to the energies of a place or other people. This stone facilitates distinguishing between true 'seeing' and appropriate psychic perceptions from wishful thinking or fear-generated prophecies and wild imaginings. It is helpful for migraines caused by psychic blockages or being too open to the emanations around you.

Raw Adularia

Gabbro with Moonstone The combination of Gabbro with Moonstone is energetically confusing to some people, the stone feels like it doesn't know whether to be deeply grounded or to float off the planet. In those who are attuned, it helps you to be 'here' and 'there' at the same time as you navigate the multi-dimensional layers of consciousness. In those that are not attuned, it may make it difficult to ground the information received in those spheres or, indeed, to return to the earth at all. If you only have a toehold in incarnation, this is not the stone for you.

Gabbro with Moonstone

Purple Moonstone A gentle heart-centred form of Moonstone that helps you to have compassion for yourself and others. May be colour infused.

Purple Moonstone

Ruby in Moonstone This dynamic combination is excellent for healing hearts broken through loss and grief. It helps you to step through your pain and develop compassion for yourself and others.

Ruby in Moonstone

MTROLITE

ALSO KNOWN AS CHROME CHALCEDONY

*Raw Mtrolite
on matrix*

COLOUR	Green
APPEARANCE	Opaque stone
RARITY	Rare
SOURCE	Canada

ATTRIBUTES Mtrolite is a calming and centring stone that enables you to ride out vibrational or situational changes with equanimity, no matter how traumatic the upheaval may be. Stimulating the ability to cope, it instils serenity in the midst of turmoil and assists with calm acceptance of current circumstances. Mtrolite helps you to be open to change and at the same time to live in the present moment. If you rail against your current situation, meditate with Mtrolite to find the soul intention behind your experience. You can accept it or, if more appropriate, change it and move on. Mtrolite calms the whole auric field. A heart chakra stone, Mtrolite is the perfect crystal to bring peace and harmony into your world.

Mtrolite reputedly supports those practising homeopathy or herbal medicine. Mtrolite is a chrome chalcedony and traces of chromium are required by the body for correct assimilation of glucose, which regulates the metabolism of fats and proteins. As we get older, the ability to assimilate chromium diminishes and may need supplementing. One way to do this is to wear Mtrolite in contact with the skin so that a homeopathic resonance dose is transferred.

HEALING Placed over the site, Mtrolite may assist backache and other pains. Said to detoxify and strengthen the liver and nervous system and may assist with stabilizing blood sugar imbalances.

POSITION Hold, position or place as appropriate or disperse gem essence around the aura.

OBSIDIAN: **FIRE**

Polished

COLOUR	Black with scintillating rainbow flashes
APPEARANCE	Dense black stone until the fire flashes
RARITY	Rare
SOURCE	Oregon, United States

ATTRIBUTES: The fire effect in Fire Obsidian is created by thin layers of Magnetite within the stone that catch the light when carefully cut and polished. This stone helps you to hone your soul to its brilliant best. A natural glass formed when hot lava bubbles out into water, Obsidian is known for its grounding, protective, releasing and penetrating metaphysical qualities. It absorbs and transforms darkness within itself. Combine this with the powerful attraction properties of Magnetite and you have a stone that draws metaphysical energies to you and fires up the transformation process for your spiritual being. This is a stone with a very high spiritual vibration.

HEALING Fire Obsidian assists energetic recovery from serious illness or psychosomatic dis-ease* but works mainly beyond the physical body to transform the soul.

Mahogany Sheen

POSITION Place over the lower chakras to ignite spiritual creativity and kundalini* rise. Disperse gem essence around the aura.

ADDITIONAL STONE

Mahogany Sheen This variation on Mahogany Obsidian carries a lighter, more refined vibration that gently brings issues to the surface and transmutes them. It offers powerful protection to the aura and the lightbody* and helps your soul to shine.

Spider Web This pretty Obsidian helps you to recognize the patterns that hold you in the past, the controls you put in place and how you manipulate yourself and others to protect the status quo. It symbolizes the web that you wove in order to survive. Like all Obsidians, Spider Web brings into light all that you have previously hidden. Helping to break all the patterns of the past, it strips you bare and reveals the beauty at the heart of your soul. With its assistance you bring your innermost designs to the surface and consciously create a web of light that supports what you most desire. Grid Spider Web Obsidian to support the energetic meridians of the subtle* or physical body or the earth, giving strength in time of need. It reportedly strengthens the knees and hips and supports speech therapy. It also alleviates dark moods.

Spider Web

NUNDERITE

Tumbled

COLOUR	Grey-brown with green-blue
APPEARANCE	Opaque stone with stripes or splodges
RARITY	Rare
SOURCE	New South Wales, Australia

ATTRIBUTES A combination of Jadeite and Feldspar, Nunderite is an excellent grounding stone. It provides a calm, still centre in which to anchor your energies during times of turmoil, change or multi-dimensional journeying*. Showing you creative ways to obtain your goals, Nunderite encourages co-operation and draws like-minded people towards you. The Feldspar component gets things moving, literally shifting energies to a different frequency and helping you to negotiate amplitude shifts as the vibration powers up. The Jadeite portion helps you to face the change with equanimity. The combination assists in balancing the new energies and putting them to work. This stone moves out of your orbit anyone who is not for your highest good.

Nunderite facilitates multi-dimensional psychic protection, creating an impenetrable interface at the outer layers of the aura. It is highly effective if you have been under prolonged psychic attack. It also cleanses the aura and charges it with light. If you are the target of emotional vampirism, Nunderite helps you to seal your aura and protect your spleen, de-energizing* cords and hooks so that you retain your own energy rather than feeding it to someone else.

Nunderite is a useful stone for those who lack self-confidence as it imparts emotional strength and the courage to move forward. Encouraging you to be self-sufficient but not selfish, it helps you to move forward into who you may be rather than what you fear you are.

This stone is traditionally helpful for weather magic, bringing rain to drought-stricken areas or the sun to dry out an excess of water.

HEALING Nunderite is soothing for the kidneys, spleen and over-stressed adrenals. It may assist the water balance within the body and the acid-alkaline balance.

POSITION Grid, hold or place as appropriate. Tape over the spleen chakra to prevent energy loss to psychic vampires. Disperse the gem essence around the kidneys and over the spleen and solar plexus.

OCEANITE

ALSO KNOWN AS BLUE ONYX

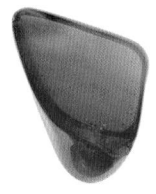

Tumbled

COLOUR	Blue
APPEARANCE	Veined stone
RARITY	Rare
SOURCE	Argentina

ATTRIBUTES Strengthening for the physical body and the soul, Oceanite provides support during challenging times. It aligns your will with your soul purpose and accesses guidance from your Higher Self. It helps to heal trauma, including that from past lives, and to communicate your feelings more clearly. Useful if you need to resolve inherent contradictions, such as conflicting past life personas, it brings dualities into harmony.

HEALING Oceanite is particularly useful if you suffer from overwhelming anxieties, fears or phobias as it calms your emotional body.

POSITION Wear, hold or grid as appropriate. Disperse gem essence into the aura. *NOTE: Blue Onyx Oceanite is energetically dissimilar to the faceted gemstone of the same name.*

OOELITHIC AND CRINOIDAL LIMESTONE

Raw

COLOUR	Varies
APPEARANCE	Varies according to type
RARITY	Found all over the globe
SOURCE	Worldwide

ATTRIBUTES Limestone was created from trillions of small creatures that died, fell to the sea floor and were resurrected as rock over an immense period of time. The stone still retains its essential lifeforce. When first excavated Limestone is soft and can be carved but the outer casing hardens over time. It represents how our soul is shaped

212

throughout its long journey and helps to weather the changes by creating an interface* with the outside world that protects your core stability.

Meditating with the stone, or living in a building created from it, helps you recognize the immense significance of how you were shaped by the people and the environment around you over aeons of time. If necessary, Limestone assists you in moving away from this ingrained patterning to follow your own script. It encourages you to live a balanced lifestyle that encompasses sufficient activity and appropriate stillness to ensure peace and happiness. The ancient Egyptians used Limestone to construct the pyramids and built a huge solar battery that stored the sun's rays and facilitated inter- and multi-dimensional travel and communication.

Crinoidal Limestone was created from crinoids, primitive echinoderms with five or more feathery arms radiating from a central disk. As with all fossils, this stone helps you to explore your roots and deep-seated issues, and to find core stability.

HEALING Limestone assists with healing the ancestral line*. Physically it restores energetic balance and supports the skeletal system. It may assist abdominal dis-eases caused by energetic blockages in the base or sacral chakras.

POSITION Grid, hold or place as appropriate.

Crinoidal limestone

213

OPAL: **ETHIOPIAN**

*Raw Orange
Ethiopian Opal
in matrix*

COLOUR	Red, orange, yellow, green, brownish, white
APPEARANCE	Fiery opalescent crystal within a nodule matrix
RARITY	Rare
SOURCE	Ethiopia

ATTRIBUTES This beautiful high vibration stone is a crystal of infinite expansion that burns off the karma* of the past and opens the way to rebirth. Carrying extremely high vibrations and ancient wisdom, Ethiopian Opal stimulates all the metaphysical gifts. It carries a soul holograph giving access to past, present and future and offering protection while journeying through multi-dimensions or within your Self.

A stone of great insight, Ethiopian Opal is a vehicle for the fire and earth elementals, bringing about purification through an inner 'fire walk' and grounding the transmutation into the physical body. As such it helps you to face your deepest fears and transform them into your greatest gifts. The stone co-operates with your soul to engineer situations that release and de-energize* deep layers of repressed emotions, fear and trauma, opening the way for new patterns to be laid down.

Ethiopian Opal exfoliates the soul, gently unpeeling encrusted layers so that new growth occurs. Program it to bring about the changes you need to make – holding the Opal facilitates your Higher Self communicating exactly what these are and how best they can be brought about. Meditating with it reveals the past life causes of situations, facilitating healing these by moving to a higher soul perspective in the inter-life.

Ethiopian Opal carries positive dragon energy*: personal and planetary. It unites, cleanses and activates the base and sacral chakras to stimulate your creativity and unites them with the dynamic unconditional love of the higher heart chakra and the refined mental capacities of the alta major chakra, so that you manifest your highest will on earth. Placed at the base and top of the spine it ignites kundalini* power and, on the base of the skull, opens the alta major chakra. Placed midway up the skull, it assists in transmuting anger into joyful, active will and a desire for inner and outer peace. Placed on power points on the earth it assists environmental cleansing and regeneration, stimulating fertility and realignment of the earth's meridians* and creating a shield against negative vibrations.

Ethiopian Opal has been shown to assist weight loss by addressing the underlying psychological causes, particularly where these relate to feelings of vulnerability or deep rage. It brings all the subtle bodies* into equilibrium, releasing blockages and imprints, so that the whole body functions harmoniously inducing well-being. However, being a fiery stone, it has been found that the healing virtue of Ethiopian Opal is rapidly discharged, especially during a traumatic healing or when making a gem essence, and the stone may need considerable recharging before working again. Cleanse depleted stones thoroughly after use: rest them and place in the sun on Quartz for a long period to recharge.

Working with this stone regularly helps to enhance your energetic sensitivity and awareness so that you become more attuned to crystal, personal, earth and planetary energies. You may need to use a shielding stone such as Healers Gold that facilitates working at interface* if the sensations become too acute.

HEALING Ethiopian Opal works best at the subtle* or psychosomatic soul level of healing. It purifies and strengthens the biomagnetic field* and the emotional body, and brings the etheric blueprint* into balance so that changes manifest in the physical body. It may assist with skin conditions, especially those with a psychosomatic base.

POSITION Place, grid or position as appropriate or disperse gem essence around the aura. Cleanse and recharge frequently.

SPECIFIC COLOURS
As with other varieties of Opal, each colour carries specific properties.
Rainbow flash brings about soul transmutation.
White flash carries the soul imprint for the current lifetime.
Orange flash stimulates creativity, dissolving karmic blocks, hooks or implants in the lower chakras.
Purple or pink flash carries the violet flame of transmutation and purifies high vibration chakras.

Raw red flash

Green flash assists interdimensional travel and kything*.
Red flash carries dragon energy, stimulating the earth's kundalini flow and creativity on all levels.
Brown flash assists with de-energizing* and reprogramming patterns that detrimentally affect physicality and manifestation.
NOTE: Make essence by indirect method.

OPAL: **HONEY**

Raw

COLOUR	Rich honey and cream
APPEARANCE	Opaque, like solidified honey
RARITY	Rare
SOURCE	Unconfirmed (it has been suggested it may be synthetic)

ATTRIBUTES Joyful Honey Opal helps make the most of opportunities. Assisting recovery from emotional heartache, it facilitates giving and receiving love. Holding this stone encourages speaking about what could not be spoken of previously. Honey Opal softens prickly, defensive people who have suffered mental, physical or emotional abuse, in any timeframe. Bringing the issues gently to the surface so that they are de-energized* and released, it restores self-confidence and awareness of innate worth.

217

This gentle stone is excellent for sensitive people who find other crystals too strong. Program the stone to radiate peace and harmony out into your environment and dissolve dis-ease* in whatever form it may take.

HEALING Honey Opal is said to be a natural antibiotic for fevers, colds and flu.

POSITION Hold, grid or position as appropriate. Disperse gem essence into the aura especially around the heart and solar plexus. *NOTE: Make essence by indirect method.*

ADDITIONAL STONE

Lavender-Purple Opal is a very gentle form of Opal that cleanses the third eye, soma and higher crown chakras to open insight and spiritual vision.

Lavender-Purple Opal in matrix

OPAL: **LEMURIAN GOLD**™

Raw

COLOUR	Deep golden yellow
APPEARANCE	Translucent shimmering opaque stone
RARITY	Rare
SOURCE	Madagascar

ATTRIBUTES Said to be connected to ancient Lemuria, high vibration Lemurian Gold Opal™ enhances your energetic sensitivities and heightens your awareness of vibrational change. This is a powerful stone for enhancing your intuition and linking into knowledge from the far past, when energy and matter were less solidified than they are now. This is an Opal from the time when the soul was 'lightly clothed in skin', and as such it brings forward memories of the light that was carried into incarnation in those distant times.

Meditating with the stone assists you to reconnect to your awareness from ancient times and to the multi-dimensional extravaganza that is your soul. Knowing who you are in your entirety enhances your trust in yourself and your universe, calming anxiety about change and reducing stress levels.

HEALING Lemurian Gold Opal™ works best at the energetic level of healing, restoring harmony and reprinting a pattern of light into the cells.

POSITION Grid, place or disperse gem essence around the aura. *NOTE: Make essence by indirect method.*

Polished Honduras Opal

ADDITIONAL STONE

Honduras Opal is a gentle stone ethically hand-mined out of seams of basalt, which is cut to form a matrix to support the stone and to reflect the scintillating colour. Gazing into a Honduras Opal helps you to see the spirit shining within your inner being. Mining this opal subsidizes the income of the local people and draws abundance to you.

OPAL: **MACEDONIAN GREEN**

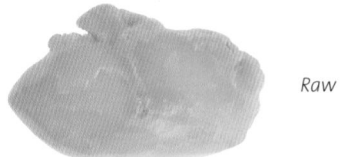

Raw

COLOUR	Green
APPEARANCE	Opaque, resin-like stone
RARITY	Rare
SOURCE	Serbia (near Macedonian border)

ATTRIBUTES Stimulating the heart chakras, Macedonian Green Opal heals emotional wounds from any timeframe. Dissolving memories held in subtle bodies*, it brings in light. Helpful in treating depression and spiritual apathy, it disperses negative energies and turns anger into joyful self-assertion. Promoting confidence and stimulating creativity, it helps express yourself in the world. Macedonian Green Opal provides a burst of physical energy to overcome depletion and promotes healthy diets. It is helpful during convalescence and prolonged periods of stress.

HEALING Macedonian Green Opal is reputed to be helpful for colds, flu, and fevers and for strengthening the immune system.

POSITION Grid, position or hold as appropriate. Place over the thymus to stimulate the immune system. Disperse gem essence into the aura or environment. *NOTE: Make gem essence by the indirect method.*

OPAL: **MOUNT SHASTA**

Raw

COLOUR	Blue
APPEARANCE	Vitreous stone in matrix
RARITY	Rare
SOURCE	Mount Shasta, United States

ATTRIBUTES An Opal that comes from one of the seven major energy vortexes of the world, Mount Shasta Opal has a deeply nurturing, high vibration that is gentle and extremely healing in its effect. This stone puts you in touch with the spiritual protection afforded by archangels and higher beings. Meditate with this stone to invoke assistance or hold it to connect to the chakra vortex energy of the site. It links to Archangels Gabriel and Michael, and to the ascended master St Germain. A powerful shamanic stone, Mount Shasta Opal helps you to travel stealthily during metaphysical workings of all kinds but is particularly helpful for lower world journeys and soul retrieval*.

Mount Shasta is said to be one of the last outposts of ancient Lemuria and meditating with this Opal assists you to reconnect to those times and to open a cosmic portal through which ancient knowledge and star healing passes. However, before opening such a portal it is wise to check that beings granted access to our earth have only our highest good in mind. Not all star beings are beneficial companions who wish to assist consciousness evolution. Program Mount Shasta Opal to only allow through the portal energies that are beneficial for the evolution of our world.

Opening and purifying all the chakras, but especially the heart and higher heart, Mount Shasta Opal infuses love into the emotional body and the mind to create a calm quiet inner space. Useful for emotional healing at any level, it disperses stress. Placed at your throat it helps communicate clearly and with focused intent. It is a stone of faithfulness and loyalty.

HEALING Mount Shasta Opal may assist insomnia and ameliorate the effects of stress.

POSITION Hold, position or grid as appropriate. Disperse gem essence around the aura or environment. *NOTE: Make gem essence by the indirect method.*

OPAL: **OWYHEE BLUE**

*Raw crystal
on matrix*

COLOUR	Blue (colour may change on exposure to air)
APPEARANCE	Opalescent stone
RARITY	Rare
SOURCE	United States

ATTRIBUTES The celestial blue of high vibration Owyhee Blue Opal connects you to the highest angelic guidance and to your own guides. A dream-stone, it opens metaphysical abilities and strengthens intuition. It has long been used for shamanic journeying* and multi-dimensional exploration, as it provides protection and shielding during the journey and makes you more receptive to what you find. This particular Opal connects the throat with the third eye chakra to facilitate kything* and communication with higher beings.

Owyhee Blue Opal dispels shyness and anxiety, helping you to be more confident and decisive, and to reach the goals you set for yourself. It aids in activating and drawing on your own personal power without being bombastic or arrogant. If you suffer from mental confusion, place this Opal between your third eye and soma chakras or on the back of the skull. It clears negative mental patterns and expectations, and instils clarity.

Blue stones assist communication and at a physical level this stone is reported to be beneficial for over-strained vocal cords and to assist singers and public speakers. It assists in finding exactly the right words for a given situation.

HEALING Owyhee Blue Opal may energetically assist throat ailments, especially bacterial or viral infections, and Parkinson's disease. Owyhee Blue Opal soothes the eyes and may regularize blood sugar.

POSITION Place, position or grid as appropriate or disperse gem essence around the aura. *NOTE: Make essence by indirect method.*

ADDITIONAL COLOUR AND TYPE
Green Opal is particularly useful for overcoming chronic sickness and excessive mucus. It gives support and vitality during convalescence.

Raw Green Opal

ORANGE KYANITE

Natural formation of Orange Kyanite with mica

COLOUR	Orange
APPEARANCE	Striated, sparkling stone
RARITY	Becoming more easily available
SOURCE	Tanzania

ATTRIBUTES A stone of immense creativity, Orange Kyanite's colour comes from manganese within its core, its sparkle from mica flakes incorporated within its striations. The stone does not hold negative energy which it instantly transmutes. It is a powerful chakra* cleanser and opener, pouring light into the energy body as it does so. This is a useful stone for opening sensitivity to your gut instincts, your instinctive *knowing*. It opens your psychic channels and your kinaesthetic sensing.

226

Orange Kyanite is a great stone for stimulating your personal power. Working with it reminds you what gives you pleasure. Taking you inside yourself to reconnect to your own resources rather than going outside for support, it energizes your libido and renews your passion for life.

Orange Kyanite hooks out other people's energy, especially from the base and sacral chakras. It releases you from the energetic residues of prior sexual encounters and dissolves karmic* blocks. At a physical level, Orange Kyanite reprograms your approach to being in physical incarnation, releasing energetic dis-ease*.

HEALING Orange Kyanite reputedly assists anorexia, bulimia, addictions, sexual dysfunction, PMS, depression and increases fertility. It is helpful for lifting black depression and increasing libido. It may regulate blood sugar imbalances.

POSITION Place Orange Kyanite over your sacral chakra, grid or hold or disperse gem essence around the aura. *NOTE: Make essence by indirect method.*

PARGASITE

Raw crystal in matrix

COLOUR	Lime-green, brown to black, green-blue
APPEARANCE	Distinctive crystal in a matrix or grainy stone
RARITY	Rare
SOURCE	Finland, Pakistan, United States, Chile, Italy, Sweden, UK, United States

ATTRIBUTES Pargasite has a gentle energy that provides emotional guidance and support. Softening the hardest of hearts, it dismantles defences built up over many years and de-energizes* the issues that lie behind them. Pargasite releases blockages in the emotional body and opens the heart chakras so that you empathize, expressing compassion and forgiveness for yourself and others. Valued for its ability to control jealousy or envy, Pargasite helps with low self-esteem and self-image.

HEALING Pargasite is beneficial for psychosomatic conditions of the heart, throat and circulation. It is reputed to assist skin diseases.

POSITION Hold, position, grid or disperse gem essence around the aura.

PENTAGONITE

Tumbled

COLOUR	Turquoise blue
APPEARANCE	Long needles or tumbled opaque stone
RARITY	Easily obtained
SOURCE	India

ATTRIBUTES The brilliant colour of Pentagonite opens the third eye and activates inner sight, expanding consciousness. Activating the soma chakra, it allows you to journey to higher dimensions to communicate with beings that inhabit those realms and consciously bring back wisdom. If you suffer from emotional turmoil, meditating with Pentagonite gently soothes your soul. Place tumbled stone under the pillow to alleviate night terrors and induce pleasant dreams.

HEALING Pentagonite may assist with the eyes and throat. At an energetic level it harmonizes the immune and endocrine systems.

POSITION Grid, place or position as appropriate. Disperse gem essence around the aura. *NOTE: Make gem essence with a tumbled stone by the indirect method.*

PERUMAR™

ALSO KNOWN AS BLUE RHODOCHROSITE

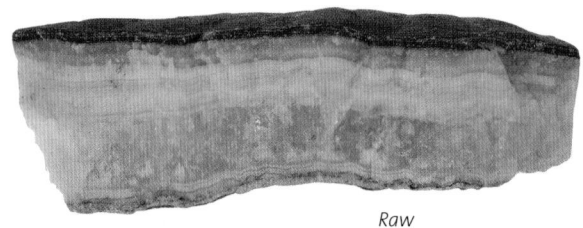

Raw

COLOUR	Light sky blue
APPEARANCE	Opaque stone with veining and bands
RARITY	Rare
SOURCE	Peru

ATTRIBUTES Blue Rhodochrosite, (Perumar™) has a gentle energy that heals the heart and instils selfless love and compassion. Its tiny flaws remind us to be forgiving and compassionate to the imperfections in our own and others' characters. Perumar™ encourages a positive take on the future. Meditate with this stone on your third eye or soma chakra to get in touch with ancient wisdom of the Incas and their sacred sites.

HEALING Perumar™ acts as a filter to remove negativity from energetic bodies, enlivening the physical body with peaceful well-being.

POSITION Wear, hold, grid or disperse gem essence into the aura, especially around the heart.

PETRIFIED WOOD

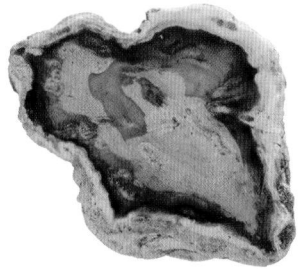

Polished slice

COLOUR	Brown, yellow, red, pink, black, white
APPEARANCE	Tree-like banded stone
RARITY	Easily obtained
SOURCE	Worldwide

ATTRIBUTES Protective Petrified Wood is invaluable for grounding high vibrations into the earth. This stone formed when a living tree fell into water and elements such as manganese, iron and copper were alchemically absorbed. In many cases the wood turned to shining silica and the stone often contains Aragonite, a powerful earth healer*. Each mineral produces a specific colour: carbon, black; copper, cobalt and chromium, green-blue; iron oxides, red, brown, and yellow; manganese, pinkish-orange and manganese oxides black and yellow. Each trace element has a specific energetic effect so choose your Petrified Wood according to its feel.

The power of Petrified Wood lies in its ancient wisdom and long service to the planet. Connect with it to find a mentor. Legends abound of the healing properties of trees and the stone is helpful in past life work as it can be read like a book, with each ring revealing a page of the Akashic Record*. Helping you to feel at home on the earth, it reminds you that you are more than spirit trapped within the material world and that one day you'll rise again to take on another form of being but that, in the meantime, there is service to give to our earthly home.

Petrified Wood supports the soul during challenges and tribulations of spiritual evolution and reveals the soul-gifts at their heart. It facilitates peeling back the layers encrusting your core being, releasing that which no longer serves while retaining that which does. With this stone's assistance you walk upon the earth with grace, honoring the wisdom of the ages.

A calming stone, Petrified Wood helps you to worry less especially about things of little importance. It helps you to accept serenely things you cannot change, to make changes that are possible and instils the wisdom to know the difference. Use this stone to be all that you may be.

Hugely supportive for the body, Petrified Wood assists mobility on all levels. If DNA potential has been blocked by ancestral genetic memory, or if a disorder has manifested, Petrified Wood de-energizes the old cellular information field and activates potential in the new. It reactivates 12 strand DNA. This stone assists you when you are in the chronic or recovery stage of dis-ease* or are facing a progressive illness, especially in old age.

Petrified Wood helps to stabilize the environment and is said to be good for people living in old buildings, especially those with structural problems. A stone for archaeologists, historians and librarians, it is reputed to counteract ageism in the workplace and to help others recognize the wisdom and value of old age.

HEALING Petrified Wood is beneficial for the immune system, joints, muscles, bones, feet, back, nervous system and the lungs. Said to assist motility and halt the aging process, disintegration and calcification and to help overcome obesity. It may be beneficial for disturbed sleep patterns, Chronic Fatigue Syndrome and genetic disorders, assisting recovery from serious illness.

POSITION Hold, position, grid or disperse gem essence around the aura or environment.

ADDITIONAL STONE
Peanut Wood is an Australian fossilized wood. It assists those who have difficulty in walking on the earth, whether physically or energetically, and helps you to feel at home on the planet. As with all Petrified Wood, it is an excellent aid to grounding energy into the physical body and keeping that body anchored to the earth. A stable, calming stone it supports during trauma and healing or emotional

Peanut Wood

challenges. A useful stone for past life healing, it facilitates previous life exploration and going to your soul's roots. It reputedly helps weight loss and is useful in cases of incontinence or, placed behind the ears, tinnitus and poor hearing.

PHENACITE ON FLUORITE

Raw

COLOUR	White on coloured matrix
APPEARANCE	Crystalline
RARITY	Rare combination
SOURCE	Unconfirmed

ATTRIBUTES This is an amazing combination for awakening your connection to the universal mind and for ensuring that communications from other dimensions are of the highest order. It instils clarity, clears confusion and helps you to make intuitive connections as it harmonizes your brain to a higher level of functioning.

HEALING This combination works beyond the physical but is excellent for removing mental confusion. Place at the base of the skull to enhance neural pathways and brain hemisphere integration.

POSITION Place on the higher crown and soma chakras, third eye or past life chakras.

PHLOGOPITE

*Natural crystal
on matrix*

COLOUR	Light brown, greenish, yellow, colourless, grey
APPEARANCE	Layered, plate-like stone
RARITY	Rare
SOURCE	Greenland, Siberia, Russia, Canada

ATTRIBUTES Phlogopite energetically filters electromagnetic pollution. It opens metaphysical abilities and activates all chakras. Use it to find the gifts hidden in the darker corners of your soul or to remove blocks to spiritual development. It connects to the four cardinal directions and is ideal for Medicine Wheel or Earth Mother ceremonies and kything*.

HEALING Phlogopite keeps the subtle* and physical bodies free of pollutant energy. Its high magnesium content energetically strengthens bones and tooth enamel, assists nutrient and vitamin assimilation, enzyme function, energy transfer, and correct working of the body.

POSITION Grid, place or hold with care as appropriate. *NOTE: If making gem essence do so by the indirect method.*

235

PHOLOCOMITE

Raw slice

COLOUR	Blackish-purplish-silver, greenish, yellowish, brownish, grey
APPEARANCE	Sparkling, mica-like layers
RARITY	Rare
SOURCE	Russia, Finland, Greenland, Canada

ATTRIBUTES This gentle stone helps you to peel away layers of mental or emotional conditioning, including those from past lives, to reveal your pure core being and helps you to access your soul's purpose for the present lifetime. It releases mind control and mental implants from any timeframe or dimension.

HEALING Pholocomite works on the subtle energetic causes of dis-ease.

POSITION Hold, position or grid. Disperse gem essence around the aura. *NOTE: Make essence by indirect method.*

PHOSPHOSIDERITE

Polished

Tumbled

Raw

COLOUR	Orchid, purple, red, brown
APPEARANCE	May be obtained as a polished gemstone, may be veined
RARITY	Rare
SOURCE	Chile, Argentina, Germany, United States, Portugal

ATTRIBUTES A stabilizing stone, Phosphosiderite opens higher chakras and subtle bodies* to assimilate downloads of high vibration energy. It has immense energy and power. Phosphosiderite accesses the Akashic Record* and past lives, facilitating objectively viewing the events of the past rather than getting caught up in emotional dramas. It de-energizes* anger or negative emotional responses, infusing joy into the karmic body.

HEALING Iron-rich Phosphosiderite reportedly treats skin and hair.

POSITION Hold, position, grid or disperse gem essence around the aura.

PINK LAZURINE™ AND RUBY LAVENDER QUARTZ™

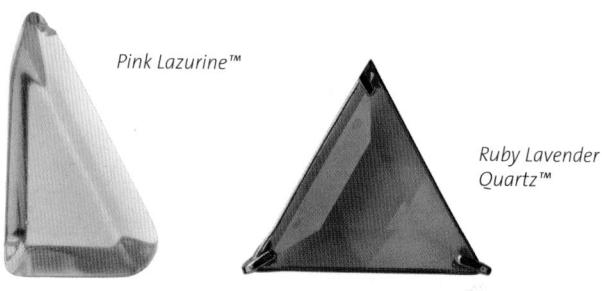

Pink Lazurine™

Ruby Lavender Quartz™

COLOUR	Pink to magenta, deep lilac-purple-red
APPEARANCE	Transparent to translucent glass
RARITY	Easily obtained
SOURCE	Optical laboratory-made glass

ATTRIBUTES Reputedly Pink Lazurine™ and Ruby Lavender Quartz™ are from the same source but Pink Lazurine is rarely faceted, simply smoothed to shape and was created with platinum. Ruby Lavender Quartz™ is faceted to reflect its bi-colour. Created from ground Quartz and rich in the rare-earth element neodyium, these immensely powerful stones carry knowledge from Atlantis and beyond. There are many myths circulating about their creation and how they came to be healing crystals. Due to refraction, the crystal changes colour when viewed from different angles, giving you alternative views into facets of yourself and others. Pink Lazurine™ or Ruby Lavender Quartz™ heighten the intuition and assist the ascension process. Use it to connect with your Higher Self/angelic beings.

These compassionate crystals activate the higher heart chakra with universal love and open the core of your being to your gaze. Helping you to both receive love and give love to yourself and others, these are stones of infinite forgiveness and reconciliation. Lazurine is excellent for healing abuse or lack of love in childhood. Meditating with it feels like being washed in a fountain of divine love that dissolves any emotional dis-ease* or trauma to create a tranquil, centred core.

Ruby Lavender Quartz™ carries an exceedingly high vibration and the transformational violet flame of St Germain, linking to the angelic realms and ascended masters. It connects the higher spiritual dimensions with the earth-plane. Ruby Lavender Quartz™ holds the flame of eternal love. With a strong power of energetic amplification, it filters energies so that exactly the right spectrum reaches you. This stone heightens your intuition and can be used as a lens through which to view the aura. Working with it releases deeply embedded emotional trauma or blockages from previous lives and de-energizes* patterns held in your karmic* blueprint.

Many people regard these crystals as having the highest of vibrational frequencies. Channelling unconditional love, both stones encourage you to open your higher heart and heart seed chakras, creating openheartedness and compassion for all. They assist if you lacked mothering or nurturing, connecting you to the divine feminine.

HEALING Pink Lazurine™ works beyond the physical to heal the soul and maintains the energetic meridians* and harmony between all the Quartz™ bodies. Ruby Lavender Quartz™ healing takes place at the micro-cellular level and through energetic fields in the body.

POSITION Wear, place, position, grid or disperse gem essence around the aura.

Purple Lazurine™

239

PINK SUNSTONE

Tumbled

COLOUR	Pinkish-yellow
APPEARANCE	Translucent stone
RARITY	May be found among yellow Sunstones
SOURCE	United States and elsewhere

ATTRIBUTES The colour in Pink Sunstone comes from a hematite infusion within the basic stone. This highly energetic, bright stone brings joy and regeneration whenever you hold it. Use it if you feel depleted. It helps you to link to higher guidance, restoring your confidence in life and your soul's path.

HEALING Anecdotal evidence suggests that Pink Sunstone may rectify a diminished blood count and balance out blood sugar swings. It is excellent for overcoming depression and Seasonal Affective Disorder, lethargy and associated insomnia.

POSITION Hold, place or grid as appropriate. Disperse gem essence around the aura or environment.

PLANCHEITE

Raw

COLOUR	Bluish-green, blue
APPEARANCE	Silky, translucent stone
RARITY	Rare
SOURCE	Zaire

ATTRIBUTES Copper based Plancheite may be confused with Shattuckite. Helpful for astrologers and diviners, it assists in connecting to the stellar and planetary beings in our solar system and beyond. This stone imparts great mental strength, especially during intellectual discussions and its ability to heighten intuition enables you to think outside the box and come up with innovative solutions.

HEALING May assist conditions such as arthritis and reputedly clears intercellular blockages and blood clots.

POSITION Hold, grid or position as appropriate. Place Plancheite on a birthchart to assist with astrological healing. *NOTE: Make essence by indirect method.*

POLDERVAARITE

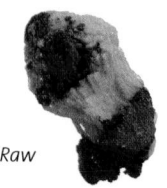

Raw

COLOUR	Light pink to brown
APPEARANCE	'Frilly', botroydal or drusy opaque stone
RARITY	Becoming more easily available
SOURCE	South Africa

ATTRIBUTES Discovered in 1997, Poldervaarite was found in the manganese fields that produce Sugilite, a stone of unconditional love. Peaceful Poldervaarite has emerged to teach that unconditional love is not passive, enabling or abuse-tolerant but rather is dynamic and active, setting appropriate boundaries whilst still accepting someone exactly as they are and giving them space to behave as they wish, not as you perceive they could be. It demonstrates how to stand quietly by without judgement while someone follows their own path of growth – and how to independently follow your own path to enlightenment.

A highly creative stone, Poldervaarite helps find a way through difficult situations and shows how to express your essence in each and every moment. It instils mental clarity and helps you to focus your intent.

HEALING Poldervaarite is reported to assist insomnia and mental confusion. It works mainly beyond the physical level but its high calcium content means that it may assist the skeletal system, teeth and joints.

POSITION Place, grid or hold as appropriate. Spray the environment with gem essence (make by the indirect method).

POLLUCITE

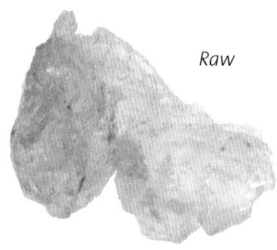

Raw

COLOUR	White or pale greyish
APPEARANCE	Translucent to opaque, luminous stone
RARITY	May be obtained via the internet or specialist dealers
SOURCE	Pakistan, Canada, Afghanistan, Pakistan, Elba, Italy

ATTRIBUTES This stone of regeneration assists Reiki* practitioners and other healers as it stimulates a rapid, deep response to healing energies. Use it to recharge all the chakras, including those above the crown. It assists you to access the angelic realms and make contact with spirits who have passed over. Reputedly the aim of Pollucite is to bring all nations together in peace.

HEALING Works beyond the physical level of healing to regenerate the etheric blueprint* and infuse energy into cellular and electrical processes.

POSITION Hold, position or disperse gem essence around the aura.

PORPHYRITE

ALSO KNOWN AS CHINESE LETTER STONE

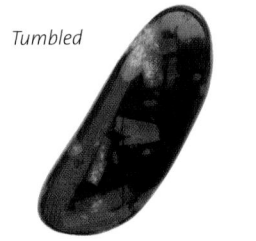

Tumbled

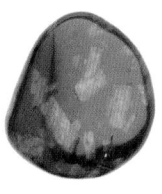

Tumbled

COLOUR	Dark and light green, blue
APPEARANCE	Striped, opaque stone
RARITY	Rare
SOURCE	China

ATTRIBUTES Porphyrite restores trust in your Higher Self, your inner self, your soul and other people. It encourages you to speak your truth no matter how afraid you may be. If you have doubted your own intuition, it helps listen to and trust your inner guidance. De-energizing* patterns, evasions and denials that have prevented you from facing up to a truth you have been avoiding, Porphyrite teaches you that real truth comes from deep within your soul.

If you have had issues or doubts about your own integrity in the past, Porphyrite helps you to be more trustworthy in the present moment. Porphyrite also assists you to deal with ancestral issues that have passed down the family line, especially where these involve family secrets and lies. With the assistance of this stone, the energetic matrix that supported the false façade is dismantled so that the truth emerges. Healing, forgiveness and reconciliation can take place.

At an emotional level, Porphyrite lifts depression by deconstructing negative emotional or belief patterns and lifting 'heavy' energies that weigh on the soul. It is excellent for karmic* emotional healing as it works without necessarily needing to know the cause, although it assists in reading the Akashic Record* if required.

HEALING Porphyrite works mainly beyond the physical to heal soul issues.

POSITION Hold, place or grid as appropriate.

PREHNITE WITH EPIDOTE INCLUSIONS

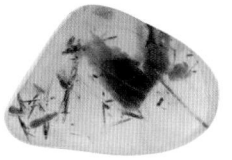

Tumbled

COLOUR	Apple-green and brownish-black
APPEARANCE	Translucent, opaque crystal with streaks
RARITY	Easily obtained
SOURCE	Mali

ATTRIBUTES Gentle and nurturing, radiating unconditional love. Epidote enhances perception and intuition, increasing personal power and spiritual awakening. Prehnite brings joy to the heart and peace to the mind. Stimulating the ability to look to the future, the combination creates an inner healing sanctuary enabling you to recognize your true self and look to the future. Over the solar plexus, it clears blockages and heals karmic* wounds. Rejuvenates body and mind after extreme exhaustion, overwork or trauma.

HEALING Prehnite with Epidote reportedly assists the kidneys, bladder, lungs, thyroid and thymus. It loosens joints and shoulders, benefits the brain and supports the skin and nervous system.

POSITION Hold, grid or disperse gem essence around the aura.

PROPHECY STONE

ALSO KNOWN AS LIFE STONE

*Natural
formation*

COLOUR	White or brownish
APPEARANCE	Knobbly, somewhat shiny opaque stone
RARITY	Rare
SOURCE	Sahara, Botswana

ATTRIBUTES Found in deserts this stone, as the name suggests, enhances your metaphysical abilities including reading the Akashic Record*, kything* and the ability to access the future. The whiteness of the stone carries intuitive moon energy and the brownish parts earth energy so that the two dimensions are united. It connects the third eye, crown and soul star chakras so that guidance is channelled from a very

248

high source and brought to earth. With the assistance of this stone you manifest your dreams and, when meditating with it, travel through multi-dimensions so that you understand your soul's purpose. Prophecy Stones bring together like-minded people with a common purpose, facilitating working for the planet in quiet service.

This stone harmonizes all the subtle bodies* and anchors the lightbody* into the physical. It is particularly useful for creating a shamanic anchor to hold the body safely in incarnation.

HEALING Prophecy Stone works mainly at the metaphysical level but may assist with varicose veins and energetically dissolve concretions within the body, supporting the respiratory and circulatory systems.

POSITION Place, position or grid as appropriate. Gaze into the stone when meditating.

Stone of Solidarity

ADDITIONAL STONE

Stone of Solidarity This stone brings like-minded people together and makes a group. A bridge-builder, it is of assistance when gridded to resolve conflict as it highlights agreements rather than points of dissent. It is also helpful if you want to find new friends. Use this stone to express the divine within yourself and to open unity consciousness*. The Stone of Solidarity energetically assists the body's oxygenation processes and supports the immune system.

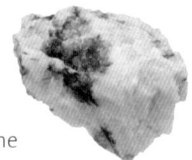

PYRITE: **FEATHER**

Tumbled

COLOUR	Silvery-gold with black
APPEARANCE	Feathery or spider-web pattern on opaque metallic stone
RARITY	Rare
SOURCE	East Harz Mountains, Germany

ATTRIBUTES In Feather Pyrite the energy is gently separated into layers, which radiate out into the body or the environment to harmonize subtle energy* meridians* and bring the whole into harmony. It creates an energetic shield on each individual layer of the aura, forming an intricate web that cannot be penetrated by negative energies. This stone imparts confidence and the stamina to succeed.

HEALING Feather Pyrite helps blood, capillaries, cell walls, lymphatic channels and neural fibres to transmit Qi* around the body and bring it to optimum functioning. Pyrite may assist bones and cellular processes and boost blood supply to the organs.

POSITION Hold, grid or position as appropriate. Disperse gem essence around the aura. *NOTE: Make essence by indirect method.*

ADDITIONAL STONES

The following Pyrites have further specific properties in addition to the generic.

Snakeskin Pyrite A great Pyrite for anyone undergoing energetic change or who is stuck in the past, scaly Snakeskin Pyrite enables you to rapidly shed your old energy imprints and protects you while in that vulnerable space. Having scoured away the residue of many lifetimes, it reveals the new pattern waiting to emerge from beneath the dross.

Snakeskin Pyrite stimulates beneficial change and imparts the necessary vigour for moving forward again. Keep one on your desk if you are looking for promotion or new opportunities. It is particularly helpful for getting to the root of karmic* and psychosomatic dis-ease. Anecdotal evidence suggests it repairs DNA damage, aligns meridians, strengthens the digestive tract and neutralizes toxins, benefits the circulatory and respiratory systems and boosts oxygen in the bloodstream.

*Snakeskin
Pyrite*

*Iridescent
Sun Pyrite*

Iridescent Pyrite Believed to be 350 million years old, rare blue-green Iridescent Pyrite Suns enhance metaphysical abilities and provide a protective shield during journeying*. Gazing into it helps you to focus your intuition and move through multi-dimensions while remaining fully present in everyday

251

Iridescent Pyrite

reality. Use it if you find returning to your body difficult or depressing. Excellent for protecting against psychic vampires* and shielding from people who exhaust you, it creates an energetic interface* that allows you to perceive what is going on without taking their issues on board. It assists in gently turning the situation back so that the person becomes aware of what has been going on. Wear one or keep it nearby.

Pyrite in Magnesite An exceedingly strong combination that protects and grounds the physical body, holding the subtle bodies* safely attached. Use it to anchor yourself if you have a tendency to float off during metaphysical working as it gives you a route back to your body.

Psychologically, Pyrite in Magnesite relieves anxiety and frustration and boosts your self worth and confidence. Helpful for men who feel inferior as it strengthens confidence in your masculinity, the Magnesite lessens any tendency to macho aggression and supports self-assertion. It helps women to overcome servitude and inferiority complexes and to step into their own power without undue ego or aggression. This combination supports people who are nervous and fearful and helps to overcome irritability and intolerance.

Pyrite in Magnesite (tumbled)

Magnesite contains a high level of magnesium and aids absorption in the body. Said to detoxify the body, it acts as an antispasmodic and muscle relaxant. Pyrite in Magnesite is reputed to assist with bone growth, tooth problems and cellular processes and to activate energetic meridians in the subtle and physical body. It boosts the oxygen supply to the organs. Magnesite brings a calming effect to the emotions, helping to tolerate emotional stress. This combination may treat menstrual, stomach, intestinal and vascular cramps and the pain from gallbladder and kidney stones. Traditionally, Magnesite is used to treat epilepsy and this combination may stabilize seizures. The combination aids headaches, especially migraine, and slows blood clotting, but speeds up fat metabolism and is said to disperse cholesterol, preventing arteriosclerosis and angina. Due to the high magnesium content, it is a homeopathic preventative for heart disease. It has a dual action on body temperature, lessening fevers and chills.

Pyrite in Quartz A powerfully energetic combination, Pyrite in Quartz blasts out even the most entrenched of blockages or intransient attitude. This combination also helps protect you when you have to venture into dangerous places, physical or energetic. A stone of health and well-being, it increases vitality and overcomes fatigue, blocking energy leaks from the physical body and the aura. In healing, this combination is extremely fast acting, bringing up the cause of the dis-ease to be examined and released. Pyrite is helpful for melancholy and deep despair. It increases the oxygen supply to the blood and strengthens the circulatory system.

Pyrite in Quartz facilitates tapping into latent abilities and unlocking potential, stimulating the flow of ideas. It speeds up evolutionary development and increases the stamina to succeed. Anecdotal evidence suggests that this combination speeds up the repair of DNA damage, aligns the meridians and aids sleep disturbed due to gastric upset. It strengthens the digestive tract and neutralizes ingested toxins, benefits the circulatory and respiratory systems and boosts oxygen in the bloodstream. Pyrite in Quartz is beneficial for the lungs, alleviating asthma and bronchitis.

Pyrite in Quartz

Pyrite with Sphalerite A useful combination for blasting out entrenched physical, emotional or mental blockages, although other crystals may be needed to heal the system once release has been achieved, Pyrite with Sphalerite teaches how to see behind a façade to what is really going on and aids diplomatic handling of a situation. It is also helpful to caregivers or healers as it helps to prevent cross-infection at an energetic level. Pyrite with Sphalerite is an excellent energy shield. It blocks out geopathogens and pollutants at all levels, protecting the subtle* and physical bodies, deflecting harm and danger. Mental activity is accelerated by Pyrite as it increases blood flow to the brain and Sphalerite adds clarity and careful planning to the mix. It can heighten your intuition too and warn you of deception or deceit. This combination improves memory and recall. Keep it near you if you want to follow your vocation. Pyrite in Sphalerite is rich in zinc, sulphur and iron ore which stimulates the immune system and the brain and neutral transmitters and yet calms the nerves.

Pyrite with Sphalerite

PYROMORPHITE

Natural formation

COLOUR	Golden-brown, green, orange, white
APPEARANCE	Distinctive crystal cluster of metallic stone
RARITY	Rare
SOURCE	Germany, Mexico, United States, Spain

ATTRIBUTES Pyromorphite is a lead based stone with excellent shielding power. Best kept in the environment to deflect polluting energies, it is available as a striking faceted gemstone that can be worn for protective purposes. Pyromorphite repairs the energetic structure of the aura and meridians* of the subtle bodies*, clearing blockages from each interpenetrating layer. Placed over a site of disturbance or attachment, it detaches entities, thought forms, energetic imprints or hooks from the subtle or physical body. Grid or wear to prevent reattachment.

HEALING As is suggested by the shape, Pyromorphite energetically stabilizes the energetic, cellular and skeletal formations in the body.

POSITION Place, position or grid as appropriate. Place around the bed at night or in a meditation or healing space. *NOTE: Toxic. Make gem essence by indirect method only.*

PYROXMANGITE

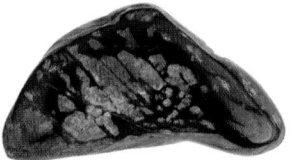

Tumbled

COLOUR	Reddish pink
APPEARANCE	Vitreous, pearly, translucent or transparent
RARITY	Rare
SOURCE	Brazil, United States, Japan, Australia, Sweden

ATTRIBUTES This beautiful, powerful and highly energetic crystal is available as a faceted gemstone or tumblestone, or as a less attractive raw stone which is equally suitable for healing purposes and may be more appropriate to place on or around your body. With its high manganese content, Pyroxmangite carries heart-healing properties and can be used in conjunction with Rhodonite, Rhodochrosite or Tugtupite to open the higher heart and heart seed chakras and invoke an infusion of divine love into the lightbody*. Placing Pyroxmangite over the heart extends these heart chakras out through the subtle bodies* and enables you to live within your own etheric heart chamber. When you live from a place of love, you cannot be anything other than in balance and harmony with your soul and your life purpose.

HEALING The manganese in Pyroxmangite may energetically assist heart disease or circulatory problems that have an underlying psychosomatic cause.

POSITION Hold, place or grid as appropriate. Disperse the gem essence around the heart chakras. *NOTE: Make the gem essence by the indirect method.*

Raw

QUARTZ: **AGNITITE**™

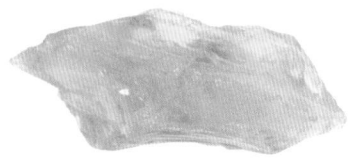

Natural crystal

COLOUR	Clear to milky with red tinge or inclusion
APPEARANCE	Translucent, silky quartz
RARITY	Rare
SOURCE	Africa

ATTRIBUTES Named after the Sanskrit for fire, Agnitite Quartz™ is hematite-based Quartz that has been designated one of the highest vibration stones for spiritual transformation and transfer of higher dimensional energies. This powerful Quartz lights your inner fire. When placed on the base chakra, power flashes up the spine and shoots out of the top of your head to open the higher crown chakras before falling back through the body to fertilize your cells. It needs to be used with care unless you have already worked with high vibration crystals. Too rapid a kundalini* rise causes physical and spiritual imbalances, 'blowing your mind' or your cells causing physical disturbances, so other stones such as Mohawkite or Smoky Elestial Quartz may be needed to assist with integration and grounding of these new energies. Having

258

heightened the frequency of the physical body, Agnitite Quartz™ integrates the lightbody and raises the energetic resonance of the whole.

This crystal stimulates personal creativity and group connection. If Agnitite Quartz™ accesses a soul or group connection, the resulting fire in the base chakra may, initially, be misinterpreted as lust for physical contact. It may be wise to refrain until the energies have settled as that may not be the purpose of the contact, but simply the recognition of an old soul partner from the past with whom there is a new purpose in the present life. Too precipitate an action may subvert or override that purpose.

When you are prepared, however, this is an excellent stone to rapidly awakening your own higher vibrational energies. It functions at a cellular and a celestial level, bringing high vibration light into the cells. With its assistance you raise the consciousness level of your cellular structure so that your body resonates with higher dimensional frequencies. This energy passes through the earth star chakra beneath your feet to fertilize the rising energies of Mother Earth. It is a useful environmental healer for the earth's meridian grid, firing it up in places where it has been damaged or become dormant.

HEALING Agnitite may assist blood and the cells.

POSITION Hold or place as appropriate particularly over the base and Earth Star chakras or place as a grid on the ground or on a map or disperse gem essence around the aura.

QUARTZ: AJO

Polished

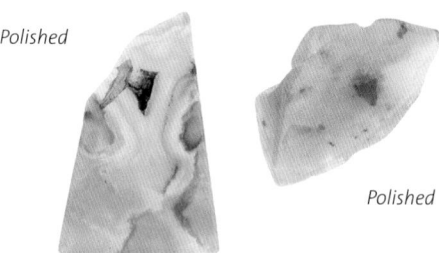

Polished

COLOUR	Bluish-white
APPEARANCE	Translucent stone
RARITY	Rare
SOURCE	USA, South Africa, Zimbabwe

ATTRIBUTES Containing the essence of Ajoite, one of the highest vibration crystals for the New Age, Ajo Quartz brings this beautiful energy into a gentle vibration that everyone can handle. It is excellent for stimulating your spiritual evolution and for facilitating contact with higher guidance or angelic beings. Placing it on the higher crown chakras opens these and aligns them to the lightbody* so that energetic downloads are transferred to the physical plane with ease. Placing it over the throat chakra facilitates communication of spiritual experiences and insights to others. Gridding* Ajo Quartz creates a safe sacred space in which to meditate to enter expanded consciousness and join with All That Is*. The stone is immensely peaceful and creates harmony wherever it is placed.

The Ajoite in the Quartz has agatized, creating a strongly grounding stone with powerfully protective, compassionate properties. This Quartz invokes goddess energy and calls in the divine feminine and unites this with the Earth Mother. It is an emotionally supportive stone for women of all ages as it contains the essence of pure love. The stone removes implants from Atlantean or Lemurian lives and heals the site with light.

HEALING Ajo Quartz works mainly at the spiritual level to bring healing to the soul, especially of karmic* wounds and emotional blockages, but it may assist cellular memory* and cellular structures within the physical body.

POSITION Hold, position or grid as appropriate. Disperse gem essence around the aura.

QUARTZ: **AURORA**

ALSO KNOWN AS ANANDALITE™

*Natural
formation*

COLOUR	Clear or white with rainbow iridescent flashes
APPEARANCE	Clear to milky small points on a matrix
RARITY	Rare
SOURCE	India

ATTRIBUTES Aurora Quartz, known by its trademarked name as Anandalite™, is a naturally iridescent, exceptionally high vibration crystal that activates the soul star and stellar gateway chakras and beyond. It integrates duality into unity and takes you into the interconnectedness of all life, expanding consciousness and harmonizing the new vibration so that the whole benefits from a quantum uplift. Swept from the base chakra to the crown and back again to ground the energies, Aurora Quartz purifies and aligns the

262

whole chakra system to higher frequencies. This stone strips you down to the bare bones of your soul and patiently rebuilds your energy patterns to accommodate a massive energy shift into enlightenment here on earth.

Aurora Quartz introduces you to the limitless possibilities of multi-dimensional being, taking you travelling through the cosmos and beyond. Meditating with it reveals that we have operated within a very narrow band of awareness. Our world is bounded by our five senses and expanded by the sixth, metaphysical, sense which appears to transcend the limits of time and space. But Aurora Quartz shows that this sixth sense too can be transcended to move into a quantum field that is non-local, everywhere and nowhere at once. Consciousness is omniscient and omnipresent, seeing all, knowing all and creating all. Aurora Quartz demonstrates what it is to be a particle that is a wave and a wave that is a particle, to travel backwards or forwards through time and realize that there is no time at all. It shows that you create the event being observed. Immersing you in a quantum field: the holographic universe; multi-dimensional consciousness and mystical inter-connection called bliss or unity consciousness, Spirit or Source.

Aurora Quartz activates the body's natural healing mechanism and constructs an energy grid* for bioscalar waves*, plant spirit essences, crystal beings or intentions to anchor into and pass through the biomagnetic field*, etheric* and physical bodies. In so doing it de-energizes* and deconstructs any detrimental older energy structure.

Disharmony created when subtle bodies* fail to integrate higher consciousness causes spiritual or physical dis-ease*, which Aurora Quartz reharmonizes. It facilitates kundalini* awakening but if kundalini rises in an undirected, disconnected way, it can create physical imbalances. Aurora Quartz gently facilitates the integration process and releases any emotional blockages in the way of spiritual awakening.

HEALING Aurora Quartz works mainly beyond the physical to activate and harmonize the lightbody* into the earth vibration and prepare the central nervous system for a vibrational shift. However, Aurora Quartz activates both the psychic and physical immune systems and bioscalar waves have been shown to unclump red and white blood cells, improving the circulation and flow of fluid in the body. They reduce swelling in injuries and activate better all-round health.

POSITION Hold, place or grid as appropriate. Disperse gem essence around the aura.

SPECIFIC COLOURS

In addition to the generic properties, specific colour flashes have further attributes.

Blue amplifies the biomagnetic field* of a person or a place. It shines a bright, luminescent beam into an area to bring peace and harmony. As might be expected, Blue Aurora Quartz connects to the element of water. Assists in purifying polluted water and earth healing* for islands.
Brown connects to the element of earth and carries a rainbow light that harmonizes and purifies the biosphere. It brings shadows into light. This colour carries demonic and angelic energy and assists in accessing the beings that are overseeing planet earth.
Green connects to the cool, calm, rational air element and accesses the multi-dimensions of consciousness.
Gold reconnects and recharges the healing circuits and the flow of bioscalar waves within the physical body or the planet (*see also* Rainbow Mayanite page 287).
Red connects to the creative fire element and revitalizes and re-motivates the soul on its journey of manifestation.

QUARTZ: **APRICOT**

ALSO KNOWN AS PAPAYA QUARTZ

*Natural
formation*

COLOUR	Apricot
APPEARANCE	Transparent to milky Quartz points or masses
RARITY	Rare
SOURCE	Brazil

ATTRIBUTES Apricot Quartz has a powerful energizing effect. Activating the sacral chakra, it clears blockages that prevent you from expressing your creativity or fertility. Use Apricot Quartz to heal sexual, physical or emotional abuse from any lifetime. It deconstructs the memory, replacing it with self-worth and loving compassion for yourself.

265

HEALING Iron-rich Quartz has a purifying effect on the blood and stimulates the energetic meridians* of the body. With its high iron content, Apricot Quartz assists in recovering from prolonged psychic attack or chronic dis-eases.

POSITION Hold, position or grid as appropriate. Disperse the gem essence into the aura.

ADDITIONAL STONES

Cat's Eye Quartz Popular for jewellery and traditionally used as a talisman for abundance and against the evil eye, Rutile inclusions in Cat's Eye Quartz create the characteristic chatoyant shimmer.

The stone helps children concentrate when studying and also gives them a sense of security and safety. Cat's Eye Quartz strengthens willpower and helps timid children to be more confident. It should be worn or kept in a pocket at all times. The stone is particularly helpful if children are undergoing bullying or feel alienated from their peers, as it affords the courage to stand up for themselves rather than going along with what the group wants. At the same time, however, it helps them to create harmony within the group. The stone can strengthen family ties and make the child feel more secure and well-loved.

Cat's Eye Quartz (tumbled)

Traditionally, Cat's Eye Quartz has been used to develop the ability to see in the dark and to negotiate dark places with ease and safety.

Cat's Eye Quartz is beneficial for eyes, muscles, bones, joints, nerves and motor skills. It is used to heal bronchial tract dis-eases and to relieve neuralgia and cramps. It is reputed to be helpful for digestive problems and constipation. The stone is traditionally used to reduce blood pressure.

Epiphany Quartz has a light, high vibration that induces a spiritual epiphany in which you recognize your purpose on earth and your place in the universe. Meditate with it to discover whether your soul's intention is in harmony with your reason for incarnating on earth. If not, the crystal reattunes you.

Day and Night Quartz This bi-coloured Quartz is extremely helpful for reconciling dualities and moving into unity consciousness. It weaves together masculine and feminine, dark and light, past and present, the Self and the Other. Day and Night Quartz Brings shadows into light and assists humanity to value differences and to recognize the singularity of spirit that binds us all together. With its assistance we can act as one to save our planet.

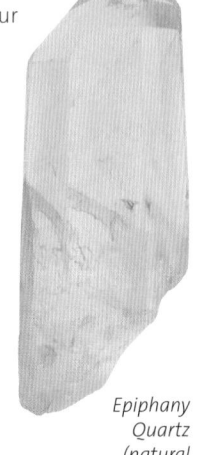

Epiphany Quartz (natural formation)

Day and Night Quartz

QUARTZ: **CELADONITE PHANTOM**

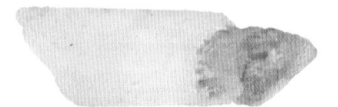

*Natural
formation*

COLOUR	Green in white or colourless
APPEARANCE	Phantom in clear Quartz point
RARITY	Fairly easily obtained
SOURCE	United States, Italy

ATTRIBUTES Celadonite brings peace and harmony to your life. Opening your intuition, it tunes into your soul's wisdom or guidance from higher beings. A manifestation crystal, Celadonite attracts all that you desire but reminds you that it is your deepest beliefs that will manifest. If you don't believe you deserve abundance, you cannot attract it. It assists in de-energizing previously hidden or outdated programs that secretly run your world. Use Celadonite to attune to the fullness of universal abundance and to your divine right to receive.

HEALING Celadonite works beyond the physical to restructure energy patterns.

POSITION Hold, grid or meditate with the stone to access your subconscious programming. Disperse the gem essence around the aura and environment.

QUARTZ: **CHAMPAGNE AURA**

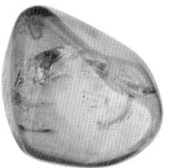

Tumbled

COLOUR	Yellowish-brown
APPEARANCE	Translucent clear crystal
RARITY	Easily obtained
SOURCE	Alchemicalized natural Smoky Quartz

ATTRIBUTES A high vibration stone of transmutation alchemicalized with gold and indium, Champagne Aura Quartz helps you to ground energetic and psychological changes into your body and to put your spiritual ideals into practice. It opens your third eye, grounds you in your subtle bodies*, and protects during multi-dimensional journeying* and other metaphysical work. Gold amplifies, regenerates and attracts so the combination enhances the basic properties of the underlying Quartz and this is a useful stone for those just beginning high vibration crystal work.

Purifying Smoky Quartz forms the base so this is excellent for drawing off and transmuting negative energy into positive. It carries dark, luminous light that encourages hidden parts of the self to emerge, and carries the energy of Lucifer, the much maligned archangel who came to earth to bring light into dark places and who goes where others fear to tread. Working with this crystal helps you to understand

and embrace shadow parts of yourself and to accept without judgement alienated outsiders and scapegoats for society, the 'sin eaters' who absorb negativity and are the focus for the projections of others. The importance of their work is rarely recognized.

Champagne Aura Quartz guards against negative energies of all kinds, including electromagnetic stress, and assists with earth healing* and transmutation. Helpful where dis-ease* is caused by emotional or physical toxicity, it assists in reconciling different viewpoints in yourself or others and settles conflict. It assists in all situations where negotiation is required and encourages philanthropy and charity. Indium assists the organs of the body to find balance (especially the thyroid) and increases assimilation of minerals, supporting optimum metabolic function and hormonal balance. It is reported to be anti-carcinogenic.

HEALING Champagne Aura Quartz may assist the thyroid and endocrine system and clear the pituitary and pineal glands where there has been depletion or blockage caused by environmental toxins and excess fluoridation. It relieves headaches, especially sinus or psychically based, and releases pain or tension in muscles and joints.

POSITION Place, grid or position as appropriate especially over the third eye and soma chakras. Place over the site of toxicity and cleanse after use. Disperse gem essence around the aura.

QUARTZ: **FIRE AND ICE**

ALSO KNOWN AS RAINBOW QUARTZ

*Heat-treated
shaped point*

COLOUR	Clear
APPEARANCE	Crackled and cracked with inner planes and inclusions
RARITY	Rare
SOURCE	Brazil (thermally shocked crystal)

ATTRIBUTES This powerful light bringer with an exceedingly high vibration has its own story to tell. Although looking like Crackled Quartz, it has been subjected to thermal shock – heated and rapidly cooled – but the underlying Quartz has a high vibration that released its innate power to fertilize the earth and the soul. This created a crystal characterized by fractures, flaws and inclusions that contain numerous rainbows and which activates expanded awareness. Carrying cosmic fire, it is inspirational, facilitating ignition of spiritual purpose.

This Quartz contains images of the Tree of Life, sacred geometry and figures that draw on shamanic medicine. The symbols can be read to give soul advice on transformation. Fire and Ice Quartz links polarities and integrates the full spectrum of consciousness. It has a particular resonance with the heart chakra of the Andes. Fire and Ice Quartz cleanses and aligns all the chakras in the physical body and activates the soma, soul star and stellar gateway.

A crystal for lightworkers*, Fire and Ice resonates with the left hand but does not work from the dark side. It harmonizes dualities and encompasses dark energy to balance light. It carries the energy of Buddhist diamond healing and links to Raphael, the archangel of healing. In past life healing, it connects to ancient Egypt and resolves misuse of power from that life.

Fire and Ice Quartz contains the spirit of life and of pure love. Self-cleansing, it is particularly useful for spiritual manifestation, having a strong resonance with the law of attraction. It is a stone for new beginnings and profound growth, cutting through the old to reveal the soul's purpose, which is achieved through acceptance of the creation of personal reality. Opening the third eye and assisting kything*, it facilitates perceiving different timelines, endless possibilities and the beauty of all through its interconnectedness to multi-realities and dimensions.

Fire and Ice Quartz recalibrates the resonance of all Quartzes to a higher level, and moves to a higher vibration itself so that it restores equilibrium. It acts as a battery for the earth's grid and, when the energy is taken to the heart of Mother Earth, it fertilizes our planet providing a power source for earthly transformation. You need to feel worthy to work with this crystal, which assists but does not do the work for you. It gently brings up your own issues for transmutation and supports during the process. It is a stone of joy and happiness, resurrection and rebirth.

Fire and Ice Quartz carries bioscalar waves* for multi-dimensional, intercellular healing at all levels. The crystal stimulates the pineal and pituitary glands, reconfiguring the endocrine system. It facilitates healing for the reproductive and urinary tracts, activating the kundalini* to sweep through the kidneys in a purifying process. Healing the etheric*, causal and higher spiritual bodies, Fire and Ice Quartz opens the central channel* and ignites the higher kundalini energy in the lightbody*.

HEALING Fire and Ice Quartz energetically assists the pineal and pituitary glands, endocrine system, reproductive and urinary tracts. It purifies and realigns the subtle* and causal biomagnetic* bodies.

POSITION Meditate with the crystal, place or hold as appropriate. Place larger pieces where the light of the sun energizes it during the day and each evening visualize that light beaming into the heart of the earth. Disperse gem essence into the aura or environment.

QUARTZ: **WITH GARNET**

Raw

COLOUR	Red or orange and clear or smoky
APPEARANCE	Small crystals on Quartz matrix
RARITY	Rare
SOURCE	China, Honduras

ATTRIBUTES Bringing together two highly energetic master healers for the heart, Garnet on Quartz is excellent for emotional healing and past life work. It lifts out dis-ease* and dysfunctional patterns, de-energizes memories, and instils joy and hope. This is an excellent combination if there is energetic depletion and re-vitalization is required. It can stimulate kundalini* rise. A first aid measure in a crisis, it helps overcome trauma.

HEALING Garnet on Quartz reputedly assists the heart, circulation and energy systems of the body.

POSITION Grid, hold or place as appropriate.

274

QUARTZ: **WITH GOLD**

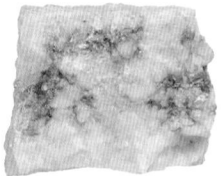

Raw

COLOUR	Gold and white
APPEARANCE	Streaks or small nugget in white Quartz matrix
RARITY	Rare
SOURCE	United States, UK, Peru, Sierra Leone, Sudan

ATTRIBUTES The amplifying and regenerative qualities of Gold lift Quartz to an even higher vibration, ensuring rapid transmutation and transmission of energy. Gold supplies pure inspiration and helps you to let go of superficiality, finding the depth in your experiences. Grid Gold in Quartz around your home to activate the law of attraction and draw abundance to you.

HEALING Gold in Quartz works mostly at the energetic level of healing to rebalance the subtle bodies* and infuse energy into the cellular matrix.

POSITION Hold, position or grid as appropriate. Disperse gem essence around the aura.

QUARTZ: GOLDEN HEALER

Shaped

COLOUR	Golden yellow
APPEARANCE	Coated and internally coloured Quartz
RARITY	Easily available
SOURCE	Brazil, Akansas, United States

ATTRIBUTES Carrying the divine essence of All That Is* and high concentrations of the universal life force or Qi*, Golden Healer Quartz has an exceedingly high vibration that takes the master healing power of Quartz to another level. Using this Quartz raises your vibrations to meet those of the crystal. It is a catalyst for profound spiritual activation and opens the alta major chakra.

Golden Healer Quartz is incredibly active, the iron oxide in the stone amps up the power exponentially and creates a multi-dimensional energy grid around our planet. This Quartz has the iron content within the crystal itself or between the layers of the Quartz as well as a dusting or coating on the crystal. Accessing multi-dimensional, interstellar healing power and bringing Christ Consciousness down to the earth, it makes healing more potent on all levels. This is a wonderful tool to prepare the lightbody* for an influx of cosmic energy that expands awareness. Using it helps you to walk in Christ Consciousness on the earth so that your whole being helps the planet to ascend.

Golden Healer Quartz carries natural bioscalar waves* that heal at multi-dimensions and intercellular levels. It purifies, aligns and re-energizes the chakras and rapidly releases ancient emotional conditioning held in the solar plexus. The crystal harnesses the personal will held in that chakra with that of divine will held in the chakras above the crown, so that the Higher Self becomes the guiding light rather than the ego. This stone facilitates making profound changes in your life with minimum fuss and effort.

Place a large Golden Healer Quartz under a healing couch, or grid small ones at each corner to experience multi-dimensional cellular healing for the physical, subtle* and light bodies*. You can dedicate your Golden Healer Quartz to send peace and healing into our world.

HEALING Golden Healer Quartz are master, multi-purpose healers for all conditions. They restore the whole system to energetic wholeness and optimum functioning.

POSITION Hold, position, grid or disperse gem essence around the aura as appropriate. Spraying with the gem essence daily helps to maintain optimum health.

ADDITIONAL STONES
Drusy Golden Healer A drusy coating overlaid on a Golden Healer Quartz lifts off encrustations, attachments*, implants, hooks, entities, mind control, mental conditioning, emotional patterning and the like

and gently scours the soul so that it shines as brightly as can be. If you want to let your inner light shine, work with a Drusy Golden Healer Quartz, one of the highest vibration Golden Healer Quartz of all.

Golden Healer Phantom This rare form of Golden Healer Quartz with pyramidal planes is excellent for breaking and de-energizing entrenched old patterns wherever they are held. It goes back to the karmic* and etheric blueprints* to heal the blockages of lifetimes.

Gold and Silver Healers Soothing iridescent Gold and Silver Healers do an excellent deep repair work on the lightbody, biomagnetic field* and intercellular structures and are extremely useful for crystal workers who need to replenish their own energy. Gold and Silver Healers gently dissolve ties and undue influence and remove entities sending them to the light – even at a distance. Full of bioscalar waves, these healers are appropriate for beginners or those with particularly sensitive auras and biomagnetic fields. Not as incisive as Rainbow Mayanite Blades, there is no danger the aura will disintegrate as these Healers work slowly and carefully, repairing and reweaving the auric field.

Drusy

Silver Healer Quartz

Phantom

Drusy Phantom
Golden Healer Quartz

Golden
Healer
Quartz

See also Rainbow Myanite, page 287

278

QUARTZ: **LODOLITE**

Polished

COLOUR	Clear with green, pink, yellow, brown, white or red
APPEARANCE	Clear with inclusions resembling landscapes
RARITY	Rare, one source
SOURCE	Minas Gerais, Brazil

ATTRIBUTES Lodolite inclusions vary greatly and each adds to the effect of the stone. Resembling a land or seascape through which you can journey to find serenity, peace, insight, communication with higher beings or spiritual growth, this gentle loving stone emanates harmony. A metaphysical enhancer and awakener, use it to explore your past lives or the multi-dimensions in which your consciousness exists. Program Lodolite to bring you all that your heart desires as this is a powerful manifestation crystal.

HEALING A useful all round healing stone. Placed around the hips, Lodolite is reported to ease PMS and to support during menopause.

POSITION Hold, place or grid as appropriate. Disperse gem essence around the aura.

QUARTZ: MADAGASCAR AMETHYST AND SMOKY

Shaped

COLOUR	Purple and brown with clear patches
APPEARANCE	Transparent crystals with internal areas of colour
RARITY	Fairly easily obtained
SOURCE	Madagascar

ATTRIBUTES This high vibration combination is an excellent gridding*
stone to create a safe sacred space as it brings together the protective
energies of Smoky Quartz and Amethyst and their ability to enhance
metaphysical work of all kinds. It is also useful for creating a calm and
serene atmosphere in your workplace or your home as it soaks up and
transforms negative vibes. If you place three of the stones in a triangle
and sit in the centre, or meditate holding one of them, it assists in
opening your psychic abilities and enhances your intuition.

Reputedly Madagascar is one of the original colonies of Lemuria and this stone carries knowledge that can be accessed from that time. It is helpful in past life healing for those who carry karmic* imprints from the far distant past, especially for those who through events at that time learnt not to trust their own intuitive abilities or who saw the consequences of the misuse of psychic powers and became afraid to exercise their power. The Madagascan Smoky and Amethyst de-energizes* that ancient pattern and instils a sense of trust in your own abilities. Use it if you need to reclaim your power from any occult or esoteric source whether it was given away or stolen from you. With this stone's assistance you learn to stand firmly in your power once again.

HEALING Amethyst and Smoky Quartz are both excellent all-round cleansing and healing stones but this particular combination is extremely effective for the karmic* blueprint and for restoring your etheric blueprint* to pristine condition so that dis-ease* is then dissolved in the physical body.

POSITION Hold, grid or place as appropriate.

ADDITIONAL STONE

Smoky Quartz with Aegerine Smoky Quartz has a powerful purifying and detoxifying energy that combines well with the earth healing* and regenerating properties of Aegerine. This stone accompanies you on a quest for your true self and facilitates safe shamanic journeying* through multi-dimensions to reintegrate lost parts of your soul. It has great integrity and power that insists you follow your own truth. Smoky Quartz with Aegerine energetically supports cellular memory, the immune, metabolic and nervous systems and detoxifies all the organs of the body.

Smoky Quartz with Aegerine

QUARTZ: **MADAGASCAR CLOUDY**

Shaped and polished

COLOUR	Slightly pinkish, cloudy white
APPEARANCE	Translucent as though filled with mist
RARITY	Fairly easily obtained
SOURCE	Madagascar

ATTRIBUTES Madagascar Quartz often tends to be milkier than Quartz elsewhere but it has a powerful, earthy energy that restores vitality and soothes the soul. Meditating with serene Madagascar Cloudy Quartz instils a profound sense of spiritual well-being that cannot be shaken. It creates an inner space of peace and calm around which turmoil may whirl but cannot enter. Cloudy Quartz assists with karmic* healing of imprinted issues from Lemuria and Atlantis and elsewhere. The Quartz helps to pull out from the karmic blueprint blockages and imprints that

282

were laid down in Lemuria or Atlantis, de-energizing the site and replacing it with a more constructive energetic matrix* that facilitates moving confidently into the future.

HEALING Madagascar Cloudy Quartz is excellent for grounding energy into the physical body. It regenerates and restores, containing bioscalar waves* and master healing energies for health and well-being.

POSITION Hold, place, position or grid* as appropriate. Disperse gem essence into the aura or the environment, especially around the head.

ADDITIONAL STONE
Madagscar Finger Quartz helps to pull out from the blockages and imprints that were laid down in the karmic blueprint in Lemuria or Atlantis. It is excellent for pin-pointing the site of psychosomatic disease* and repairing the etheric body*. If anyone points the finger this stone assists in getting to the truth of the matter.

QUARTZ: **MESSINA**

Raw

COLOUR	White with green, blue, grey
APPEARANCE	Clear Quartz with opaque powdery coating
RARITY	Fairly easily obtained
SOURCE	South Africa

ATTRIBUTES This peaceful coated Quartz is from the same region as Ajoite. It carries a gentle frequency suitable for those who are beginning crystal work or who are extremely sensitive to crystal energies. A cleansing stone, it helps you connect to the pure flame of compassionate being and to express that out to the universe and to yourself. This is a very forgiving stone. Use it whenever there is a need to overcome guilt or anxiety.

HEALING Messina Quartz with its copper component is beneficial for cellular memory*, joints and cell structures.

POSITION Hold, grid or position as appropriate. Disperse gem essence around the aura or environment.

QUARTZ: **MOLDAU**™

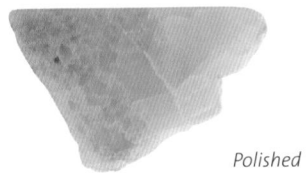

Polished

COLOUR	Milky white to yellowish
APPEARANCE	Opaque stone
RARITY	Becoming easily available but expensive
SOURCE	Czech Republic

ATTRIBUTES Blending heaven and earth, Moldau Quartz™ comes from the same region as Moldavite. Nondescript until you meditate with it, it carries the energetic frequency of Moldavite and has a high vibration suitable for beginners. This stone increases intuition, strengthens healing and enhances your life force. Promoting inner clarity and releasing emotional trauma, it shows you the truth in your heart.

HEALING Moldau Quartz™ carries the master healing power of Quartz combined with the ability of Moldavite to get to the source of dis-ease*.

POSITION Hold, wear, position or grid as appropriate. Disperse gem essence around the aura.

QUARTZ: **PIEMONTITE**

Raw

COLOUR	Red, red-brown-black, crimson, yellow in white
APPEARANCE	Veined, vitreous to dull opaque Quartz
RARITY	Rare
SOURCE	New Mexico, Italy, Japan

ATTRIBUTES Manganese-rich, Piemontite opens the heart, higher heart and heart seed chakras to an influx of unconditional love. It heals emotional wounds and de-energizes* blocks in the subtle bodies* that may be preventing you from trusting yourself and others. Meditating with this stone helps you tune into your own innate wisdom and the voice of the heart. Use it to listen to mentors.

HEALING Piemontite works on the emotional body to heal heart and allied conditions. The Manganese-rich crystals help to maintain homeostasis and are antioxidant supporting metabolic function and mineral assimilation, correct bone development and tissue repair.

POSITION Place over the heart, grid or position as appropriate. Disperse the gem essence into the aura or environment.

QUARTZ: **RAINBOW MAYANITE**

Natural point formation

COLOUR	Golden with iridescent rainbows
APPEARANCE	Layered crystal with golden coating
RARITY	Rare, one mine only
SOURCE	Cascade Mountains, Eastern Washington, United States

ATTRIBUTES Discovered in 2011, naturally iridescent Rainbow Mayanite was marketed as a support for riding out the planetary changes of 2012. A self-cleansing stone, it was recommended for rainbow chakra healing, kything* and activation of new joy, focus, purpose and stepping on to your true path. The crystal quickly revealed that its true potential was far greater. Rainbow Mayanite is a Golden Healer Quartz taken to new heights. With exceedingly high vibrations, it contains natural bioscalar healing waves*. Not a stone for the fainthearted or the inexperienced, Rainbow Mayanite de-energizes* old patterns from any source, taking out debris and karmic* encrustations from the past, and pulls out toxic dross that you have absorbed from other people or the environment that has lodged between the subtle layers of your etheric body*. It builds new, more supportive structures at every level as we move into the expanded consciousness of the New Age. The minerals that percolated deep through the Quartz to create the deep yellow coating and myriad rainbows were strongly concentrated and this stone takes you into the depths of yourself to discover your own inner rainbow treasures.

Rainbow Mayanite works in different ways according to its natural shape. In chunky, sinuously shaped pieces or points it is a gentle support for energetic change and is suitable for those who are new to high vibration crystal work. It links you to guides and angelic helpers and assists a detached perspective. Holding or meditating with this soothing form is like having silky balm poured over your aura that gently infuses itself into every cell of your body to dissolve cellular debris, past life and ancestral patterning and create a unified cellfield which is activated to its full potential. Having purified the dross, the crystal anchors your lightbody* in place. It assists you in speaking your truth and accessing your power. Placed over the solar plexus, it draws out ancient emotional pain and infuses dynamic unconditional love.

Rainbow Myanite blade

As a blade Rainbow Mayanite really comes into its own but needs to be used with delicacy, sensitivity and higher awareness in the hands of a skilled healer as otherwise auric damage may occur. This highly intelligent crystal knows exactly how to work and a Rainbow Mayanite blade simply requires the sensitive co-operation of a practitioner, not direction or control which would limit its abilities. Working at all levels simultaneously, it rapidly dissolves cords, attachments, hooks, patterns and implants from any dimension and any timeframe that are caught up in the etheric levels, and replaces destructive cellular memory* or auric imprints with a new beneficial matrix bringing about core soul healing. Releasing detrimental spiritual connections and past life jealousies and interference, it calls in co-operation, light and dynamic unconditional love. The Rainbow Mayanite then creates a non-penetrable interface around the outside of the aura to protect the biomagnetic sheath* and multi-dimensional bodies. It continues to repattern the energy field to its optimum functioning and highest frequency. If even a tiny scrap of toxic or inappropriate energy has been left in the aura, Rainbow Mayanite dissolves it, de-energizes the memory structure left behind, and replaces it with divine sparks.

Pieces that combine both shapes, blades and chunky points, work on all levels simultaneously and are perfect for gem essences for multi-dimensional and intercellular healing.

HEALING Rainbow Mayanite contains bioscalar waves* that bring about healing on all levels simultaneously. It is extremely effective as an aura spray.

POSITION Hold, grid or place points and chunks as appropriate. Grid to protect and energize your space while travelling. Use blades with extreme care and sensitivity. Disperse gem essence around the aura, feet, heart and above the head daily to dissolve old patterns and infuse the highest of vibrations. Excellent for sending distance healing.

QUARTZ: **SACRED SCRIBE**

Also known as Russian Lemurian, freeform

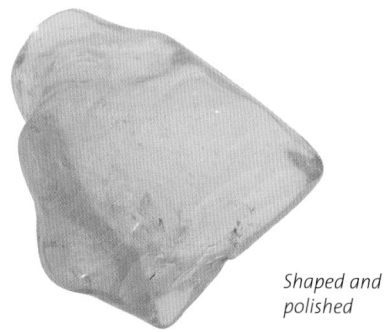

Shaped and polished

COLOUR	Clear
APPEARANCE	Sinuously shaped clear Quartz or optical glass
RARITY	Easily obtained
SOURCE	Russia (the shape has been crafted)

ATTRIBUTES Sacred Scribe Quartz freeforms can be extremely tactile. For many people, however, these shaped Russian Lemurians display an almost technological absence of feeling – a cold, rational and intelligent 'mental' energy. They greet you with a clinical and dispassionate appraisal that chimes with the Aquarian age. They are excellent for people who are overly emotional and mentally out of control as they insist on mental focus. Sacred Scribe Quartz have a clarity that there is no getting away from, it is impossible to hide the truth in their presence. For other people there is warmth at the heart of this stone.

They carry the ancient Egyptian energy of Osiris and Anubis, weighing up intention and integrity. The 'judgement' is of beliefs, concepts and how life plays out. Sacred Scribe Quartz assist with balance and seeing things from all sides.

This stone is an incredible tool for those sensitive enough to attune to the esoteric information they carry. Placed on the soma chakra it reseeds ancient knowledge. Placed around the head as a 'helmet' from the ears to the crown, these Russian Lemurians act as outposts or guardians of a grid that creates a still point for the mind. This tunes in to silence in which an enormous amount of information is downloaded without the need for thought. It is a total switch off from earth. These stones take you to the forty-fourth chakra – a plane of existence rather than a chakra as we currently know them. The stone has a powerful connection with binary fission, fusion and the core energies of creation. Some stones are crafted from optical glass.

Sacred Scribe Quartz energy can be directed by sound or touch. Acting as a regulating valve connecting opposite and complementary processes, an energy release occurs without the need to know what or why. They enable you to see what's at the other end of the wormhole.

HEALING Sacred Scribe Quartz work at the level of the higher mind and beyond rather than for physical healing.

POSITION Grid, place or position as appropriate. Disperse gem essence around the aura, especially around the head.

QUARTZ: **STONE OF SANCTUARY**

Raw

COLOUR	White
APPEARANCE	Luminous white Quartz
RARITY	Rare
SOURCE	Canada, United States

ATTRIBUTES A 'stone for the New Age', as the name suggests the Stone of Sanctuary provides a safe haven for the soul during times of transition and dimension-shift. Meditating with this piezoelectric stone of dynamic unconditional love takes you into a place of profound inner peace, which is radiated out to our planet and all upon it. Use it whenever thoughts of the future stress you out to enable you to hold a positive vision for the future of humankind and our planet.

A useful adjunct to Reiki*, despite its tranquillity the stone is highly energetic and counteracts the depletion that arises from being too open and using your own energy for healing rather than channelling higher vibrations to the earth. Its purity teaches you how to be a conduit for divine light and love and for inspiration and guidance from higher sources.

HEALING The Stone of Sanctuary works at a subtle* level to induce well-being through inner peace and harmony.

POSITION Grid, place or position as appropriate. Disperse gem essence around the aura. Place under the pillow during sleep.

ADDITIONAL STONE

Sulphur in Quartz is a geological impossibility that should never have formed, as the sulphur should have been consumed. It helps you to solve paradoxes and contradictions. With its strong negative electrical charge, Sulphur is a powerful energetic cleanser that draws out negativity from the body or the environment and replaces it with positive energy. In Quartz, it purifies the energetic bodies and quickly brings issues to the surface for resolution. Sulphur is traditionally used for skin eruptions, inflammation, fevers and joint problems.

Sulphur in Quartz

QUARTZ: **TANGEROSE**

Natural point

COLOUR	Luminous pink with orange flush
APPEARANCE	Clear crystal
RARITY	Rare but fairly easily obtainable
SOURCE	Brazil

ATTRIBUTES Tangerose was created by Hematite laid down on a Quartz crystal in the latter stages of its development. It brings together the powerfully loving and yet gentle heart healing energy of Rose Quartz with the much more buzzy healing energy of Tangerine Quartz. A high vibration crystal, Tangerose is prized for its ability to ignite passion and creativity through the sacral chakra and to bring dynamic unconditional love into any relationship through the heart chakra.

A useful stone for those who find it difficult to love themselves, Tangerose promotes re-evaluation and self-acceptance. Offering support during challenging times, it helps you to feel less isolated and alone by reconnecting you to All That Is*. Meditating with the stone feels like being wrapped in a cloak of unconditional acceptance in which any emotional stumbling blocks are instantly dissolved, to be replaced by loving warmth and a peaceful heart.

The ideal soul rescue remedy, Tangerose heals shock and trauma and is especially useful in past life healing and soul retrieval. It helps soul fragments to purify and reintegrate themselves into the incarnated portion of the soul and be welcomed home. Tangerose dispels unwarranted fears and shows you the origin of negative thoughts and expectations. By helping you to feel less vulnerable, it instils the strength and courage to move forward calmly and with equanimity, no matter what changes may occur. This makes Tangerose an ideal accompaniment for personal and planetary change.

HEALING Tangerose may assist disorders of the reproductive system by releasing blockages in the base and sacral chakras and etheric blueprint* and in the circulatory system by dissolving emotional blockages in the heart and solar plexus. Said to assist production of T-cells in depleted immune systems, it provides support during traumatic or terminal illness.

POSITION Grid, place or position as appropriate, especially over the heart, sacral and base chakras.

QUARTZ: **TRIGONIC**

*Trigonic markings
on facet*

COLOUR	Clear to slightly milky white, although other crystals may exhibit trigonic markings
APPEARANCE	Quartz point with many downward triangles on the faces and a 'crumpled' base
RARITY	Expensive but fairly easily obtained
SOURCE	Brazil (New sources are opening up as trigonic markings appear on crystals from other locations)

ATTRIBUTES A soul midwife crystal, this exceptionally high vibration Quartz is characterized by cascading upside down triangles containing cosmic DNA codes. The stone takes you to the core of who you are. The power of Trigonic Quartz lies in its deep connection to the soul and unity consciousness. Working like a hive-mind, it accesses multi-dimensional, holographic awareness transcending the boundaries of earth-based perceptual reality. Everyone who works with a Trigonic

Quartz has a very personal experience as individual stones facilitate different energy and information interchanges. The triangles represent souls who are entering or leaving incarnation and this stone takes you instantly into multi-dimensions to gain an objective overview on your soul's journey. Meditating with Trigonic Quartz triggers a theta brainwave state that enables deep healing and restructuring of body, beliefs and realities in addition to multi-dimensional journeying*.

The crystal brings up unresolved personal or group conflicts for resolution. It is essential to have released all blockages from the chakras and toxicity from the physical and energy bodies and open the higher dimensional chakras to prepare for an influx of higher energies. The process cannot be short circuited or evaded as Trigonic Quartz bring up personal, unresolved issues for resolution and may induce a dramatic catharsis. It is a profound tool for personal and planetary evolution.

Trigonic Quartz made themselves known to facilitate the transition to expanded awareness. They need compatible, harmonious human consciousness to facilitate their work. Part of a coherent information field, they communicate over vast distances with each other and those who are in contact with them. Their stated aim is to dissolve the war-gene encoded within the human DNA system and to help humanity move from everyday reality* into unity with All That Is*. This stone has a playfulness about it – and more than a touch of the trickster energy. They are transceivers, transmitting and receiving, and create a feedback system that goes to all souls in the group (human and crystal). Strongly connected to the cosmic tides and to the earth's poles and currents, Trigonic energy flows through the body in waves and is experienced at different temperatures according to body type.

Trigonics expand your soul to rejoin the holographic oversoul that is consciousness. Creating a calm core around which everything rushes and flows, it is the perfect stone if you feel trapped on earth.

A Trigonic Quartz facilitates reconnection to your higher purpose. Calling back and reintegrating soul fragments, it renegotiates soul contracts.

Teaching that awareness is never lost, Trigonics facilitate moving between different levels of reality with grace and ease and is the perfect tool for soul midwives. Once you have experienced the totality of All That Is* your vibratory rate is permanently changed to a higher frequency that enables you to facilitate shifts of consciousness in others.

A Trigonic is helpful in any confrontational or conflict situation whether it be internal or external, personal or collective, individual or racial. Trigonic Quartz is particularly helpful for dissolving shame and de-energizing* emotional blockages that you didn't know you were carrying, replacing them with dynamic unconditional love, acceptance and forgiveness for yourself. It is helpful for holding intent and sending distant healing. Trigonics carry natural bioscalar waves* that give cells greater energy and an enhanced response to healing and immune processes.

HEALING Trigonic Quartz energetically assists the brain, circulation and lymphatic systems, fluid balance and swollen joints but its main work is at the level of the soul, subtle and light bodies. Trigonic infused water made in a deep toned Tibetan bowl has a potent healing power. Sounding the bowl instantaneously transfers the vibration to the water.

POSITION Hold over the higher chakras or place the Trigonic where it radiates its energy into the environment. Put essence into bathwater, or disperse into aura. If making a gem essence do not leave in the water for a long period. *NOTE: Other high vibration crystals may display etched triangular trigonic markings and can be used as a stepping stone to multi-dimensional reality.*

QUE SERA

ALSO KNOWN AS VULCANITE

Tumbled

COLOUR	Pink, blue, black and colourless combination
APPEARANCE	Opaque stone with clearly distinguished patches of colour
RARITY	Rare
SOURCE	Brazil

ATTRIBUTES A powerful, synergistic combination with extremely high and yet deeply earthy vibrations, Que Sera contains quartz, feldspar, calcite, kaolinite, iron, magnetite, leucozone, and clinozoisite and carries those energies even when not visible. Linking to the megaforces that created our multi-dimensional universe and which still drive cosmic evolution, Que Sera acts like a battery to activate your personal power. With this stone, you truly create your own reality. This stone energizes the Earth Star, base, sacral and stellar gateway chakras and, placed below the navel, activates the higher sacral chakra that sits in the dantien*. Holding it lights up every cell in your body.

This stone creates an awesome power source for higher creativity and spiritual evolution. With its assistance you attune to the Akashic Record* of your soul's purpose and view all possible pathways with their outcomes. Que Sera insists that you stand in your own power. If you took on duties or unconsciously assumed a role or obligations so the world would perceive you as 'a good person', Que Sera releases you. The stone teaches that such an act of 'service' is actually selfish and self-serving. If you find it impossible to say no when asked to do even more, keep Que Sera in your pocket.

If you have a tendency to dwell on problems this crystal helps you find constructive solutions and to be confident about your actions. With Que Sera there are no mistakes, only learning experiences. Although Que Sera means 'what will be', this stone helps you co-create your own future. It encourages you to take the most appropriate pathway for your evolution, which can be instantaneous.

Physically a powerful carrier of Qi* and an excellent all round healer, Que Sera has strong, readily accessible bioscalar wave* energy. This stone is an excellent shield against Wi-Fi emanations and other electromagnetic pollutants and geopathogens*. It recharges and balances the meridians* and organs of the subtle* and physical bodies. Place it wherever dis-ease* or depletion exists. The stone activates neurotransmitters to optimize the energetic circuit. Assisting a healer to see into the recipient's energy matrix, Que Sera highlights areas of dis-ease, twitching as it moves over places that need healing.

HEALING An all-round healer and re-energizer carrying strong bioscalar waves, Que Sera assists the energetic systems and meridians of the subtle and physical bodies and energizes all the organs and systems of the physical body. It may energetically remove mercury dental amalgam from the system, especially after removal of fillings.

POSITION Place the stone over a site to dissolve dis-ease and restore the body's cellular and energetic structure. Hold, wear or place under your pillow. Disperse gem essence around the aura. *NOTE: Make essence by indirect method unless the stone has been tumbled. Que Sera is sold as Vulcanite but there is a copper mineral with this name.*

ADDITIONAL STONE

Texas Llanite (Llanoite) is similar in appearance to Que Sera, as it is a similar combination from South Africa, but is unawakened and earthier. It carries energy deeper into the present earth vibration whereas Que Sera goes to the level to which we are shifting. Placing the two crystals together ultimately

Texan Llanite

brings Llanoite up to the same high vibration as Que Sera. These stones assist those who feel compressed into physicality when they return to everyday reality after journeying* through multi-dimensions. Llanoite helps you to see the bigger picture. This stone is said to be an excellent companion for those who find themselves embroiled in constant arguments as it promotes co-operation and harmony, offering the gifts of diplomacy and tact.

RAINBOW COVELLITE

Raw

COLOUR	Dark blue with rainbows
APPEARANCE	Iridescent stone
RARITY	Rare
SOURCE	Italy, United States, Germany

ATTRIBUTES Rainbow Covellite is attuned to the Higher Self and helps you to connect to the Akashic Record* for your soul. If you need to de-energize* past patterns, place this stone over the past life or alta major chakra at base of skull for fifteen minutes. It may need to be followed with a high vibration light-carrier.

HEALING Covellite is traditionally used for detoxification and to overcome dis-eases* caused by irradiation or fungal or parasitic infestations.

POSITION Hold, grid or place as appropriate.

REALGAR AND ORPIMENT

Raw Orpiment and Realgar on matrix

COLOUR	Red and yellow
APPEARANCE	Crystalline
RARITY	Rare
SOURCE	Peru, United States

ATTRIBUTES Realgar and Orpiment stimulates anything sluggish. Clearing the base and sacral chakras, it strengthens your physical energy and combats energetic depletion at any level. Use it if you have put your spiritual or intellectual development on hold. A stone of intellectual clarity, it assists the left side of the brain, promoting rational analysis and constructive thought. A great help when studying, it facilitates retaining information.

HEALING Realgar reputedly clears dis-eases* associated with blockages in the base and sacral chakras.

POSITION Grid or position as appropriate. *NOTE: Combination is arsenic based. Wash hands after use. Make essence by the indirect method only.*

RENIERITE

Raw

COLOUR	Bronze-pink, orange-bronze
APPEARANCE	Lustrous metallic, may be tarnished
RARITY	Rare
SOURCE	Peru, Congo/Zaire, Alaska

ATTRIBUTES Magnetic Renierite is believed to contain germanium, an oxygen catalyst that raises oxygen levels in cells, improving cellular metabolism and homeostasis. Germanium is an antioxidant, electro-stimulant and immune enhancer used to support cancer patients in their healing process. Renierite delivers a homoeopathic energetic dose.

HEALING Reported to assist immune system, normalize high blood pressure and cholesterol, protect against cellular disintegration and heart disease, alleviate rheumatoid arthritis and Reynauds, and normalize physiological functions.

POSITION Grid, position or place as appropriate. *CAUTION: Toxic, wash hands after handling and make gem essence by indirect method.*

RHODOZITE

Raw, natural points

COLOUR	Brownish-white
APPEARANCE	Dodecahedron-shaped tiny opaque stone
RARITY	Easily obtained
SOURCE	United States, Madagascar

ATTRIBUTES A master crystal in a very small package, Rhodozite packs a powerful punch especially when used for earth healing*. This stone combines potassium, cesium, beryllium and aluminium and was born out of oxygen catalization. It is extremely effective gridded around a site on a map or on the ground for earth healing. It rarely needs cleaning so can be left in situ to do its work. Placed in a grid, Rhodozite enhances the effect of other crystals.

In meditation this stone assists in entering a state of 'no-mind', switching off the chatter and taking you into stillness. It facilitates journeying* and out of body experiences. Reputedly this is a favourite stone of the Madagascan shamans when making weather magic.

A useful stone for de-energizing* blockages, Rhodozite cleanses, activates and powers up all the chakras. Place or wear it over the solar plexus to release emotional blockages causing psychosomatic dis-ease*. The stone is excellent for past life regression as it assists in linking a previous life to its effect on the present. Rhodozite can also be placed on or around a person who is passing on so that the karmic* and etheric blueprints* are cleansed and no dis-ease is carried forward. They assist with a gentle transition and may ameliorate pain.

Physically, this is a highly energetic stone that can add vitality to the body and stimulate the flow of Qi*. It is an excellent booster for any type of healing.

HEALING Rhodizite is reported to be helpful for cancer, tissue inflammation, cellular diseases and pH balance in the body and is said to stabilize brain function and to be a pain reliever especially for eyes, headaches or migraine.

POSITION Place, hold or grid as appropriate. Disperse gem essence around the aura or environment.

Rhodozite in Feldspar

COMBINATION STONE
Rhodozite in Feldspar
This combination accelerates the effect of Rhodozite as Feldspar speeds up the process and grounds the energy into the body or the environment.

RIEBEKITE, SUGILITE AND BUSTAMITE

*Riebekite,
Sugilite and
Bustamite*

COLOUR	Purple-pink-black
APPEARANCE	Opaque tri-coloured stone
RARITY	Rare
SOURCE	South Africa

ATTRIBUTES Riebekite is a Granite so the gentle combination of Sugilite and Bustamite is energized and earthed more intensely, clearing blockages on all levels. It nourishes sensitive souls who find it difficult in incarnation. Strengthening spiritual intuition and connectedness, deepening insights and awareness, it draws-like minded souls together encouraging the application of a group's talents.

HEALING Reportedly improves circulation and respiration and assists skin, nails and hair. It is helpful for stress related dis-ease*, headaches or migraines with a psychic cause and anxiety.

POSITION Hold, grid or place as appropriate, especially over the base of the skull. Disperse gem essence around the aura.

RICHTERITE

Tumbled

COLOUR	Whitish-yellow, blue
APPEARANCE	Opaque translucent stone
RARITY	Rare but fairly easily obtained
SOURCE	Finland, Afghanistan

ATTRIBUTES Although high vibration, Richterite's greatest power lies in assisting the body to withstand constant stress or sudden trauma. It imparts strength to the physical, mental and subtle bodies*. A profoundly calming stone, it deepens relaxation and meditation, turning off the mind and all anxieties to create a quiet space so that the body switches on its own natural healing mechanisms and rebalances itself. If you need to 'unfrazzle' yourself, meditate quietly for ten to 15 minutes with Richterite about a hand's breadth out over your higher heart chakra and then tap each side of the breastbone with the stone to stimulate the immune system.

Physically, Richterite boosts well-being by reducing stress and allowing the body to relax so that the adrenals shut off the 'fight or flight' mechanism that pumps adrenaline into the system. Constant adrenaline overload causes dis-ease* on many levels, including high blood pressure and circulatory problems. It may also create mental confusion and dizziness. Richterite is said to be particularly helpful when dealing with Post Traumatic Stress Disorder or great shock. With Richterite's assistance you face life calmly and let go any feeling of being wound-up by events or by other people. It strengthens the body's psychic and physical immune systems, boosts the thymus and increases production of T-cells to fight diseases and infections.

HEALING Richterite reputedly assists the endocrine glands, particularly the thyroid which it rebalances, and the pineal and hypothalamus which it purifies. An energetic detoxifier for the blood, cells and lymph, it may assist the kidneys, liver, adrenals and pancreas, and remove excess mucus from the respiratory system.

POSITION Wear constantly or position as appropriate. Disperse gem essence into the aura or put a few drops in the bath.

ROSELITE

*Raw Roselite
on matrix*

COLOUR	Pink to fuchsia-pink
APPEARANCE	Lustrous, crystalline or drusy
RARITY	Rare
SOURCE	Peru

ATTRIBUTES Roselite is rich in cobalt although it may also have traces of manganese. Beautiful Roselite is helpful for opening the higher heart and heart seed chakras and for clearing energetic blockages from the physical heart and emotional bodies. Meditate with it to draw in unconditional love.

HEALING Roselite may assist circulation and the heart, especially when dis-ease* has a psychosomatic basis.

POSITION Hold, place or position as appropriate. *NOTE: Make gem essence by indirect method.*

RUTILATED KUNZITE

Shaped and rutilated

COLOUR	Blue-green with gold
APPEARANCE	Threads within opaque crystal
RARITY	Rare
SOURCE	Unconfirmed

ATTRIBUTES Rutilated Kunzite is an extremely high vibration stone as the rutilation lifts the underlying crystal to a new level. It is excellent for drawing off negative energies and impediments to spiritual growth that are held in the subtle bodies*, higher chakras or the soul. The stone then channels refined spiritual energy through the higher chakras into the physical body, filling it with unconditional love, raising the frequency of the whole.

HEALING Rutilated Kunzite heals the spiritual dis-ease* that eventually manifest in the physical. It repairs the etheric blueprint* and removes energetic encrustations from the karmic blueprint.

POSITION Hold, place or position as appropriate. Sweep around the aura and chakras.

SANDSTONE

Polished

Opalized

Raw

COLOUR	Sandstone
APPEARANCE	Coarse grained stone
RARITY	Easily accessible
SOURCE	Worldwide

ATTRIBUTES Sandstone is an abrasive stone that has been through enormous changes in its long lifetime and so helps with soul scouring and cleansing the etheric bodies*. With an abundance of Qi*, it enhances acceptance of change and going with the flow. Psychologically, this stone helps to reduces anger. Opalized Sandstone with its rainbow light brings the stone to a higher level of transformation.

HEALING Sandstone may assist general healing or broken bones and is reputedly beneficial for hair and nails and to maintain flexibility and elasticity of tissue and joints.

POSITION Grid, position or place as appropriate.

SCHALENBLENDE

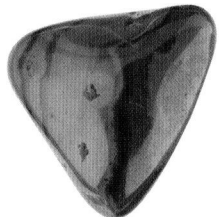

Tumbled

COLOUR	Brown-black-grey
APPEARANCE	Opaque, banded or veined stone
RARITY	Easily obtained as tumbled stone
SOURCE	Germany

ATTRIBUTES Promoting peace, Schalenblende is a combination of Sphalerite, Pyrite, Wurtzite and Galena. A protective stone that keeps you grounded and functioning optimally on the earth, its best known property is that of energetically regenerating and strengthening the physical body. It is an excellent stone to overcome physical or mental weakness and exhaustion. Use it when you feel you have no resources left with which to cope with what life is throwing at you. The stone supports you in replenishing your inner reserves so that you move forward confidently knowing that the energy never runs out.

This stone is used by shamans and metaphysicians to provide a shield during journeying* and out of body working and to assist the soul in returning to the physical body. It encourages you to put into practice your highest ideals. Schalenblende supports the mind by increasing concentration and analytic abilities while at the same time encouraging the use of intuition. It brings spontaneous solutions through the integration of the intuition and the intellect. This stone is an effective communication enhancer, facilitating interaction and solution-finding between those who are not of like-mind or between different species.

If you lie awake at night worrying, place Schalenblende under your pillow to switch off your mind and bring about a good night's sleep. The situation looks different in the morning.

HEALING With its strengthening effect on the immune and endocrine systems, Schalenblende has been found to assist diabetes and stabilize pancreatic function and the prostate gland, and may assist HIV and AIDS. It is used to speed up wound and cellular healing and to support processes within the brain. It reportedly assists the prostate, testicles and ovaries, the retina and the sense organs.

POSITION Place, grid or position as appropriate or disperse gem essence around the aura.

SCHEELITE

Raw

COLOUR	Orangey-yellow, golden
APPEARANCE	Translucent crystalline
RARITY	Becoming more easily available
SOURCE	United States, China, Czech Republic, UK, Bohemia, Switzerland, Japan, New Zealand

ATTRIBUTES Scheelite encourages being spiritually grounded. It heightens intuition and opens the third eye, assisting in journeying*. This incisive stone turns the head and the mind around. It is helpful for people stuck in patterns of mental negativity who constantly – by situations and by retelling the story – repeat their own and other people's negative experiences. They anchor the story back in by retelling it after a clearance as though they cannot bear the positive state. Scheelite 'closes the gap' so that the old pattern cannot reattach and assists a positive mental suggestion to be implanted so that the outlook changes and the past falls away. It harmonizes the mental body to the new positive vibration and encourages creative thinking. Scheelite assists you in identifying appropriate goals for yourself that are in accordance with your soul purpose and with putting these into action.

Scheelite is particularly useful for healers and therapists who hold onto their client's experience. If a therapist doesn't let go it is as though it is still activated in the client, as the therapist carries it for the client. Scheelite helps both parties to let go. Keep a piece in the therapy room. Place Scheelite in a toilet cistern to flush the old patterns out after release. Scheelite removes past life mental patterning that has been carried over in the etheric blueprint*. It clears the past life chakras of mental soul overlays* and quietens mind chatter so that a new inner voice is heard. Overcoming self-sabotage, it helps the mind to function analytically rather than emotionally.

Lymph and other fluids act as a medium for carrying negative messages to the appropriate part of the body so that it reacts psychosomatically to an old stimulus. Scheelite releases the pattern so that the cells reprogram positively. It assists with EFT and other tapping or meridian*-based therapies. It is a useful stone for aligning the subtle bodies* with the physical and re-energizes all levels. The stone balances an excess of yang or masculine energy, especially in a female.

Scheelite brings out the good in someone's heart who has struggled to manifest their positive intentions. It acts as a spiritual support for those who are unsure of their future pathway. Scheelite harmonizes with Amphibole Quartz to call in angelic guidance.

HEALING Physically Scheelite would appear helpful in cases of heart failure where the body, especially the lungs and heart, becomes water logged and makes breathing difficult as it energetically stimulates fluid release. Scheelite assists the parathyroid and the fluid balance throughout the body (especially the lungs), reversing dehydration, and may treat inflammation of the bladder and urethra. It assists the lower back, nerves, muscles and blood vessels and restores energy when you are depleted.

POSITION Place or grid as appropriate or disperse gem essence around the aura, particularly around the navel.

SCOLECITE

*Raw natural
formation*

COLOUR	White, clear, yellow
APPEARANCE	Translucent, ribbed crystal
RARITY	Easily obtained
SOURCE	India, Iceland

ATTRIBUTES Scolecite is a gentle, high vibration stone that promotes inner peace and opens all the heart chakras, especially the heart seed, connecting it to the third eye and soma chakra. Similar to Natrolite, Scolecite has a slightly earthier vibration. It is appropriate for people new to high vibration crystals or with a particularly sensitive energy field. The inner light carried by Scolecite infuses peace into the core of your being, connecting you to the highest energies in the universe and multi-dimensional realms. An excellent journeying* crystal, this serene stone assists with lucid dreaming and dream recall. Meditate with it to reach the deeper meaning of significant dreams or connect to higher guidance or benign extraterrestrials and star beings.

Place Scolecite on the chakras along the back and Natrolite on the front to accommodate a download of high vibrational energies or to realign the physical body with the lightbody*. Wearing Scolecite ensures a healthy auric field and heals holes, splits or fragmentation where negative energies or entities* could attach. Scolecite assists in restructuring thought patterns and shaping everyday reality into a positive outcome. It hooks out the last remnants of detrimental patterns or beliefs, clearing the etheric blueprint* and the mental body. Scolecite is extremely calming, encouraging unselfish love of one's self and inner contentment. It dissolves anxiety and fear, instilling a quiet confidence that faces life with equanimity.

Grid Scolecite to create an area of total peace. It calms disturbed energies and creates a safe, sacred space in which to live, work and have your being. This crystal harmonizes the energies between lovers and loved ones and helps those whose heart has been turned to stone to gently release the traumas of the past and love again. Physically Scolecite resonates with the nerves and neural pathways, bringing the body back into equilibrium and encouraging control of autonomous processes.

HEALING Anecdotal evidence suggests Scolecite is effective for MS and neurological rebalancing, and for realigning the spinal column and associated nerves. It further suggests an anti-seizure effect and that it may help benign tumours of the brain. The calcium component energetically strengthens bones. Scolecite is used for intestinal conditions including parasites and IBS, and supports the circulatory system and lungs.

POSITION Place or grid as appropriate or disperse gem essence around the aura.

SEDONA STONE

Shaped

COLOUR	Reddish-grey
APPEARANCE	Smooth opaque pebble or grainy raw stone
RARITY	Easily sourced, especially as beads
SOURCE	Sedona, United States

ATTRIBUTES The red rock of Sedona is pure crystallized energy. Sedona is a powerful cluster of multi-dimensional vortexes where spiritual energy is fiercely concentrated and the stone links you into that energy from afar. It enhances metaphysical abilities, especially if placed over the soma chakra, and powers journeying* and sacred ceremonies. The vortex also takes you deep within yourself to explore your inner dimensions.

HEALING Sedona Stone heightens your sense of physical and spiritual well-being as it downloads energy stored in the stone to effect multi-dimensional healing.

POSITION Place, hold, grid or meditate with the stone as appropriate.

SERPENTINE IN OBSIDIAN

Tumbled

COLOUR	Black-grey-green
APPEARANCE	Banded opaque stone
RARITY	Unusual combination
SOURCE	Mexico

ATTRIBUTES A powerful combination of earthy stones that raise kundalini* power, Serpentine in Obsidian grounds and protects the physical body, strengthening energetic boundaries and creating an interface between your biomagnetic sheath* and the outside world. Knowing that you are safely shielded paradoxically enables you to be more open and receptive to others. It provides a protective shield during shamanic journeying* and metaphysical activity.

Obsidian brings deep-seated emotional issues to the surface for resolution and may result in a catharsis, but the gentler energy of Serpentine regulates this process so that it is never more than can be handled and emotional balance is maintained. If you are unsure of exactly what is causing a feeling or situation, meditate with this stone to find and release the hidden cause. With its assistance you find your emotional strengths and overcome any weaknesses or outgrown patterns. If you continually beat yourself up over your mistakes, this stone helps you to turn things around so that you perceive these as learning experiences that helped you to grow.

Spiritually, Serpentine opens the third eye and Obsidian has traditionally been used for crystal gazing, so this combination helps you to access the past, present or future. The combination assists in reading the Akashic Record* of previous lives and is beneficial in past life healing with an emotional or psychosomatic component. It overcomes fear and instils a deep sense of inner security and safety within the physical plane. The combination may open the flow of kundalini up the spine and help to channel it productively so that you become more creative in the multi-dimensions of being.

HEALING Useful for removing energy blockages, Serpentine in Obsidian directs healing to precisely where it is required. It may assist with kidney, stomach or digestive disorders and facilitate the energetic expulsion of parasites. It is used to stabilize blood sugar imbalances and the pulse, bringing calcium and magnesium assimilation into energetic balance. It reputedly improves circulation and aids the lungs. Placed over muscles it may relax cramp and over the uterus PMS.

POSITION Hold, place or grid as appropriate or disperse gem essence around the aura.

SHUNGITE

Raw

COLOUR	Black
APPEARANCE	Dusty, graphite-like stone that may have a metallic lustre
RARITY	Becoming more easily available
SOURCE	Russia

ATTRIBUTES A profoundly earthy and anti-geopathogenic* stone, Shungite is found only in Karelia, northern Russia. At least two billion years old, Shungite formed before organic life was established and yet carbon-based minerals normally arise from decayed organic matter such as ancient forests. It may have been instrumental in creating life on earth. It has been suggested that an enormous meteorite hit the earth and created the crater in which Lake Onega later formed. It is postulated that micro-organisms were swimming in a soupy-sea and that the seabed formed the Shungite deposit. What is known is that although the lake is highly polluted, the water that pours from it has been purified by the Shungite bed. The water has been used as a healing spa for hundreds of years.

Shungite contains virtually all the minerals in the periodic table. It has phenomenal shielding power that arises from its unique formation. A rare carbon mineral it is composed of fullerenes, otherwise called 'Buckyballs' (spherical) or 'Buckytubes' (cylindrical). Each tiny, hollow Buckyball has from 20 to 500 carbon atoms. Fullerenes empower nanotechnology, being excellent geothermal and electromagnetic conductors, and yet they shield electro-magnetic frequency emissions. A group of English scientists was awarded a Nobel price in 1996 for their discovery and the full potential of this mineral is being investigated by scientists around the world. Wear Shungite or place on the source of electro-magnetic frequency (EMF) emissions such as computers and cell phones to eliminate their detrimental effect on sensitive human energy systems (cleanse frequently).

Psychologically, Shungite clears out mental or emotional pollutants so that fresh patterns imprint. At the same time, it encourages keeping the wisdom of the past and applying to the present to create a new future.

At a physical level, Shungite transforms water into a biologically active life-enhancing substance, whilst at the same time removing harmful micro-organisms and pollutants. Research has shown that Shungite absorbs that which is hazardous to health whether it be pesticides, free radicals, bacteria and the like, or EMF, microwave and other vibrational emissions. It boosts physical well-being and has a powerful effect on the immune system. Restoring emotional equilibrium, it transmutes stress into a potent energetic recharge. Shungite infused water is traditionally drunk two or three times a day to eliminate free radicals and pollutants, as an antibacterial and antiviral, and for prevention or lessening of the symptoms of the common cold and other diseases. A Shungite pyramid placed by the bed counteracts insomnia and headaches and eliminates the physiological effects of stress.

HEALING A traditional cure-all, anecdotal evidence and scientific research suggest that Shungite assists cellular metabolism, neurotransmitters, immune, digestive and filtration systems, enhances enzyme production and provides pain relief. It is a detoxifier, antioxidant, antibacterial, anti-inflammatory and antihistamine. Shungite Water treats sore throats, burns, cardio-vascular diseases, blood disorders, allergies, asthma, gastric disturbances, diabetes, arthritis and osteoarthritis, kidney and liver disorders, gall-bladder dysfunction, auto-immune diseases, pancreatic disorders, impotence and chronic fatigue syndrome.

Shungite (polished)

POSITION Place, wear, hold or grid as appropriate, especially in the presence of EMF frequencies. Drink activated Shungite Water several times a day. Shungite has to be immersed in water for at least 48 hours to therapeutically activate the water. *NOTE: As Shungite is a rapid absorber of negative energy and pollutants it needs to be cleansed regularly and placed in the sun to recharge.*

SILLIMANITE

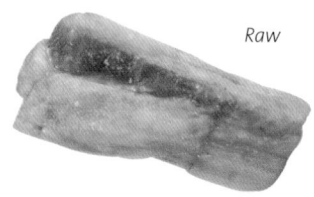

Raw

COLOUR	Blue-grey to white, olive green, brown
APPEARANCE	Striated, fibrous silky opaque stone
RARITY	Fairly easily obtained
SOURCE	United States

ATTRIBUTES Excellent for purifying, energizing and connecting the chakras, high vibration Sillimanite aligns the subtle bodies* with the physical, facilitating a free flow of energy throughout the whole. A stone of self-mastery, if you suffer from lack of self-discipline it helps maintain your intention and concentrate on the job in hand. Linking the personal mind to the universal, it attunes to concepts that run the universe at a higher state of consciousness and brings those to bear on the present three-dimensional everyday reality.

HEALING Sillimanite reputedly contributes to overall well-being and creates an endorphin rush that overcomes depression.

POSITION Grid, position or wear as appropriate. Disperse gem essence around the aura.

STEATITE

ALSO KNOWN AS SOAPSTONE

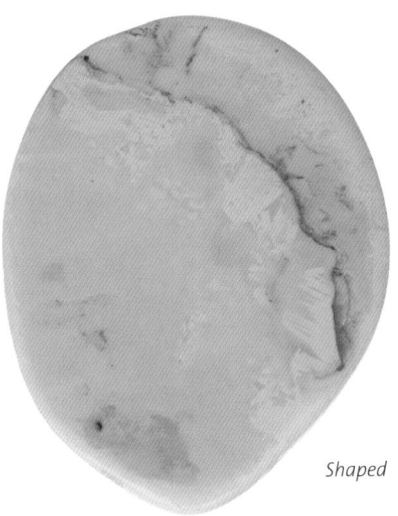

Shaped

COLOUR	White, grey, green, brown
APPEARANCE	Opaque, soapy stone
RARITY	Rare
SOURCE	Cornwall, UK, United States, China

ATTRIBUTES Rare and prized by stone carvers, the White Steatite pictured above is found in the Serpentine deposits on the Lizard Peninsula in Cornwall. Cornwall is steeped in Arthurian legend and the stone carries the mystic presence of The West and the Blessed Isles to which the souls of the dead passed. This mysterious county is where the magic of Merlin lies and where an ancient king waits to be awakened in time of need. White Steatite is useful for rebirthing and renewing rituals and supports the adventurous in their exploration.

Meditating with Steatite puts you in touch with the mythical, chivalrous past, helping you to ground the knowledge that you find there. It facilitates finding learned guides and the higher knowledge that you seek. Especially when placed in the west, whether in a medicine wheel or on an altar, Steatite encourages introspection and going within. Showing you the value of quiet, fallow times, it teaches that all you need to know is already within yourself.

Steatite from other locations connects you to the mythical past of its location and the knowledge carried by the ancient peoples who inhabited the land. It assists in dissolving racial memories of conflict, offering forgiveness and the opportunity to move on.

This calming, earthing stone has a strengthening effect on the physical and subtle bodies*, particularly when you are involved in challenging experiences. It helps you to move forward confidently in whatever direction life takes you no matter how unexpected that may be.

HEALING Steatite may assist the skeletal structure and tendons of the body and the organs of elimination, and aids digestive problems with a psychosomatic basis.

POSITION Place, grid or position as appropriate or disperse gem essence around the aura.

STICHTITE AND SERPENTINE

Polished

COLOUR	Purple-lilac
APPEARANCE	Speckled, mottled opaque stone
RARITY	Rare
SOURCE	South Africa

ATTRIBUTES At a very deep level Stichtite and Serpentine changes your core relationship with yourself, helping you to love and fully accept who you are. It nourishes body and soul so that emotional energy and spiritual intent flow freely in harmony. This gentle stone has an extremely soothing effect, grounding and centreing the body and anchoring it to the earth so that your true self reveals itself in the physical dimension and, simultaneously, operates in multi-dimensions and time-frames.

Stichtite and Serpentine helps you to trace the source of emotional and psychosomatic dis-ease* and to de-energize the events underlying it, no matter from which lifetime it arose. Once this energy drain is cleared, new patterns of positive self-regard and optimism are put in place. It is particularly helpful for eating disorders or self-destructive, self-deprecating behaviour as it enhances self-love and dissolves patterns of self-abuse arising out of a deep sense of inferiority and poor self-image. If you have never been able to speak about what has happened to you, this stone gently encourages you to verbalize and release what has been blocked for so long.

If spontaneous, uncontrolled kundalini* rise occurs, Stichtite with Serpentine helps to rebalance all the subtle bodies* with the physical, attuning all the levels of your being and opening mystical consciousness and connection to All That Is*.

This stone comes from the other side of the ocean to Australian Atlantasite but has a similar connection to the ancient continents of Lemuria and Atlantis, helping you to explore your connection with those civilisations.

HEALING This combination provides pain relief as it gets to the energetic core of a problem. It may assist diabetes (balancing hypoglycaemia and sugar imbalances), stabilize blood pressure and harmonize the nervous system. It is reported to treat Parkinson's and dementia.

POSITION Grid, place or hold as appropriate.

STONE OF DREAMS

Raw

COLOUR	White
APPEARANCE	Crystalline opaque stone
RARITY	Rare
SOURCE	Canada

ATTRIBUTES The Stone of Dreams assists in attaining something that you have dreamed of for years. If you have plans that you never fulfil, or aspirations which always seem out of reach, meditate with this optimistic stone and program it to bring the plan to fruition. Opening and clarifying your mind, it shows the way forward, offering inspiration and support and enabling you to think outside the box. This stone encourages you to be all that you may be.

HEALING The Stone of Dreams is said to be useful for overcoming pain and allergies. It energetically strengthens bones and may improve calcium uptake and lactation.

POSITION Wear, grid, position or place as appropriate. Disperse gem essence into the aura.

STROMATOLITE

Polished

COLOUR	Brown, grey, green
APPEARANCE	Swirling bands of colour
RARITY	Becoming more available
SOURCE	United States, Russia, Madagascar, Australia

ATTRIBUTES Created from fossilized algae, one of the earliest life forms and believed to have created the oxygen on our planet, Stromatolite carries eternal knowledge. It helps you to read the Akashic Record* of your previous lives, and yet looks to the future. This stone is an excellent support during evolutionary change as it has weathered billions of years of chaos, catastrophe and transformation.

Stromatolite is a useful aid to processing and learning from all your experiences. It instils flexibility and the ability to 'let go' or to opt out of disagreements while still maintaining your own point of view and fulfilling your personal and planetary goals. Extremely effective for learning from past experiences, it helps you to stand in your own power acting only on your soul's directions. Meditating with this stone acts as a portal to the far past of the earth, delving deep into its history, evolution and closely guarded secrets. If you have been imprinted with mental programs that are no longer relevant or which insist you conform to someone else's agenda, Stromatolite helps you to release these. It assists in being less emotionally stressed and brings comfort and friendship to the lonely of heart.

Stromatolite resonates with the oldest part of the brain stem and the autonomic processes of the body. Placed in the hollow at the base of the skull it removes blockages, patterns and programs that have been deeply ingrained and encourages assimilation of new patterns, instilling flexibility of mind. It assists meridian*-based tapping therapies such as EFT, increases brain function and enhances the workings of neurotransmitters. Encouraging healing at the cellular level, it strengthens the body's structures. Hold the stone to assist recovery from serious illness or psychosomatic dis-ease*. Stromatolite assists the passage of fluid through the body and brain, regulating the flow as appropriate, and, like all fossils, helps to maintain the skeletal system and brain hemispheres. It encourages the elimination of toxins through the kidneys and blood-rich organs. Environmentally, Stromatolite assists with earth cleansing and healing*. Grid to repair and activate the earth's meridians and song lines, and to improve fertility in the earth and the physical body. The stone supports photosynthesis in plants and increases oxygen output.

HEALING Stromatolite reportedly assists the thymus and throat and is traditionally used for hands and feet. It may be beneficial for Parkinson's and brain stem dis-ease. It energetically strengthens bones and teeth and supports the kidneys and bladder.

POSITION Grid, place or position as appropriate or disperse gem essence around the aura, particularly at the back of the head and the feet.

STRONTIANITE

Raw

Raw

COLOUR	Yellow, grey, green, brown, white
APPEARANCE	Striated opaque to transparent stone
RARITY	Rare
SOURCE	Austria, Scotland, Germany

ATTRIBUTES Strontianite shares properties with Aragonite, a powerful earth healer*. This stone offers you strength, confidence and self-awareness without egotism. Strontianite assists energy to move through the body, increasing physical vitality and helping you to feel comfortable within your body.

HEALING Calcium-rich Strontianite may energetically assist bones, teeth and joints and is said to restore elasticity to discs and tendons and to prevent muscle spasms.

POSITION Grid, place or hold as appropriate.

TANTALITE

Polished

COLOUR	Reddish-brown to black
APPEARANCE	Metallic pitted opaque stone, shiny when tumbled
RARITY	Rare
SOURCE	Australia, Afghanistan, Namibia, United States, Nigeria, Canada, Europe, Brazil, Madagascar

ATTRIBUTES A useful stone of protection, Tantalite soaks up negative energy and guards against psychic vampirism* or environmental pollution. Blocking invasion by alien or adverse forces, it creates an energetic grid around the body to 'repel boarders'. Clearing the effect of psychic attack or ill-wishing, Tantalite removes hooks, attachments, implants, mental imperatives and core beliefs* lodged in the etheric* or physical body, in the present or previous lives, that created dis-ease* and

335

Tantalite (raw)

vulnerability to fresh attacks. It shields the body so that nothing else attaches. Grid or wear Tantalite to deflect radiation and other adverse energies.

Tantalite reverses obsession. Reining in excessive behaviour, it supports in overcoming addictions and cravings. Where such obsessions result from past life excess or depletions, Tantalite dissolves underlying patterns in the etheric blueprint* and may facilitate insightful dreams or retro-cognition into the karmic* causes.

This stone stabilizes the environment. Grid in areas of negativity or imbalance. Placed at the four corners of a house, it creates a quiet equilibrium that reflects in those who inhabit the space. Tantalite has been found to overcome chemical pollution as it energetically removes the consequent disharmony at a cellular and etheric level.

Excellent for decision making, Tantalite instils a sense of purpose and direction, facilitating planning for the future but reminding you not to disregard the present or the influence of the past. If you are impetuous it reminds you to hold back until the full picture is obtained, and if you are over-cautious, it urges you to move forward confidently once an informed decision is made.

Tantalite's stabilizing properties helps ADHD or a butterfly mind that cannot settle. It provides focus and assists in suspending judgements that have their base in the past rather than the present. A useful stone if enthusiasm has waned or lethargy set in, Tantalite revitalizes a sense of purpose and direction.

This stone re-establishes equilibrium in extreme mood swings and counteracts pessimism. It promotes passion and love of life that radically transforms depressive tendencies and stimulates the creative forces within you.

A stone of strength, Tantalite is rich in manganese, an important physiological constituent with a powerful antioxidant and metabolic function. Correct balance of manganese is essential. Tantalite works at a homeopathic level to maintain an appropriate level and to raise core stability and physical endurance.

Spiritually, Tantalite assists in feeling nurtured and guided by higher beings and in negotiating the earth-plane during times of vibrational change. Meditating with it facilitates knowing your purpose in taking on incarnation at such a time and shows the way forward.

HEALING Manganese-rich Tantalite energetically supports correct bone development and assimilation of minerals and may assist in tissue and cellular repair, easing pain and discomfort in joints. It acts as a first-aid measure during shock, trauma or the onset of dis-ease. Tantalite assists in overcoming food, drug or nicotine cravings.

POSITION Place or grid as appropriate. Disperse gem essence around the aura.

ADDITIONAL STONE
Columbite *is a niobium and tantalum ore closely related to Tantalite that shares many of its properties.*

Columbite

TERRALUMINITE™

Raw

COLOUR	Pink, black and white
APPEARANCE	Speckled granular opaque stone
RARITY	Rare
SOURCE	Vermont, United States

ATTRIBUTES Terraluminite symbolizes bringing divine light to the planet. A mixture of Quartz, Feldspar and Mica, it opens the heart to universal love and spiritual insight. Dissolving deeply embedded, outgrown or destructive emotional patterning, it reframes situations and fills the emotional body with divine light so you live from your heart as part of All That Is*. Stimulating tantric union between the Sky God and Mother Earth to fertilize new growth, Terraluminite is excellent for earth healing*.

HEALING Terraluminite brings harmony and balance into the subtle bodies* to increase core stability. Activating the meridians*, it enhances the flow of Qi*.

POSITION Meditate with the stone, hold, place over the heart or grid* as appropriate. Disperse gem essence around the aura.

THOMPSONITE

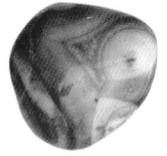

Polished

COLOUR	White, yellow, pink, brown, green
APPEARANCE	Bubbly botroydal transparent to translucent crust
RARITY	Rare
SOURCE	Australia, Scotland, United States

ATTRIBUTES Thompsonite helps you to be in grounded in incarnation. Creating a strong connection between the mental and emotional bodies, it anchors you to the physical. Psychologically this stone softens a brash or harsh personality and motivates a lazy one. It removes mental fog and confusion, imparting greater clarity and acuity.

HEALING Thompsonite may assist fevers, cysts, oral fungus and support the thymus.

POSITION Hold, grid* or place over the thyroid.

THUNDER EGG

ALSO KNOWN AS MOUNT HAY AGATE

Polished slice

COLOUR	Variable
APPEARANCE	Opaque, veined stone with star-like markings
RARITY	Easily obtained
SOURCE	Australia

ATTRIBUTES Thunder Eggs are powerful spherical stones created when mineral-laden gasses became trapped in volcanic lava and were then ejected. As with all stones that have been through the plutonic process, they assist with survival issues and hold you safe within your incarnation body, providing a haven for your soul*. Thunder Eggs create an impenetrable shield around the subtle bodies* with a strong outer edge that resists energetic incursion of any kind. The stone is useful for drawing off negative energy and for breaking down the energy imprint of an ingrained thought, or attitude. They also assist if you come under mind control.

Thunder Egg facilitates realigning the energetic connections between the physical and subtle bodies, and between the personal energy body and that of the planet. Traditionally used as amulets by the Aboriginal nation, Thunder Eggs help to overcome fear and anxiety, especially when you travel. They can be helpful for adjusting to the earth's magnetic grid especially in areas of high geomagnetic, electromagnetic or geothermal activity that conflicts with the earth energy frequency of your home. They may assist jet lag arising from conflicting earth energy patterns or time zones.

Thunder Eggs open the earth star chakra and connect it deep into the core of the planet, giving you an unshakeable bond with Mother Earth. Use for earth healing* and to stabilize and realign the earth's energetic grid. Thunder Eggs are an excellent receptacle for healing power. The stone can be charged up for the recipient to keep in their energy field to provide a continuous healing source.

HEALING Thunder Egg infuses the body with strength and power, helping to overcome or resist dis-ease* in any form. It overcomes dis-ease created by geopathogenic* events.

POSITION Hold, grid or place as appropriate.

NOTE: Thunder Egg may be cut and sold as Uluru Stone *(see page 348).*

TINGUAITE

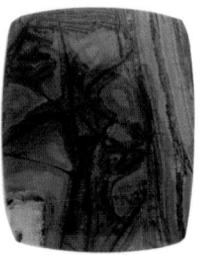

Polished

COLOUR	Pale to dark green
APPEARANCE	Tortoise-like markings or striations on opaque stone
RARITY	Rare
SOURCE	Russia, Brazil, Sweden, United States

ATTRIBUTES Tinguaite is helpful when you have 'something on your back', whether this is a burden, an attachment, a mental imperative or a structural malfunction. Releasing constraints and repatterning the energy field, it helps you to stand straight again, confident in your own power. This is a stone of integrity and sincerity that enhances your self-esteem.

HEALING Tinguaite may assist the skeletal system and nerve endings, particularly those radiating out from the spinal column.

POSITION Grid, hold or place as appropriate.

TITANITE (SPHENE)

Polished gem

COLOUR	Green, white, colourless, grey-black, pinkish-red (Greenovite)
APPEARANCE	Translucent crystal, may be faceted or tumbled
RARITY	Rare
SOURCE	Brazil, Switzerland, Austria, Russia, Canada, United States

ATTRIBUTES This high vibration crystal is soothing and yet highly energetic. Meditate with or wear Titanite (Sphene) to speed up your spiritual development as it unlocks all the chakras, including the highest crown. Connecting with higher beings, it assists out of body journeying* and expands consciousness, especially when placed on the third eye. Titanite (Sphene) is said to facilitate understanding of Oracles and divination tools such as Tarot or numerology. Sharpening sense perception, it promotes mental flexibility and intuition.

Titanite is helpful during past life work as it brings insights to the surface and assists you to de-energize* and reprogram the karmic* blueprint. Use Titanite if you find it difficult to listen to other people or to speak in public as it encourages opening yourself up to give and receive information without mental overwhelm. Encouraging emotional recovery and balancing mood swings, placed over the heart and solar plexus Titanite removes the blockages that prevent loving yourself and which, if left untreated, could create psychosomatic dis-ease*.

Titanite is helpful for plant healing, put one into the pot or place in the ground at the roots. It also helps you to bond with animals.

Raw Sphene in matrix

HEALING Titanite reputedly assists the immune system, sinuses, bones, skin, mouth, gums, teeth, muscles and cellular tissue.

POSITION Place, hold or grid as appropriate. Disperse gem essence around the aura.

TORBERNITE

*Raw crystal
on matrix*

COLOUR	Green
APPEARANCE	Striated opaque stone
RARITY	Rare
SOURCE	United States, Czech Republic, France, Mexico

ATTRIBUTES Torbernite is rarely used in crystal healing, but in the hands of an experienced crystal therapist may be useful for energetically ameliorating the effects of radiation and X-rays, or for earth healing* grids at sites of pollution. Said to open and purify the heart chakra and dissolve blockages to connection with All That Is*, opening metaphysical abilities.

HEALING Use under the guidance of a qualified practitioner.

POSITION Use as appropriate. *CAUTION: Radioactive, handle with care. Keep wrapped in foil and store with Malachite or Smoky Quartz.*

TREMOLITE

Raw crystal in matrix

COLOUR	Green, grey, white, pink, brown
APPEARANCE	Opaque stone
RARITY	Fairly easily obtained
SOURCE	United States, Tanzania

ATTRIBUTES A stone of higher knowledge and connection on many levels, Tremolite draws people to you and helps you to stay in contact with people who are far away. Projecting a mental picture of a person onto the crystal brings the person closer, whether in spirit or in body. Stimulating the pineal gland, and the third eye, Tremolite also connects you to higher beings, drawing guidance and support from other dimensions. It assists in reading the Akashic Record* for your soul*.

Enhancing innate trust and helping you to stay in the present moment, Tremolite offers strength and courage to people struggling with a difficult situation, especially those of a nervous disposition. It eases anxiety or panic wherever it arises and clears emotional baggage, breaking through denial. Useful for emotionally sensitive children who don't feel they fit in, it helps everyone to feel more secure. Placed under the pillow, it assists children who suffer from nightmares or night terrors.

Grid Tremolite in disturbed environments to restore peace and tranquillity.

HEALING Tremolite may strengthen the lungs and is reportedly beneficial for respiratory difficulties such as asthma and shortness of breath due to panic attacks. It also stimulates neurotransmitters.

POSITION Place, position or grid as appropriate, especially around the bed. Wear over the thymus. Disperse gem essence around the aura.

ULURU AMULET STONE

ALSO KNOWN AS ALCHERINGA STONE

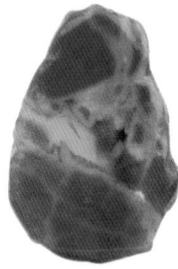

*Slice sold as
Uluru Amulet Stone*

COLOUR	Beige-orange-red
APPEARANCE	Trisected opaque stone
RARITY	Rare
SOURCE	Australia

ATTRIBUTES Uluru Amulet stone is sacred to the Aboriginal people and must be treated with the greatest respect. Since the Uluru (Ayers Rock) site was returned to its traditional guardians it has not been possible to pick up stones there, but an Amulet Stone is available from a location nearby and carries the same vibration. Some 'Uluru Amulets' are sliced Thunder Eggs from locations further afield but they still connect with the energies of this most sacred site. The stone from Uluru is divided into three distinct sections by lines on the surface. Known as Acheringa or Uluru's Children, it is believed to ensure a harmonious relationship between all creatures, nature and the earth itself.

Uluru is the solar plexus chakra of the world and the stone helps us to make an emotional reconnection to the earth so that we can feel its song lines and powerful earth energies with our hearts rather than our heads. With Uluru Amulet Stone we know that our planet is a sacred, living being and must be treated with the utmost reverence and care.

The stone can be used to enter the dreamtime and to connect to the wisdom and myths of the ancients. It has powerful protective qualities and assists in earth healing*, especially where there has been great sadness around loss of land rights to sacred sites, as occurred at Uluru.

Physically the stone is said to give the wearer resistance to diseases and to increase vitality.

HEALING Uluru Amulet Stone reputedly cleanses the blood and protects connective tissue and skin from disease, rashes, and eczema. Said to alleviate migraines, painful joints caused by weather conditions and to have a beneficial effect on the lining of the stomach, stabilizing the metabolism and helping circulation by stimulating the nervous system.

POSITION Place, grid or position as appropriate.

NOTE: The stone shown on the right was said to have been gathered near Uluru many years ago and may not be true Uluru Amulet Stone. The one above left is from a location nearby and is sold as Uluru Amulet Stone. See also Thunder Egg (Mount Hay Agate) *page 340.*

Natural formation

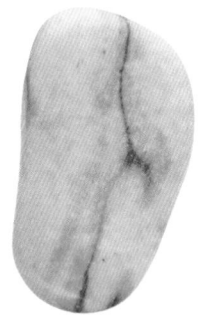

UVITE TOURMALINE ON MAGNESITE

Raw

COLOUR	Green on white
APPEARANCE	Transparent crystals on matrix
RARITY	Rare
SOURCE	Unconfirmed, believed to be Brazil

ATTRIBUTES A potent crystal mix uniting the earth star, heart and crown chakras, the combination anchors the soul to the body providing grounding during metaphysical work. Balancing the brain hemispheres, it helps you know who you truly are. Uvite Tourmaline on Magnesite brings you deep peace, stimulates visualisation and helps you to love yourself. Excellent for sending unconditional love to anyone on a self-destructive pathway, including yourself, it de-energizes* detrimental patterns.

HEALING Uvite Tourmaline on Magnesite works beyond the physical to reprogram destructive patterns in the karmic* and etheric blueprints*.

POSITION Place or grid as appropriate. Disperse gem essence around the aura or air. *NOTE: Make essence by indirect method.*

VALENTINITE AND STIBNITE

Polished

COLOUR	Silver-grey
APPEARANCE	Opaque, somewhat shiny stone
RARITY	Rare combination
SOURCE	China

ATTRIBUTES Handled with care, Valentinite and Stibnite is a valuable healing and journeying* stone. Connecting all the chakras and separating pure energy from toxic dross, it releases entity attachment and creates a shield so that nothing can re-attach. Valentinite is said to be the writer's stone, assisting in having your work published. It provides support if you self-publish and promote yourself via technology.

HEALING This stone may assist cellular memory and dissolve rigidity.

POSITION Grid, position or place as appropriate. *NOTE: Toxic, handle with care and wash hands after use. Make gem essence by indirect method only.*

VICTORITE

Raw

COLOUR	Red to violet with black and white
APPEARANCE	Speckled crystals in a matrix
RARITY	Rare
SOURCE	South India

ATTRIBUTES Victorite combines red or violet Spinel with black Biotite and Snow Quartz to produce a revitalising package. Red Spinel stimulates physical vitality and imparts strength and stamina. It arouses the kundalini* and opens and aligns the base chakra, stimulating creativity. Violet Spinel kick-starts your spiritual development and facilitates out of body journeys and psychic sight.

Biotite helps your body and your aura to detoxify and release negative energies, so that the whole system realigns and energy flows freely through the physical and subtle bodies* and the psyche. The Snow Quartz component is quietly energetic, giving stability and stamina to the body as it re-energizes the meridians and chakras.

Victorite stimulates all the chakras from the root to the crown, encouraging the rise of kundalini power, and opens the higher crown chakras to accommodate downloads of high vibration energy. It puts you in touch with your soul and facilitates discovering your life purpose. This unique combination gives you spiritual protection and direction, and helps to anchor the lightbody* into the physical dimension.

HEALING Victorite is concerned with revitalizing and rebalancing the body rather than specific ailments or organs, although it may assist the reproductive organs. It is an excellent stone for convalescence and for recovery from trauma as it imparts physical and emotional energy.

POSITION Place, grid or position as appropriate.

VOEGESITE

Tumbled

COLOUR	Brown-grey-white
APPEARANCE	Opaque stone with coloured patches
RARITY	Fairly easily obtained
SOURCE	China

ATTRIBUTES Dubbed the 'stone of innocence', Voegesite encourages unity in diversity and helps you to get along with others. It offers support, guidance and wisdom for life's journey: leading you step by step, hand in hand, soul* to soul. Helping you to find out where you've been, where you are now, where you are going and exactly who you are travelling with, it also shows you why you are on this pathway. It is a stone to heal inner scarring and to release feelings of being tainted or unclean. Voegesite is perfect for deep acceptance work, especially the withdrawal of projections and embracing the shadow side of your nature to find the gifts that lie within the rejected and repressed part of yourself. It helps you to see how and why people are demonized and how easily motives can be misunderstood, bringing forgiveness and the ability to reframe past events.

Related to the Fool in the tarot, this stone takes you back to the innocent child who was born into the present life, but it goes further back to the original innocent being that set out on the soul's journey. It is excellent for past life healing of issues that have carried forward across lifetimes. Not every soul is born so innocent, many carry a soul scarring burden of guilt or shame from other lives. Voegesite releases this burden. If you feel that your childhood was stolen, it facilitates letting this go, creating the warmth of a happy childhood by nurturing your inner child*. It also attunes you to the cosmic and inner parents who unconditionally nurture and love you so that you learn to do this for yourself.

HEALING By dealing with issues from pre-birth, birth and childhood, Voegesite releases psychosomatic dis-ease* at all levels. It energetically stabilizes the reproductive system and kidneys.

POSITION Hold, position, or grid as appropriate. Disperse gem essence around the aura, especially around the heart, solar plexus and sacral chakras.

WINCHITE

Raw

Raw

COLOUR	Yellow-white-purplish patches
APPEARANCE	Opaque stone
RARITY	Rare
SOURCE	Unconfirmed

ATTRIBUTES Supportive Winchite is the 'stone of tolerance' that helps you to deal patiently with life's vicissitudes and with other people's foibles. Encouraging you to listen to the voice of your intuition, Winchite helps you to recognize the value of lessons learned in your life through tribulations, strengthening your spiritual perceptions.

HEALING Winchite is said to overcome auto-immune dis-eases*, supporting the immune and metabolic systems. It is believed to be helpful for joints and teeth.

POSITION Hold, grid or place as appropriate.

WONDER STONE

ALSO KNOWN AS DR LIESEGANG'S STONE, BRUNEAU JASPER

Bruneau Jasper

Dr Liesegang's Stone

COLOUR	Brown to burgundy
APPEARANCE	Opaque banded stone
RARITY	Becoming more easily available
SOURCE	Grand Canyon and other areas, United States

ATTRIBUTES A type of Rhyolite Jasper, also known as Dr Liesegang's Stone or Bruneau Jasper depending on location, this banded stone carries the power of the water element and illustrates the need to bring swirling emotions to a point of stillness so the soul can attain its true potential. It is helpful for past life regression and deep meditation.

HEALING Rhyolite fortifies the body's natural resistance. It traditionally treats veins, rashes, skin disorders and infections, and improves assimilation of B vitamins. It may dissolve stones and hardened tissue. As a gem essence, Rhyolite gives strength and improves muscle tone.

POSITION Place on forehead for past life regression (under the direction of a skilled therapist) and solar plexus for emotional release.

XENOTINE

Raw

COLOUR	Brownish orange
APPEARANCE	Opaque stone
RARITY	Rare
SOURCE	China

ATTRIBUTES Xenotine helps heal the wounds of the past and stand on your own feet. It stimulates your personal will so that projects manifest in the here and now rather than remaining a dream. If people do not support your highest good or drain your energy, program Xenotine to remove them, or improve the interaction. Use it to neutralize the energetic imprint of former sexual partners, especially where this is causing dis-ease*. Helpful if you have a co-dependent nature and find it difficult to break away from an abusive or addictive partner, wear it if you are absorbing or giving away too much energy. Keep with you if you are afraid of doing or saying the wrong thing as it supports your confidence and helps you negotiate difficult situations.

HEALING Xenotine assists the bowels and reproductive organs.

POSITION Hold, grid or disperse gem essence.

358

Z-STONE

Raw

COLOUR	Blackish-brownish-grey
APPEARANCE	Knobbly, opaque stone
RARITY	Rare
SOURCE	Sahara

ATTRIBUTES A concretion found only in the Sahara, Z-stone opens the third eye and links it via the soma chakra to the crown and higher crown enabling journeying and the expansion of consciousness into multi-dimensions. Acting as a bridge between one level and another, it links to elemental beings as well as extraterrestrials. Focused intent is required for working with this stone, which may be assisted by combining Z-stone with other crystals such as Tugtupite to open the heart seed chakra to provide an anchor for expanded awareness. It works well with Rhodozite, Brandenberg or a Trigonic Quartz.

HEALING Z-stone works beyond the physical but can assist with earth healing*.

POSITION Hold, grid or position as appropriate. *NOTE: Make gem essence by indirect method.*

QUICK REFERENCE

In this section essential information facilitates working with your crystals, showing how to cleanse and activate them. You will also find chakra associations and two chakras of which you might not be aware: the palm or manifestation and the alta major, together with the physical and subtle anatomy without which you cannot efficiently position a crystal. Instructions on how to finger dowse help you select appropriate stones.

Gem essences are an excellent way to use crystal energy. They can be dispersed around a room, rubbed on the wrist or over an organ, or taken as instructed by a qualified crystal healer or essence therapist. These gentle energetic essences work at a subtle level to effect change, usually at the emotional or psychological levels, but they are excellent space clearers and energy enhancers.

AWAKENING CRYSTALS

Crystals only work when they have been activated. But first they need purifying and require regular cleansing to keep them working at optimum efficiency.

CLEANSING YOUR CRYSTAL

If your crystal is not soluble, friable or layered, hold it under running water for a few minutes and place in sun or moonlight for a few hours to re-energize. Delicate crystals can be cleansed in raw brown rice, or with sound, light or a smudge stick. Salt can only be used if the crystal is not layered, friable or delicate.

ACTIVATING YOUR CRYSTAL

Hold your crystal in your hands, concentrate on it and say out loud: 'I dedicate this crystal to the highest good of all who come into contact with it'. If you want to use the crystal for a specific purpose, state clearly what that is.

STORING YOUR CRYSTAL

As delicate stones can easily be damaged, it is sensible to keep them wrapped when not in use or on display. If you display stones, remember that strong sunlight quickly fades colours.

CHOOSING YOUR CRYSTAL

If you want to choose a crystal for a specific purpose the Directory and the Index will help you to find exactly the right one. Look up possibilities in the Index and then check out the crystals themselves in the Directory. You can also pick out a crystal at random. Trust your intuition. Look out for the one that 'winks' at you when in a shop or when browsing the net or the Directory. There will no doubt be several to choose from. Handle several, allow yourself to be drawn to one, or put your hands into a tub of crystals until one sticks to your fingers. If it makes you tingle, it is the one for you. Remember that big or outwardly beautiful is not necessarily most powerful. Small, rough crystals can be extremely effective. Alternatively use a pendulum or finger dowse to help you choose the crystal which is right for you.

HOW TO FINGER DOWSE
Finger dowsing harnesses your innate bodily intuition to choose exactly the right crystal for your needs or to answer questions.

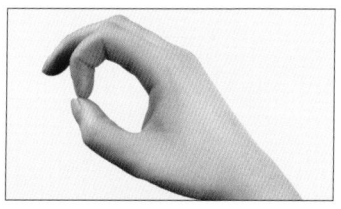

1 *Begin by looping your thumb and finger together as shown.*

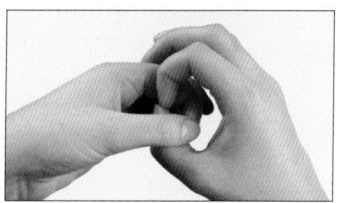

2 *Slip your other thumb and finger through the loop and close together. Hold over a crystal or photograph. Ask your question.*

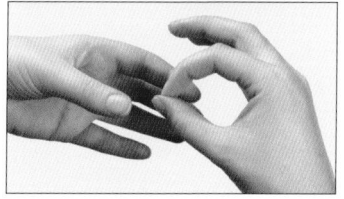

3 *Pull steadily. If the loop breaks, the answer to your question is no. If the loop holds, the answer to your question is yes.*

PHYSICAL AND SUBTLE ANATOMY

Knowing exactly where internal organs and the subtle chakras and energy meridians* of the body are located makes placing crystals for maximum effect an easy task.

PHYSICAL ANATOMY

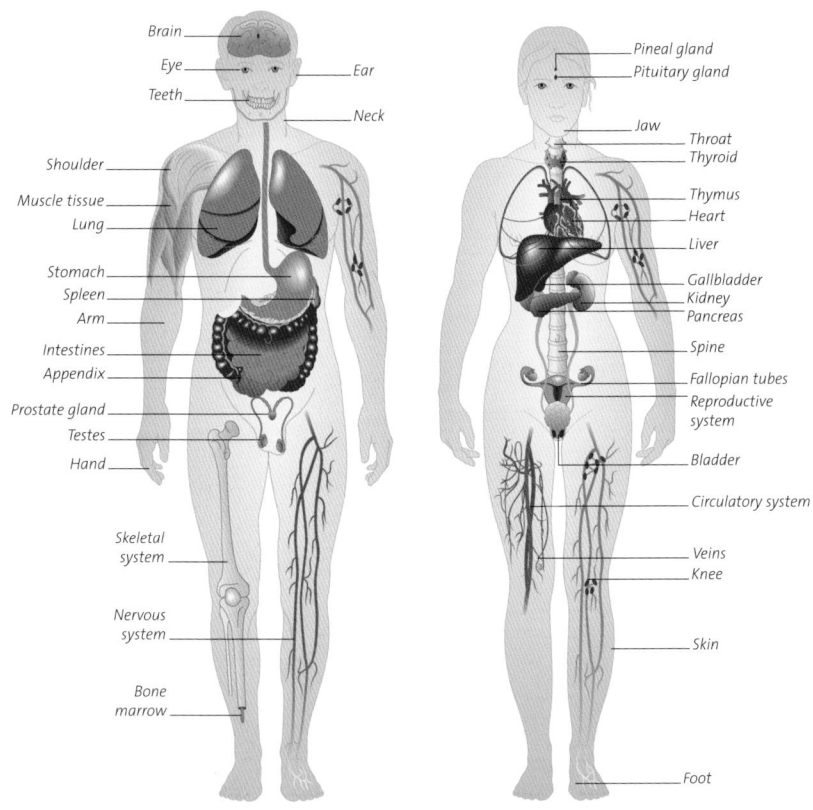

Brain
Eye
Teeth
Ear
Neck

Shoulder
Muscle tissue
Lung
Stomach
Spleen
Arm
Intestines
Appendix
Prostate gland
Testes
Hand

Skeletal system
Nervous system
Bone marrow

Pineal gland
Pituitary gland
Jaw
Throat
Thyroid
Thymus
Heart
Liver
Gallbladder
Kidney
Pancreas
Spine
Fallopian tubes
Reproductive system
Bladder
Circulatory system
Veins
Knee
Skin
Foot

SUBTLE ANATOMY: CHAKRAS AND BLUEPRINTS

1   HIGHER EARTH CHAKRA Above the feet; linkage point to earth's etheric field

2   EARTH STAR CHAKRA Between the feet; linkage point to the earth

3   BASE CHAKRA At the perineum; sexual and creative centre

4   SACRAL CHAKRA Just below the navel; the other sexual and creative centre

5   SOLAR PLEXUS CHAKRA At the solar plexus; emotional centre

6   HEART SEED CHAKRA At the base of the breastbone; site of soul remembrance

7   SPLEEN CHAKRA Under left armpit; potential site of energy leakage

8   HEART CHAKRA Over the heart; love centre

9   HIGHER HEART CHAKRA Over the thymus; centre of immunity

10 THROAT CHAKRA Over the throat; truth centre

11 PAST-LIFE OR ALTA-MAJOR CHAKRA Just behind the ears; stores past-life information

12 THIRD EYE CHAKRA Midway between eyebrow and hairline; centre of insight

13 SOMA CHAKRA At the hairline above the third eye; centre of spiritual identity and consciousness activation

14 CROWN CHAKRA At the top of the head; spiritual connection point

15 HIGHER CROWN CHAKRA Above the crown of the head; linkage point for spirit

16 SOUL STAR CHAKRA About 30 cm (1 foot) above the crown of the head; linkage point for the spiritual and subtle bodies* through which higher energies can be grounded or physical vibrations can be raised

17 STELLAR GATEWAY CHAKRA Above soul star chakra; cosmic doorway to other worlds

18 ALTA MAJOR CHAKRA In head; expansion of consciousness

19 MANIFESTATION/PALM CHAKRA Manifestation and healing

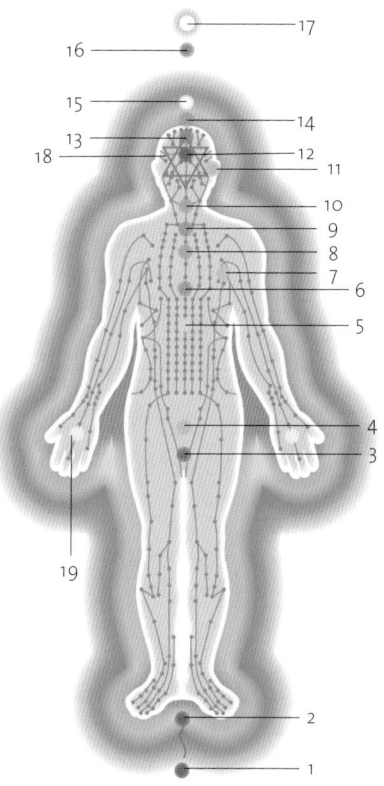

CHAKRAS ASSOCIATIONS

CHAKRA	COLOUR	POSITION	ISSUE
HIGHER EARTH AND EARTH STAR	Brown	Below feet	Material connection
BASE	Red	Base of spine	Survival instincts
SACRAL	Orange	Below navel	Creativity and procreation
SOLAR PLEXUS	Yellow	Above navel	Emotional connection and assimilation
HEART SEED	Pink	Base of breastbone	Soul remembrance
SPLEEN	Light green	Under left arm	Energy leaching
HEART	Green	Over heart	Love
HIGHER HEART	Pink	Over thymus	Unconditional love

POSITIVE QUALITIES	NEGATIVE QUALITIES
Grounded, practical, operates well in everyday reality	Ungrounded, no sense of power, cannot operate in everyday reality, picks up negativity
Base security, sense of one's own power, spontaneous leadership, active, independent	Impatience, fear of annihilation, death wish, violence, anger, over-sexed or impotent, vengeful, hyperactive, impulsive, manipulative
Assertive, confident, fertility, courage, joy, sexuality, sensual pleasure, acceptance of sexual identity	Low self-esteem, infertility, cruelty, inferiority, sluggishness, emotional hooks or thought forms, pompous, gender disorders
Empathetic, good energy utilization, organization, logic, active intelligence	Poor energy utilization, emotional baggage, energy leaching, lazy, overly emotional or cold, cynical, taking on other people's feelings and problems
Remembrance of reason for incarnation, connection to divine plan, tools available to manifest potential	Rootless, purposeless, lost
Self-contained, powerful	Exhausted, manipulated
Loving, generous, compassionate, nurturing, flexible, self-confident, accepting	Disconnected from feelings, unable to show love, jealous, possessive, insecure, miserly, resistant to change
Compassionate, empathetic, nurturing, forgiving, spiritually connected	Spiritually disconnected, grieving, needy, inability to express feelings

CHAKRAS ASSOCIATIONS CONTINUED

CHAKRA	COLOUR	POSITION	ISSUE
THROAT	Blue	Throat	Communication
PAST LIFE	Light turquoise-green	Behind ears	Anything carried over from past lives
THIRD EYE	Dark blue	Forehead	Intuition and mental connection
SOMA	Lavender	Centre of hairline	Spiritual connection
CROWN	Violet	Top of head	Spiritual connection
HIGHER CROWN	White	Above head	Spiritual enlightenment
SOUL STAR	Lavender/white	30 cm (1 foot) above head	Soul connection and highest self illumination
STELLAR GATEWAY	White	Above soul star chakra	Cosmic doorway to reach other worlds

POSITIVE QUALITIES	NEGATIVE QUALITIES
Able to speak own truth, receptive, idealistic, loyal	Unable to verbalize thoughts or feelings, stuck, dogmatic, disloyal
Wisdom, life skills, instinctive knowing	Emotional baggage, insecurity, unfinished business
Intuitive, perceptive, visionary, in the moment	Spaced-out, fearful, attached to past, superstitious, bombarded with other people's thoughts
Spiritually aware and fully conscious	Cut off from spiritual nourishment and sense of inner connection
Mystical, creative, humanitarian, giving service	Overly-imaginative, illusory, arrogant, uses power to control others
Spiritual, attuned to higher things, enlightened, true humility	Spaced-out and open to invasion, illusions and delusions
Ultimate soul connection, soul intertwining with physical body together with high-frequency light, communication with soul intention, objective perspective on past lifetimes	Soul fragmentation, open to extra-terrestrial invasion, messiah-complex, rescues not empowers
Connected to highest energies in the cosmos and beyond, communication with enlightened beings	Disintegration, open to cosmic disinformation, · unable to function

THE 'NEW' CHAKRAS

Familiarizing yourself with additional chakras greatly enhances your crystal experience. These chakras are coming on line to facilitate the assimilation of higher dimensional energy, but you may find that you have been using them for some time without necessarily being aware of it. All healers use their palm chakras and, if you meditate regularly, especially when holding high vibration crystals, you will probably find that your alta major chakra has been activated. But, if not, you can soon have these powerful energy points working for you.

CHAKRA POWER

Most people are familiar with the traditional seven chakras running up the spine (see page 365). However, there are far more chakras in many ancient chakra illustrations. Two so-called 'minor' chakras that are firmly attached to the earth-plane are far from minor in their effect. And the alta major chakra in your skull plays an integral part in expanding your awareness and your ability to reach multidimensional consciousness.

THE PALM CHAKRAS

The manifestation and healing chakras in the palm of your hand are what you use to sense crystal energies and to channel healing. These chakras are receptive (receiving energy), and expressive (radiating it). So, they are intimately connected with your ability to receive and to generate. Fully functioning palm chakras help you to receive energy from the universe – or from your crystals – and channel this into your energy field. There is a continual process of receiving and giving out and you experience expanded awareness and increased creativity.

ACTIVATING YOUR PALM CHAKRAS

The chakras are sited in the centre of your palms, but the energy radiates up to your fingertips and as far as your elbows. If you rub your hands together briskly and bring them together with fingers steepled and palms almost touching, these chakras tingle and pulsate. It is as though there is a ball of energy between your palms.

TO OPEN THE CHAKRAS

- State your intention of opening the palm chakras.
- Rapidly open and close your fingers five or six times.
- Concentrate your attention into your right hand palm and then your left. (If you are left handed reverse the process). Picture them opening like petals. The centres become hot and energised.
- Bring your hands together. Stop as soon as you feel the energy of the two chakras meeting.

- If you brought your hands together with fingers touching, reverse them so that your hands point in opposite directions. Place your right and then your left hand above the other, palms facing. You'll soon learn to recognize what works for you.
- With a little practice you'll be able to open the chakras simply by putting your attention there.
- Place a crystal point on your hand. Feel the energies radiating into your palm. Turn the point towards your arm and then towards your fingers. Sense the direction of the energy flow. (Points channel energy in the direction they face).

THE ALTA MAJOR CHAKRA

The alta major chakra is a major factor in accelerating and expanding consciousness. The anchor for the multi-dimensional energy structure known as the lightbody*, it has to do with metaphysical sight and intuitive insight, enabling you to put together the bigger picture. With its base in the cerebellum, it holds valuable information about our ancestral past and the ingrained patterns that have governed human life and awareness. This chakra contains your past life karma* and the contractual agreements you made with your Higher Self and others before incarnating in this life time. Activating it enables you to read your soul's* plan.

Closely linked to the metaphysical functioning of the pineal gland and extended awareness, the alta major creates a complex, merkaba-like geometric shape within and around the skull that stretches from the base of the skull to the crown, connecting the past life and soma chakras, hippocampus, hypothalamus, pineal and pituitary glands with the third eye and the higher crown chakras. Its link to the throat chakra facilitates expression of information from higher dimensions. Many of the new high vibration crystals activate the alta major and facilitate multi-dimensional awareness and the ability to be in several dimensions at once.

The pineal gland or third eye works in conjunction with the subtle energy* structure of the alta major. The pineal contains crystalline 'brain sand' or hydroxyapatite (found in Apatite, Fluoroapatite and other crystals) which holds crystalline information and acts as a multi-dimensional energy structure into which higher vibrational energies anchor. It has been postulated that the pineal secretes DMT, often called the 'spirit molecule'. A natural psychedelic, DMT is involved in out-of-body, near-death and other exceptional human experiences that take the soul into multi-dimensions. So, when the alta major is activated in conjunction with the pineal, or third eye chakra, metaphysical abilities, especially telepathy and far sight, function with much greater clarity.

Positive function Opening the alta major creates a direct pathway to your subconscious and your intuitive mind. It allows you to instinctively know your spiritual purpose. Reputedly the alta major chakra itself has been imprinted with 'divine codes' that will, when activated, allow divine love and cosmic evolution to be fully manifested on earth. High vibration crystals act as an activator for these codes.

Negative imbalances in the alta major chakra show themselves as eye problems, floaters, cataracts, migraine function, headaches and feelings of confusion, 'dizziness' or 'floatiness', loss of sense of purpose and spiritual depression.

HEALING GRIDS

Gridding is the art of placing stones to create an energetic net to protect and energize space. The easiest way to grid a room or other space is to place a crystal in each corner, since this creates an energy grid across the whole room. Join the crystals with a wand or long-point crystal, such as a Lemurian, to set the grid. Wands are the traditional tools of shamans, healers and metaphysicians. The magic wands of myth and legend are believed to have been used by crystal healers in the ancient civilizations of Atlantis and Lemuria. Wands have the ability to focus energy tightly through their tip, and the healing ability of wands is vastly expanded when dedicated with intent (see page 362). When using a wand, it is important to consciously allow universal healing energy to flow in through your crown chakra and down your arm to the hand holding the wand, and then into the wand where it is amplified and passed on (using your own energy for this purpose is inefficient as this makes you weak and depleted and in need of healing). Remember to cleanse and activate crystals before use, setting out your intention clearly (see page 362).

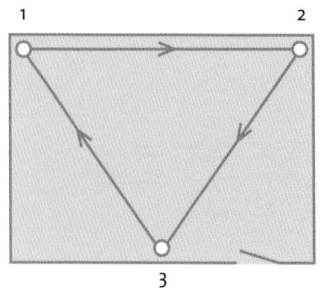

TRIANGULATION

Triangulation gridding works well to neutralize negative energy and bring in positive energy.

Place one crystal centrally along a wall and two others on the wall opposite, at an equal angle if possible. If working on a whole house, the lines of force pass through walls, so connect the points with a wand to strengthen the grid (see opposite).

ZIG-ZAG

The zig-zag layout is particularly useful for dealing with sick building syndrome and environmental pollution. Place appropriate crystals as shown on the diagram, remembering to return from the last stone laid to the first. Cleanse the stones regularly.

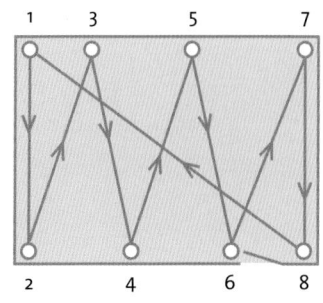

FIVE-POINTED STAR

This is a useful protection layout or caller-in of love and healing and it enhances your energy. Follow the direction of the arrows on the diagram when placing crystals and remember to return to the start crystal to complete the circuit. Like the Star of David, this layout can be used to grid around a body and also for a room or other space.

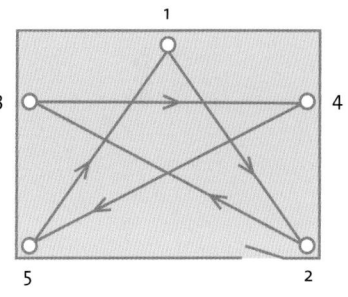

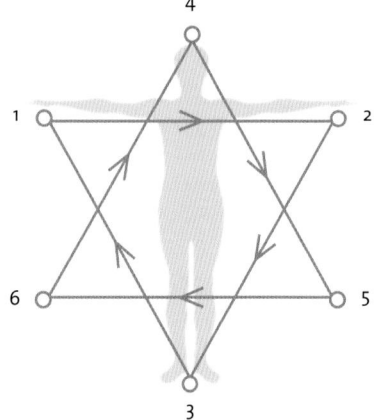

STAR OF DAVID

The Star of David is a traditional protection layout but also creates an ideal manifestation space when laid with Honduras Opal, Black Moonstone or other abundance stones. Lay the first triangle and join up the points, then lay another triangle the other way up, over the top. Join up the points. Lay Tantralite or other protective stones to neutralize ill-wishing*.

375

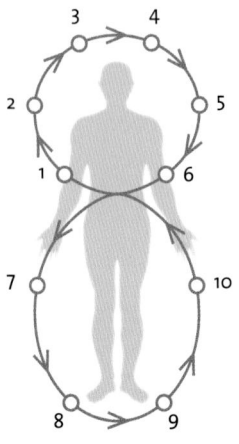

FIGURE OF EIGHT

This layout draws spiritual energy down into the body and melds it with earth energy drawn up from the feet to create perfect balance. It also opens a cosmic anchor* to ground you between the core of the earth and the galactic centre, creating core-energy solidity that equips you to ride out energetic changes and channel high-vibration energy down to earth. Place high-vibration stones, such as Auralite 23, Aurora Quartz or Trigonic Quartz, above the waist to the crown of the head, and grounding stones, such as Basalt, Dinosaur Bone or Gabbro, below the waist, down to the feet. Remember to complete the circuit back to the first stone placed.

MAKING A GEM ESSENCE

As crystals work by resonance and frequency, their vibration is easily transferred into spring water. To make an essence, cleanse your crystal and place in a clean glass bowl. Cover with pure spring water. (Indirect method: If the crystal is toxic, layered, soluble or fragile, place in an empty clean glass bowl then place bowl in water.) Leave in the sun or moon for six to 12 hours. Remove the crystal. Add two-thirds brandy, vodka or cider vinegar as a preservative. Bottle in a clean glass bottle. This is mother tincture and needs further dilution.

USING THE ESSENCE

Add seven drops of mother tincture to a small glass dropper bottle, top up with one-third brandy to two-thirds water if taking by mouth or putting on skin. If using as an eye drop, do not add alcohol at any stage.. Sip at regular intervals, rub on the skin, or bathe affected parts. A few drops of gem essence can be added to a spray bottle of water. Spritz it around your home or workspace. Disperse essence around the aura by putting a few drops on your hands and sweeping about a foot away from the body.

Place the crystal in a clean glass bowl with spring water.

Bottle in a clean glass bottle with two-thirds brandy or cider vinegar.

GLOSSARY

ALL THAT IS Spirit, the Source, the divine: the sum total of everything that is.

AKASHIC RECORD A cosmic record containing information on all that has occurred and all that will or could occur.

ANCESTRAL LINE The means by which family patterns and beliefs are passed from previous generations.

ASCENSION PROCESS The means of which people on earth seek to raise their spiritual and physical vibrations.

ATTACHED ENTITIES Spirit or alien forms that become attached to the biomagnetic sheath of a living person.

BETWEEN-LIVES STATE The vibratory state in which the soul resides between incarnations.

BLADE FORMATION: A flat-bladed crystal, extremely useful for clearing past patterns and psychic blockages: the edge removes and the point heals and seals with light. (See Rainbow Mayanite p.287)

BIOMAGNETIC SHEATH/AURA The subtle energy body around the physical body, comprising physical, emotional, mental, ancestral, karmic and spiritual layers.

BIOMAGNETIC ENERGY The human body, as with all living things including crystals, is surrounded by a subtle, organised electromagnetic energy field known as the aura or biomagnetic sheath.

BIOSCALAR ENERGY/WAVES a standing energy field created when two electromagnetic fields counteract each other which directly influences tissue at the microscopic level bringing about healing balance.

CELLULAR MEMORY Cells carry a memory of past life or ancestral attitudes, trauma and patterns that have become deeply ingrained as on-going negative programmes, such as poverty consciousness*, which create dis-ease or are replayed in the present in slightly different forms.

CENTRAL CHANNEL An energetic tube running up the centre of the body (close to the spine) linking the chakras and higher consciousness. The pathway for kundalini.

CHAKRA An energy linkage point between the physical and subtle bodies. Malfunction leads to physical, emotional, mental or spiritual dis-ease or disturbance.

CHANNELLING The process whereby information is passed from a soul not in incarnation to or through an incarnate being.

CORE BELIEFS Ancient, deeply held, often unconscious beliefs that have been passed down through the ancestral line or the soul's lineage and which powerfully.

COSMIC AND SHAMANIC ANCHOR A subtle energy tube-like conduit down the central line of the body passing through the earth chakra deep into the earth attaching to the core, and via the soul star chakra above the head, upwards to the galactic centre. It solidifies your core energy and provides a grounding cable for the lightbody, enabling riding out earth energy changes and assimilating downloads of high vibration energy and, where appropriate, grounding it into the earth.

CRYSTAL OVERSOULS Michael Eastwood of Aristia has named the hive-mind-like beings that inhabit crystals and work from other dimensions, the crystal oversouls. These beings communicate across space, time and distance and hold keys to our evolution that are activated by making contact with them through the crystals.

DANTIEN A small, spirally rotating, power-generating sphere sitting on top of the sacral chakra. If empty or depleted, creative energy cannot function fully, resulting in unbalance. Draining occurs through sexual acts that are not fully loving and supportive, through overwork and by people pulling on your energy.

DE-ENERGIZE Taking the emotional charge out of a negative emotion or mental construct to open room for a positive feeling or belief to express itself.

DIMENSIONAL SHIFT A change to a more refined frequency of energy that will open perception of the multi-dimensional levels of being.

DIS-EASE The state that results from physical imbalances, blocked feelings, suppressed emotions and negative thinking which, if not reversed, leads to illness.

DRAGON ENERGY The earth's natural kundalini or earth energy is carried by dragon currents throughout the meridian grid.

EARTH HEALING Rectifying the distortion of the earth's energy field or meridian grid caused by pollution, electro-magnetic interference and the destruction of its resources.

ELECTROMAGNETIC SMOG A subtle but detectable electromagnetic field given off by power lines and electrical equipment that has an adverse effect on sensitive people.

EMPATHY NICK A small chip or nick in a crystal means that the crystal knows what it is to feel pain and will, therefore, work all the harder to heal and rebalance. Empathy nicks may not be pretty but they are potent.

ENERGY IMPLANT Vibration, thought or negative emotions implanted in the subtle body by external sources.

ENERGETIC INTERFACE A meeting point of energy fields that may be personal, metaphysical or planetary. An interface enables healing and psychic activity to take place without draining your biomagnetic energy or invading your personal space.

ENTITY Discarnate spirit who hangs around on a plane close to earth and may attach to an incarnate being.

ENTITY REMOVAL/SPIRIT RELEASE Detaching a discarnate spirit and dispatching it to the appropriate post-death place.

ETHERIC BLUEPRINT The subtle energetic program from which the subtle and physical bodies are constructed. It carries imprints of past-life dis-ease, injuries and beliefs which present life conditions may reflect.

ETHERIC BODY The subtle biomagnetic sheath surrounding the physical body.

EXPANDED AWARENESS/CONSCIOUSNESS An expanded spectrum of consciousness that encompasses the grounded, lower frequencies of earth and the higher frequencies of multi-dimensions. Being in a state of expanded awareness facilitates accessing each and every level of reality and all timeframes simultaneously.

FUNCTIONAL REALITY The consensual, three-dimensional world view that currently prevails that veils a much wider understanding of consciousness and the metaphysics of existence.

GEOPATHIC STRESS AND GEOPATHOGENS Earth and physiological stress created by energy disturbance from underground water, power lines and ley lines and other subterranean events.

GRIDS/GRIDDING Placing crystals around a building, person or place for energy enhancement or protection – position is best dowsed for.

GROUNDING Creating a strong connection between one's soul, physical body and the earth.

HEALING CHALLENGE A temporary intensification of symptoms or cathartic release.

HUMOUR In medieval astrology and medicine people were divided into four humours, each expressing a specific personality type.

IMPOSTER SYNDROME Feeling that you are not qualified to do a job or take on a role, or are operating under false pretences.

INNER CHILD Part of the personality that remains childlike (but not childish) and innocent, or which may be the repository of abuse and trauma that requires healing.

INNER LEVELS Levels of being that encompass intuition, psychic awareness, archetypes, emotions, feelings, the subconscious mind and subtle energies.

INTERFACE Where two energy fields meet.

JOURNEYING The soul leaves the physical body and travels to distant locations. It is also known as out of body experience and astral travel.

KARMIC Experiences or lessons arising from or appertaining to a past incarnation. Debts, beliefs and emotions such as guilt are carried over into the present life and create dis-ease but past life credits and wisdom are available to heal these.

KUNDALINI Inner, subtle spiritual and sexual energy that resides at the base of the spine and, awakened, rises to the crown chakra. Kundalini is also found in the earth.

KYTHING A two-way communication with discarnate beings.

LIGHTBODY Subtle energy body vibrating at a very high frequency. A vehicle for the spirit.

LIGHTWORKER A soul who has undertaken to assist the vibrational shift of the earth by doing their own work here on earth anchoring in the new energies and, in so doing, stimulates others to evolve.

LUCIFERIAN ACCEPTANCE WORK Accepting and incorporating repressed shadow energies that have been deemed unacceptable in the past and finding the gift in their heart.

MATRIX The bedrock on which crystals are formed. An energetic matrix also interpenetrates the planet.

MENTAL INFLUENCES Effect of other people's thoughts and strong opinions on your mind.

MERIDIAN Subtle energy channel that runs close to the surface of the skin, or the planet, that contains acupuncture points.

METAPHYSICAL ABILITIES Abilities such as clairvoyance, telepathy, healing.

NEGATIVE EMOTIONAL PROGRAMMING
'Oughts' and 'shoulds' and emotions such as guilt instilled, often in childhood or other lives, remain in the subconscious mind and influence present behaviour, sabotaging effects to evolve until released.

PEOPLE PLEASE People pleasing means that you fulfil what others expect so you receive praise and validation, or that you appease other people, rather than following your own soul path.

PLANETARY GRID Subtle and invisible earth energy lines that cover the planet rather like a spider's web.

POVERTY CONSCIOUSNESS Ingrained belief that it is somehow right and meritorious to suffer poverty and lack.

PRE-BIRTH/BETWEEN LIFE STATE Dimension inhabited by the soul before birth.

PSYCHIC ATTACK Malevolent thoughts or feelings towards another person, whether consciously or unconsciously directed, create dis-ease and disruption in that person's life.

PSYCHIC VAMPIRISM Drawing or feeding on the energy of others.

QI The life force that energises the physical and subtle bodies.
Reframing: seeing a past event in a different, more positive light so that the dis-ease it is creating is healed.

REIKI Natural hands on method of healing.

SHAMANIC ANCHOR An energy conduit hooked into the centre of the earth that helps to bring earth or galactic energies into the physical body during upper or lower world journeying and provides a cord to guide the return.

SOUL Vehicle for carrying the eternal spirit. Soul parts are parts of the soul not presently in incarnation, which includes but are not limited to soul fragments that split off (see soul retrieval).

SOUL GROUP Cluster of souls who have travelled together throughout time, all or some of whom are in incarnation.

SOUL IMPERATIVE Past life agendas and unfinished business that operative unconsciously to motivate the present life. It includes past life promises and purposes that drive the soul forward from life to life and which draw past partners back into your orbit in the guise of lovers – or enemies.

SOUL LINKS Connections between members of a soul group.

Soul overlays: outdated intentions from other lives that still motivate the soul.

SOUL PLAN/LIFE PLAN: The soul's intention and learning-plan for the present life, which may have been carefully reviewed in the between-life state, or may be a knee jerk reaction to karmic causes.

SOUL RETRIEVAL Trauma, shock or abuse, and even extreme joy, can cause a part of the soul energy to leave and remain stuck at a certain point in life, or past life death. A soul retrieval practitioner or shaman retrieves the split off part bringing it back to the present life body.

SUBTLE BODIES Layers of the biomagnetic sheath.

SUBTLE ENERGY FIELDS Invisible but detectable energy fields that surrounds all living beings.

THOUGHT FORMS Forms created by strong positive or negative thoughts that exist on the etheric or spiritual level and affect a person's mental functioning.

VICTIM MENTALITY An ingrained point of view that says: 'I don't deserve this, poor me' and which takes no personal responsibility for one's thoughts or feelings.

INDEX

USEFUL INFORMATION

AUTHOR ACKNOWLEDGEMENTS

I would like to thank all my workshop participants for their assistance in exploring the stones in this book. My gratitude goes to all the crystal suppliers, too numerous to mention by name, who have introduced me to new stones and generously shared information. In particular Keith Birch and Katie Jacqueline of KSC Crystals, John Van Rees of Exquisite Crystals and Kellie Conn of Avalon Crystals USA. Many were exceptionally generous in gifting me with their precious new finds and it is much appreciated. It is a joy to me when I explore a new crystal, whether alone or with a group, and find that the results correspond to those of other practitioners, as it is to find entirely new applications. After all, we share a unity of consciousness and communication with the crystal beings. As always my gratitude to David Eastoe of Petaltone Essences without whose clearing, recharging and protection essences I could not work. My thanks also to Mike Eastwood of Aristia for the crystal oversoul mandalas and much else besides. I am grateful to Robert of Heaven and Earth Crystals for permission to use his trademarked. My apologies go to anyone whose trademarks have not been so indicated. My thanks also to Liz Dean and Joanne Wilson of Godsfield Press who made the process of publishing this third volume of *The Crystal Bible* a delight.

Crystals attuned by Judy Hall can be obtained from www.angeladditions.co.uk

PICTURE ACKNOWLEDGEMENTS

All photography © Octopus Publishing Group Limited, with the exception of the following: Alamy/David Gallimore 22; Lyroky 101. Corbis 26; Michael Eastwood 15. Octopus Publishing Group/Russell Sadur 21. Thinkstock/iStockphoto 28. Jennifer Campbell 2 (Bumble Bee Jasper), 45, 166 (Polychrome Jasper), 278 (Silver Healer), 296; Joanne Wilson 11 (Rainbow Mayanite)

Editor: Joanne Wilson
Copy Editor: Keira Price
Proofreader: Marylin Inglis
Executive Art Editor: Yasia Williams-Leedham
Designer: Sally Bond
Photographer: Andy Komorowski assisted by Ken Kamara
Production Controller: Davide Pontiroli
Picture Researcher: Jennifer Veall

FURTHER READING

Hall, Judy, *The Crystal Bible*, Godsfield, London, 2003

Hall, Judy, *The Crystal Bible Volume 2*, Godsfield, London, 2009

Hall, Judy, *The Crystal Experience*, Godsfield, 2010

Hall, Judy, *Crystal Prescriptions*, O Books, Ropley, 2005

Hall, Judy, *Good Vibrations: Psychic protection, space clearing and energy enhancement*, Flying Horse Books, Bournemouth, 2008

Hall, Judy, *101 Power Crystals: The ultimate guide to magical crystals, gems and stones for healing and transformation*, Fair Winds Press, 2011

Hall, Judy, *Crystals and Sacred Sites*, Fair Winds Press, 2012

Eastwood, Mike, *The Crystal Oversoul Cards*, Findhorn Press, 2011